TALES OF AN
AMERICAN SOLDIER

TALES OF AN
AMERICAN SOLDIER

From KP to Seeing his former Nazi
leaders in the dock at Nuremberg

—◦◦◦◦—

Werner H. Von Rosenstiel

Library of Congress Number: 00-192233
ISBN #:   Hardcover   0-7388-3914-0
                  Softcover   0-7388-3915-9

This book was printed in the United States of America.

To order additional copies of this book, contact:
Xlibris Corporation
1-888-7-XLIBRIS
www.Xlibris.com
Orders@Xlibris.com

To Marion and Anne, my two wives:
One with whom I lived this book years ago
And one who encouraged me to write it

FOREWORD

Tales of an American Soldier is my story. It maps an amazing journey that starts in Germany and winds through momentous events of our time. I briefly served as a soldier in Hitler's war machine, the Wehrmacht, and later advanced in the United States Army against all odds, as my unique background was put into the service of the Allied war effort.

Although in this book occasional references are made to events covered in earlier volumes of my memoirs, this volume stands alone as the story of my army years. My path to the tale told here started long ago. The third of six children, I was born into a family that had served the Prussian monarchy for centuries.

From 1906 to 1927 my father was Royal County Commissioner of Anklam in Prussia, a prestigious job with many perks. When the monarchy disappeared in 1918, my father's unremittingly monarchist views cost him his job. When he was transferred to a small job in Stralsund, his life lost all purpose.

For me life was still new and fascinating. From the beginning I was driven by an insatiable curiosity. But at age ten I felt the Great German Inflation. Hoping to earn enough money to buy a soccer ball, I spent two back-breaking weeks in the potato fields. My wages bought me *one* sweet roll, and then only because the shopkeeper took pity on me. I never got the soccer ball.

In 1928 my grandmother arranged for me to spend the summer with a Dutch family. My passport gave me a breathless taste of independence. I discovered ex-Kaiser Wilhelm living in exile almost next door to the family's summer home in Doorn. Still a believer in monarchy as the best form of government, I arranged a courtesy visit. The Kaiser disappointed me by asking if I was a "good republican." Not prepared for that opening, I failed to answer. The Kaiser turned to his next visitor. I left Doorn a republican. I was seventeen; things looked bright, and the name Hitler meant nothing yet.

Later while I was studying law in Berlin, Hitler became German Chancellor and I along with over a million others, saw and heard him speak on May 1, 1933 at the Templehof Airfield. I was impressed. Immature and non-political, I hoped he would save Germany from reparations and the depression.

More important than seeing Hitler was learning that I could get a scholarship to study in the United States merely by applying. To me America meant James Fenimore Cooper's *The Leatherstocking Tales*. I applied, and by the time I was accepted I had already passed my first German bar exam and completed one year of my three-year training as a law clerk in the Nazi judicial administration. By 1935 I was an exchange student at the University of Cincinnati studying political science. At my first dormitory bull session, fellow students tried to explain President Roosevelt's New Deal to me. It was a lively discussion and when someone called Roosevelt a "son of a bitch," I objected. He brought me up short saying, "Werner, you're in America now." To improve my English I subscribed to the *Cincinnati Inquirer*, where I learned much about Germany that I had never read in German papers. I had always been lucky and I didn't know it then, but luck was touching my shoulder when one day Marion Ahrens, a student in my class at the university, invited me to Sunday dinner. We would fall in love.

Early in 1936 I had a scare. As a German exchange student I was expected to visit German clubs. At one such club a member, just back from Germany had nothing but praise for the rejuvenation he'd seen and the faith in the future that Hitler had inspired. He had seen a big sign erected at the entrance to the town of Rothenberg: JEWS ARE NOT WANTED HERE. Another member turned to me and casually asked what I thought. Having forgotten all the caution that I had lived with in Germany, I said, "I think that's awful." A few days later another German exchange student contacted me. "Werner," she said, " you must have said something stupid because the consul in Cleveland called me. He wanted to know if I thought you were 'reliable'."

Suddenly I realized: *Hitler listens everywhere.* I had received my first warning, which was an eye-opener.

In January 1937 I returned to Germany after 17 months abroad. I had traveled in the U.S., worked on farms, and returned via the Far East, earning passage from Singapore to Marseilles by shoveling coal on a German tramp steamer. What I saw on my return was devastating.

Germany had become an armed camp. Soldiers, military vehicles, barracks, airfields and planes were everywhere. Returning to my clerkship in Breslau I saw Hitler's "justice." It was available to Nazis and those who had submitted to them. I was warned by my uncle, an attorney, to avoid the traps that were everywhere and to get out as soon as possible. I made a plan and confided in my father, who called it treason and insisted that I finish my legal education - two more years—before I could go.

I managed to get through those two years. I was in Berlin when Hitler annexed Austria. Then for eight weeks during the Czech crisis I was drafted into the Wehrmacht. On November 9, 1938 I was in Berlin when Goebbels organized the Kristallnacht—the Night of the Broken Glass. It was a preview of what Hitler planned for the Jews.

Good fortune remained with me and I made highest marks in my final bar exam. This brought an offer of a lifetime job in Hitler's judicial administration. I accepted the position, but asked for permission to postpone employment for 30 days while I visited the

U.S., ostensibly to improve my English language skills. Permission was granted and on March 31, 1939 I left for America. I would return not thirty days, but almost six years later during the Battle of the Bulge, as an American soldier.

Getting out of Germany and traveling to America was one thing, but being able to stay was another. Love and luck combined as I married Marion, the student I had fallen in love with in Cincinnati. Wed to an American, I qualified for a preferential immigration visa. On August 17, 1939 I arrived in Detroit, a married man with a green card. Marion didn't mind my lowly job unloading boxes for Schering, a German pharmaceutical firm in Bloomfield, New Jersey, but she insisted that I study English at night at Rutgers University. Later in New York I studied law.

Pearl Harbor instantly turned me into an enemy alien in the eyes of the Department of Justice. I was fired from my job with Schering, but later re-hired at the insistence of my friends. I was tried by an Enemy Alien Hearing Board exactly one year after Pearl Harbor. Marion, the most important witness, stood up and read a letter I had written to her from Berlin one day after the Night of the Broken Glass telling her of my shame and disgust. The board believed her and set me free. The army inducted me on March 15, 1943.

This volume relates the strange but true tale of an army private who becomes a second lieutenant, pores over the secret files of the German judicial administration and aids in the Allied effort to create the International War Crimes Tribunal at Nuremberg.

Chapter 1

Pvt. Werner H. Von Rosenstiel
ASN. 32826569

SUDDENLY, ABOUT THREE hours out of Penn Station we arrived at an enormous rail head with perhaps 30 platforms. Men in uniform were waiting for the new recruits and they herded us into trucks that drove us to barracks on the vast Fort Dix Military Reservation, teeming with military vehicles and soldiers. I recall endless rows of identical two floor, wooden buildings painted olive drab, the color which now supplanted the red, white and blue of the national flag all over America. All of them had 28 beds on each floor, a room for the non-commissioned officer who was responsible for the floor and a large bathroom with 14 wash basins, about 10 toilets and 10 cold and hot showers.

Having once been drafted into Hitler's army, sharing quarters with other men was not new to me, but sharing toilet space was a new experience. The German army and also the German freighter on which I had once worked, considered the toilet the only place where a man had a right to be alone. Now there was no privacy and since the activities related to essential body functions, my vocabulary was quickly enriched by the addition of words that I had not learned during my English courses at Rutgers. It took me some time to adjust to the toilet intimacy. The privacy of the Prussian toilet was the only change that I ever wanted to recommend to the United States military program, which compared with the drab, grim Prussian system had a country club atmosphere.

The metal construction beds with their firm mattresses were a welcome surprise. At Dix I would not be required to stuff a bag with straw as I had done in 1938, when I had been drafted in Germany. There were bed sheets, a pillow case and two wool blankets. At the foot of each bed was a footlocker with lock and key, and behind each bed, fastened to the wall, a rack to hang the clothes that we would soon receive.

The sharp sound from a sergeant's whistle brought us to attention. He said: "Men, you're in the army now. Forget everything you have learned before. I'll tell you how things are done here. First you are to learn how to make a bed. I will show you how it is done. There's only one way to make a bed, and that's the army way. I want you to learn it and be perfect right away. Every Saturday morning there is an inspection by the company commander. He is very tough and expects you to learn fast because," he added with a gleeful sneer, "if your bed is not perfect the *whole* barracks is restricted for the weekend -not just the jerk who did a lousy job." The demonstration was precise and thorough—spiced with the profanity, which now became part of our daily communication jargon.

Still in our civilian clothes, we were herded to a gigantic mess hall and given our first army meal. I remember the cooks standing behind a counter; next to each of them stood vast metal containers from which they ladled soup. Long tables with benches gave us a hurried chance to enjoy the first free meal that the army handed us.

It was not bad. The place was clean. The moment we were finished and got up a group of GI's in fatigues followed us and cleared the debris from the table to make room for the next incoming draftees. They worked fast and I was impressed. Soon I would be called upon to perform the same services.

Now the tempo sped up. . . . We were rushed to a large hall with tables and chairs and told to sit down. From a podium an officer announced over a loudspeaker that we would be given a test to determine our future. He admonished us to pay close attention, because those who did not do well on the test would not get the better jobs in the service. The army wanted to know exactly how they could use us best. He explained how the test would be given. His assistants brought us books and we marked them with the heavy lead pencils that were lying on every table. The test was timed and as soon as the time was up we turned the workbooks in and were marched to a barn-like clothing store, in which each man was measured and given a quick evaluation (fat, slender, waist, neck, length of pant legs), which in my case was amazingly accurate.

First stop was for shoes. After we had taken off our civilian footwear we stepped on a foot-measuring device. Next to it were heavy metal weights of about 40 pounds each. When we were told to lift those two heavy weights, the clerk who measured the feet observed how the added weight spread our feet and he read the specifics, which were recorded on my army record. Mine were 9 1/2 E—that was the shoe that I got and it fit perfectly. I was given two pairs of brand new shoes, which I would now have to keep immaculately shined—and pay for the cleaning supplies from my wages.

Next we passed endless racks of uniforms from which GIs in fatigues handed us socks (4 pairs), handkerchiefs (4 pairs), long underwear (2), fatigues with caps (2 sets), dress uniform, OD shirts (2), tie (1), a winter coat and visor cap, a field jacket, and a web belt with buckle. Before leaving the hall we had to sign a slip stating that we had received all of this stuff and acknowledge in writing that we were now responsible for the maintenance. If we lost something or if it was stolen, we would have to buy a replacement. We signed our names and walked back to the barracks, deposited the clothes on our beds, and immediately were marched to the hospital.

Back in the barracks, our platoon sergeant was ready to give detailed instruction on the storage of our clothes and in particular how our footlocker was to be arranged. Shirts, socks, handkerchiefs, everything had to be in precisely the prescribed place, no deviation was tolerated. Most of us had brought our own toilet kits with us. I am not sure whether the army provided us with a standard toilet kit or not. The sergeant alerted us to the necessity of keeping our toilet articles in immaculate condition at all times and a special place was provided for them in our footlocker. Invariably at the Saturday inspection the company commander would inspect this toilet kit, which had never been used, and was in reality a decoy for inspection. Praising the nice kit for its cleanliness he would then ask the soldier: "And now, soldier, show me the kit you use to shave, because I know this is just the inspection kit." The sergeant, who always accompanies the company commander at the inspection—wise to army routine, continued: "You recruits now go to your barracks bag under the bed and produce a second toilet kit which must show signs of wear and tear but must also be kept immaculately clean." And then he added: "The real toilet kit with which you shave, you keep in one of your beautifully shined shoes—and we don't give a . . . how that one looks." I always suspected that the Surgeon General of the army had stock in the Gillette Company and Burma Shave.

Our classification test and physical characteristics were supplemented by a series of interviews that gave the army a clear understanding of what they had in hand with each of us. I remember that at my interview I was, of course, immediately identified as an **enemy alien** and consequently questioned by a man of greater experience. In considerable detail he noted my German Army training and remarked that there were many places in the army where I would not be welcome. They included: infantry, artillery, cavalry, engineers, signal corps, air force, airborne troops, ordinance, and intelligence. That left the army band and the quartermaster corps as places where I could be safely used without endangering the nation. Knowing that I was incapable of producing any acceptable music, it was obvious that I was headed for a heroic career as a cook.

I suspect that my interrogator had been a personnel director of an industrial enterprise that employed a wide range of people. Before him he had a preprinted tan sheet with room for numerous essential biographical data. This would become my army record with every last detail of my performance recorded. Reading discreetly (upside down) I saw that most of my essential data had already been recorded, including an AGCT score of 147. This put me into the top layer, but in combination with my enemy alien status, made me highly suspect—perhaps a spy? The interrogator proved to be inquisitive and thorough. He wanted to know about my legal training in Germany and what I had studied in the United States. My German he did not test but he spoke a few words of French and when I answered them he listed it as a language that I could handle. He recorded the fact that I had traveled widely in the United States and the Orient. But what seemed to interest him most was what I had done in my job at Schering Corporation (a large pharmaceutical company where I had worked until a few weeks after Pearl Harbor, when I was fired because I was German). He wanted to know everything about my work as a billing clerk, how I had managed with my limited English as a sales correspondent and what I did in the area of market research. When I told him how Schering had bought one of the first IBM computers and how we had used it to derive sales results in various areas of the country, he beamed with pride and jotted down, "familiar and experienced with use of IBM equipment." How that entry could possibly help the army or me was beyond my horizon—but maybe it would gain some meaning later.

During this time we were brought to a lecture by the army's Finance Department and the Insurance Board. The finance officer told us that our pay scale of $50 per month was actually very good, because we had no expenses for food, clothing or housing and we had very good, free medical care. But with $22 withheld from my pay I was down to $28. Of course, it was pointed out, the army had to see to it that we always looked neat so they would provide a universal laundry service for the bargain price of $7.50 per month, which would automatically be deducted on payday.

And there was still one great and wonderful surprise: For the token fee of $7.40 per month we could buy a $10,000 GI life insurance policy which would guarantee, that in case of our being killed, this enormous amount would be sent forthwith to the surviving widow or parents. Here was something that was really very new. In the German army being killed was an honor and not profitable for the family unless there was a wife who was entitled to a widow's pension (very small of course). Here I could be really generous to my wife—but it would reduce my total monthly income to $13.10. When the officer explained the enormous attraction of this generous offer, and asked for a raising of hands of those who realized the tremendous benefits, I was one of those hesitant to raise my hand, because I had found that $13.10 per month for my own needs was shaving it very close—figuring that I would have to supply shoe shine and toilet articles. How would I be able to get to see my wife, Marion? The officer explaining the scheme smiled with a sigh and said he well understood our problem, but he wanted to merely mention that the army always assigned soldiers without insurance to dangerous combat duties, because it saved the army a lot of money. The second showing of hands was overwhelming.

Before we were released that day, we learned one more thing about the modalities of payment for enlisted men. Pay day would always be on the last Saturday of the month. We would always be paid off in cash in our barracks. But before we would be given our money, each one of us would be inspected to determine if we had, during the preceding month, acquired a venereal disease. Once we had been found to be clean we were deemed deserving of our pay of $13.10. Always delicate for public relations problems, this examination was called "The short arm inspection."

Before we were dismissed, an officer advised us that gambling on military reservations was forbidden. This hint alerted us to the opportunity that every pay day night, in every barracks of the United

States Army, there was a gigantic crap game. When we received our pay we were always given brand new bills, but by Monday morning most of the bills had passed through so many sweaty palms that it was difficult to find a crisp dollar bill.

The crap games were always conducted on the second floor of the barracks because it would enable the participants to remove the dice and cash before the search party reached them. A footlocker with a blanket draped over it, the essential crap table was immediately available on pay day in every barracks in the United States. The muffled sound of the rolling dice and the jubilant screams of the winners were our Kleine Nachtmusik on paydays and kept those of us who could not afford participation awake until the winner had it all.

For almost ten days, until they had collected a trainload to ship to the Quartermaster Training Center at Camp Lee Virginia, just outside of Petersburg, I was used as unskilled labor. I remember unloading hundreds of toilet bowls, wash basins, and metal beds that were to be installed in the mushrooming rows of new barracks.

By this time we had disposed of our civilian clothes and had learned to jump out of our beds at the first early morning whistle, followed by washing and dressing in our fatigues for the morning reveille where our names would be read off and names of those who would be shipped out would be announced. There followed the forming of the chow line and the passing of the table where the cooks slapped breakfast into the eagerly presented mess kits. The diet followed a rigid, never varying pattern, which invariably included: creamed beef on toast (SOS: profanity—on the shingle), oatmeal, scrambled eggs, pancakes and syrup.

The design of the mess kit was perfect for the simplest clean-up and washing procedure. With the spoon the soldier cleaned the uneaten remains of the meal into a large 20 gallon garbage barrel, which was hauled away by KPs the moment it was full and replaced by an empty one. Then followed another 20 gallon barrel filled with boiling water in which we shook the mess kit with utensils attached to the kit's handle. Next came another 20 gallon barrel in which a strong soap solution removed all traces of food and then a fourth barrel also with boiling water and some disinfectant served to sterilize our kit and protect us against all imaginable food dispensed diseases. For the next two years I became very experienced in the management of this eating technique, and it has left me with an acquired habit of reducing eating time to the minimum.

CHAPTER 2

BASIC TRAINING

IT WAS AN all day train ride from Fort Dix to the enormous quartermaster training center at Camp Lee, just outside of Petersburg, Virginia. The train consisted of worn out railroad cars that may have been used during WWI or had perhaps brought troops to Gettysburg.

The short indoctrination at Fort Dix had prepared us for what we now saw everywhere and what would become our normal environment for the next year. Barracks and arrangements were exactly the same everywhere and we were quickly sorted out into units of 56 men for each barracks. Compared to what I had experienced five years ago in Germany, life as a draftee was easy. Completely missing was the Prussian concept that every recruit is stupid and only through the most arduous, continuing humiliation can he be made into a useful soldier. It was clear that most of our non-coms had been people like us only a few months ago. They had been taught to bark and holler, but it was obvious that they were not to be taken too seriously. The major task our non-coms had to accomplish during those eight weeks of basic training was to make us look and behave like soldiers. Every morning there was reveille and roll call. After breakfast we had about 45 minutes of calisthenics. We would run to a sandy area in the nearby woods of scrub pines and then follow the routine exercises that loosened our muscles and worked up a gentle sweat. Returning to the barracks we received instructions on marching, and how to behave at reviews and inspections.

Once we were certain to react promptly and correctly to commands, we were shown how to get close to the ground at the first sign of shooting and how to slide on the ground without giving the enemy a target. I remember the curious sensation of navigating a long field on my belly and creeping under barbed wire strands without getting snagged, while machine guns were fired above me. We were told that live ammunition was used to give us the "real feeling" but I am sure it was not true.

Every good army must have a manual of arms, a prescribed way in which a rifle is gotten from the ground to the shoulder and is held when the command "Present Arms" is given. To perfect our skills in this important department each of us had been assigned a rifle (model Springfield 07). We had been instructed to give it the same tender loving care that we would give our girlfriend (raucous laughter). My German training gave me a slight advantage, because the gun was almost identical to the one that I had learned to clean and take apart.

Compared to the rigors and indignities of my prior training all of this was a wonderful physical rehabilitation course, which I found exhilarating. Since our time was occupied from morning 'til supper, I was not given to moping and in no way felt sorry for myself, but many of the men in my barracks were depressed and unhappy. To them being drafted was the worst punishment that could have been dished out. They all felt: Why me? After supper there followed the mail call, an event that we eagerly awaited and where I was rarely disappointed. Marion had very quickly realized that the exchange of letters that we had started in 1936 was a proven and certain way of helping us over our separation and so I heard from her every day. I reciprocated and the mass of letters that we exchanged has made it possible for me to refresh my memory and re-live some of those long ago events. The army was more generous than any one of us ever was ready to concede. Congress in an unusual spirit of generosity had given to soldiers the same privileges heretofore reserved to congressmen: free mailing privileges.

It was at this time that Marion set into motion a program that vastly enriched my life. She had very quickly seen that my liberal education had totally neglected English writing. My basic concept of literature was: If it was not Greek, Latin, Goethe or Schiller, it could not be worth knowing. While I studied law she thought that I had enough educational inspiration and did not mention literature. But now, seeing that I would have lots of time she made a list of what I should have read. Working in a publishing house, she managed to select my educational reading material. At no time in my life have I had such an opportunity to read and enjoy literature. And the arrival of the books provided an unexpected bonus. Many of my buddies wondered what was in the packages that I received so frequently at mail call. When they discovered they were books, many of them asked if they could borrow them after I had read them. I always gave the books away and merely asked them to send them back to Marion when they had finished them.

I cannot say that there is much new that I learned during those two months of basic training, except for two events that have stayed with me. The army was determined to educate us about the war. They wanted us to know what this war was all about. I knew it very well, but as I listened to the griping and complaints of my new buddies, I realized that they had considerable reservations about being soldiers and tackling Hitler. When I had been drafted in Germany, no time was wasted on making me recognize the need or advantages of war. That was something that had always been decided by the King and now by Hitler. We were trained to kill and not to reflect—that was a task reserved for our leaders only. I saw that in America things were done differently.

To educate us the U.S. Army had enlisted the help of talented movie makers who used modern propaganda techniques to visualize what was important. They were determined to explain to us why we had been drafted and why we must fight Hitler. The first film of this type made a lasting impression on me. I can still see it as if it were playing now. They used a German-made film showing the German Army's victory parade after the 1940 defeat of France. The film shows an arrogant German cavalry officer coming from the Arch de Triomphe with his steel helmet and prancing horse leading an endless field-grey line of victorious soldiers. Frenchmen line the street with tears streaming down their faces in a mixture of hatred and despair. Softly, background music plays: "The last time I saw Paris, my heart was young and gay . . ." a tune that in 1940 was high on the list of hit tunes. I doubt that there was ever another film strip that so eloquently brought home to me what was at stake.

But perhaps even more impressive was the educational skill with which the army taught us **what not to do,** once we got into territory that the enemy had occupied and vacated. The army knew, of course, that every soldier in every army in the world is eager to collect trophies, and if conveniently possible loot a little. It was well known that the Germans in particular had recognized this human tendency and utilized the knowledge to maim their adversaries through the skillful use of booby traps. Everything was booby trapped—we were told that they even wired dead bodies. How then could American soldiers be immunized and made impervious to this danger? The army engaged Walt Disney to make one of the most charming and effective cartoons using Mickey Mouse as an educator. Mickey Mouse observed the enemy as he wired a piano in such a manner that upon touching just **one** key the whole piano would explode. He then sat down at the piano and played a familiar tune, using a false note to avoid that critical (wired) key. In the end, one of his not-so-bright assistants, who had not understood the whole concept, rushed forward, hit the right note and blew the whole piano into the air.

When I got to France in 1944 I carried that scene with me and touched nothing in our billets or anywhere that had not been checked out by the engineers.

After about three weeks of this modified country club atmosphere we were told that there was the possibility of a one-night pass. I immediately called Marion with the good news and she made her way from New York to Petersburg, where a good friend of ours, a captain in the Dental Corps, offered to put her up.

Marion arrived radiant with the excitement with which so many American women saw their heroes for the first time in uniform. She inspected me with a critical eye and gave me whispered praise, saying, "You look much better now than in that German uniform in 1938." All wives who had come to Camp Lee were guests of the United States Army for Saturday dinner, and the army had spared no effort to dress up the spam. Battalions of KPs had hollowed out grapefruit halves and given them the appearance of Halloween decorations. These creations now served as containers for the fruit salad (from cans) that was served on tables that with paper tablecloths had acquired some semblance of a parish house supper. Our festivity was short lived.

The company commander who welcomed the women and addressed us at the dinner announced: "I am very sorry, ladies, that I must disappoint you, but all passes have been cancelled, because there has been an outbreak of flu reported and we cannot take chances. You are welcome to stay for another two hours on the post, but then you'll have to leave." It was the first of many things that I had to learn: The army knows best. Marion and I were lucky to find seats on a bench near the gate before they blew the whistle and she had to go back to New York.

Gradually as our stamina increased we were taking on more demanding activities. We learned how to pitch tents, how to walk and run with a gas mask, how to pack our field pack, and of course how to march distances of perhaps 10 miles loaded down with about forty pounds of weight. All of these necessary skills were often interrupted by assignments to KP, where I very quickly learned that re-

bellious attitudes would invariably be rewarded by the more oner-
ous tasks like cleaning out the grease traps and scrubbing pots and
pans.

Toward the end of April our fitness training was extended to
climbing high wooden fences and jumping from high towers into
sawdust pits. At one of those exercises I came down crooked and
tore the ligaments of my right ankle. I was excused from marching
and KP and given a supply of APC pills, the universal army treatment for minor discomfort, and told to report for sick call every
third day, and walk on my painful foot as much as possible. It was
an effective treatment but it was disagreeable.

The threat of a flu epidemic had been a false alarm, as we all
expected, and we were again given the promise that wives would be
allowed to see us outside the camp on a weekend. Marion was again
welcomed by our friends, who had even secured a room for us in a
tourist home. I had received my weekend pass in which I had given
my friend, Captain Vosper's address, as the place where I could be
reached in case the army required my immediate presence, which I
did not consider likely. But in my enthusiasm to see Marion I had
forgotten that on Sunday morning I was to report to the dispensary
for sick call for my gimpy ankle. Marion and I were blissfully asleep
in our modest tourist home when at 7:30 in the morning we heard
the bellowing voice of Captain Vosper: "Where is Private Von
Rosenstiel?" The frightened landlady showed him into our bedroom
where he said: "Get out of the sack, they are waiting for you at the
dispensary. You're lucky if you are not booked for being AWOL." I
jumped out of bed and into my uniform. Jack Vosper dropped me
at the dispensary and said a few good words for me. I was given a
new supply of APC pills and told: "Missing a sick call can have very
serious consequences." I came to attention, saluted, and realized
that I still had a lot to learn.

During those first eight weeks in that unit I formed no lasting
contact. We were all involved with learning the same things and
most of us were older people—between 25 and 38 years old. Many
had worked as store clerks, a few had trade skills like shoemakers

and tailors and there were several who had worked in restaurants and as truck drivers. Having an accent was no burden, and I never found that my German background created any problem for me. Our instructors had told us that the grand finale of our basic training would be the last week at the rifle range.

On the scheduled day our whole regiment equipped with field packs and rifles marched to the range. After pitching tents, we were shown how to use our brand new shovels to dig a latrine for the unit. The planning for the event was memorable. We were fed from a field kitchen, our tents were lined up as if a surveyor had laid out a pattern and our company commander admonished us that he expected every one of us to perform and be a credit to his company.

During that five-day field exercise every one would serve in the target pit, as target crew, and would have to demonstrate that we had acquired the necessary skill to hit a target and achieve a minimum score. The best performers would receive as a visible reward of their skills a decoration that identified them as **sharpshooter** or as the coveted **expert**. Having grown up with guns and always having been an excellent shot, I could hardly wait until I could again blast away at a target. But before I would have my chance, I had to be fully exposed to the elaborate rifle range procedure.

On this vast range were arranged some fifty or sixty targets which were raised for every fusillade and then lowered for the determination of the result. All of this was accompanied by a never varying ritual of the range officer intoning over a loudspeaker:

Ready on the Right   Ready on the Left
Ready on the Firing Line
Targets
FIRE

The pit crew upon hearing the word 'targets' would push the target up and now the firing followed the pace at which each soldier aimed and shot. The targets had the conventional bulls eyes and circles, which credited hits of lesser quality.

Within a few minutes all firing had been accomplished. The targets were lowered and read, and for each target the pit crew would record the hits and report them on a separate indicator giving the number of bulls eyes and the lesser scores.

After the targets were replaced with new ones the procedure was repeated until every soldier had his chance to learn how to use his weapon and how to rapidly reload his gun and shoot ten bullets at the target in less than a minute.

After two days in the pit my turn on the range came. I did extremely well, qualifying as an expert and gaining a rewarding nod from my platoon sergeant and the company commander. I shared the tent with another soldier, and was sound asleep after my successful demonstration of proficiency when somebody tapped me on the shoulder. It was my platoon sergeant. He motioned me to be silent and ordered me out of the tent. Obviously he had something important to say. He took me to the side where several of the non-coms sat around a fire and smoked. In a low conspiratorial voice he explained to me that the unit's results at the rifle range were of great importance to the company commander and all of the non-coms. If they turned in a good score for their unit this would prove that they were excellent trainers and they would stay in Camp Lee; if the results were poor they would be shipped overseas, which none of them really desired. Sometimes they had soldiers on the rifle range who could not hit a barn door at a distance of 10 feet no matter how much effort the non-coms exerted. To avoid the tragedy of such incompetencies lousing up their record as competent trainers, they had selected the best riflemen of their units to shoot at the targets in the place of those dummies to qualify them. I had been picked to pinch-hit for one of them and would go to the rifle range the next morning when the name Tyrone was called. They assured me that the company commander knew and approved the plan. I was told that I must not shoot a perfect score but one that looked good without causing suspicion. The records at the end of the rifle range exercises showed that Private Von Rosenstiel qualified as an expert rifleman and Private Tyrone qualified with an average score. I realized that I had arrived. I was really serving my chosen country.

As we all knew, within a few days after the rifle range, we would be assigned to schools for further special training as cooks or clerks, or we would be sent to jobs where our qualifications were needed. Every morning at reveille assignments were read off and the barracks was more deserted, until I was the only one left. My assignment was to the 1576th Service Unit at Fort Indiantown Gap Military Reservation, Pennsylvania—via Harrisburg, PA. I returned my rifle, packed my two barracks bags and set out to my assigned unit, wondering what a service unit might be.

CHAPTER 3

THE U.S. "FOREIGN LEGION"

FOR THE NEXT three months of my army service I was assigned to the 1576th Service Unit at Fort Indiantown Gap Military Reservation near Harrisburg, Pennsylvania. That time was the most difficult and taxing experience of my three years in the army. Nothing that I experienced before or after challenged my faith in America more than those three months.

That today I still can provide an accurate account of my thoughts and actual feelings of that time is the result of a curious habit that has often helped me during my life to put behind me matters that have deeply troubled or distressed me. Once I manage to get all of what presses down on me on paper, I can rid myself of this burden and free myself to make a new start and move on. What follows here, I recaptured from detailed notes (100 typed pages) that I wrote down in September of 1943, immediately after leaving Indiantown

Gap on August 27 of that year. The army had transferred me to the 63rd Quartermaster Laundry Battalion in Elkins, West Virginia, the army's Mountain Troops Training Center, where I spent a happy four weeks recuperating from what I have called *Camp Filter* at Indiantown Gap. This chapter contains detailed recollections of events and people who also spent time at this place—many of them with backgrounds similar to mine.

Foreign Legion
Training for Admission to U.S. Army

Of the men with whom I had received basic training at Camp Lee I was the only one who was assigned to a service unit. All the rest had been shipped to specific training schools (cooking, baking, shoe repair, tailoring) or to quartermaster units. I had no idea what a service unit was nor what or whom it served. The large, brown, sealed envelope probably held the answer but there was no way for me to see what was inside. Loaded down with my two heavy barracks bags I boarded the train in Petersburg. It was late afternoon on a Saturday at the end of May when I finally reached my destination. From Petersburg to Harrisburg is a mere 300 miles, but trains were slow and what with waiting as I transferred to different lines and buses it took 18 hours to reach my new destination.

Indiantown Gap is a military reservation of about 40 square miles roughly 15 miles northeast of Harrisburg in Dauphin County, a farming area in the foothills of the Appalachian Mountains. For many years it has served as the home base for the Pennsylvania National Guard. The bus stopped at the post headquarters. I dragged my bags up the stairs of the building, went inside and turned the envelope over to the desk sergeant. He told me to wait for the officer of the day. After a few minutes a lieutenant came, the sergeant handed him the envelope and I thought that I heard him whisper: "Another one for the Foreign Legion." The lieutenant opened the envelope, called a driver who was sitting on a chair near the door and told him to take me to the 1576th Service Unit at the old CCC camp about a mile beyond Area 10, adding: "You know that's the section marked Area 13."

The driver helped me load my bags into his small truck and I sat next to him as we took off. When I tried to find out what I was going to do here, he said that he was new and did not know; I had the feeling that he did not want to tell me. We rode in silence. It was a large camp with the familiar army barracks, motor vehicles and soldiers milling around. There were all sorts of parked armored vehicles and hundreds of tanks with their guns covered with camouflage covers. This was the real army preparing for war that I had not seen at either Dix or Lee. After about two miles we passed some older, dilapidated buildings, crossed a bridge and suddenly arrived at a row of low, prim looking buildings. The driver turned my service record over to the corporal on duty, who put the envelope in a desk drawer and asked if I had eaten. When I told him that I had been in transit for 18 hours he took me to the kitchen, and made the cooks fry me a few eggs.

I heard two of the cooks speaking German and two of the KPs, Italian. The orderly took me to a bunk in the third platoon in barracks #12 about two hundred feet from the orderly room and showed me the building where I would be billeted. The first night I could sleep in the bunk of one of the soldiers on a pass. The next day I would get bedding and all the other stuff that I would need; breakfast on Sundays was at 7:00 A.M. He showed me the latrine in a nearby building before he returned to the orderly room. There were only two soldiers at the end of the room. One of them repeated over and over "bank crash and monopolies"; he sounded like a record when the needle got stuck. After a hot shower I sank into bed and was asleep immediately. It had been a long day.

I was up early next morning and I looked around my new quarters. This was a very different unit from what I had seen before. The army had taken over the barracks that had once accommodated a large CCC (Civilian Conservation Corps) unit. The site was well chosen. Behind the camp was a small mountain lake -nice for swimming—wedged in between two wooded ranges that rose several hundred yards. There were altogether about 30 buildings in the area, most of them not in use. They were nicer than the WWII barracks models. Each housed 40 men on one floor. The barracks was immaculately clean with light wooden floors. There were the familiar, standard metal frame beds and footlockers and behind each bed a rack for uniforms. Unlike previous beds I had inhabited, here each had a small metal frame at the foot end with the typed name of the occupant, his rank and serial number. Two round potbelly stoves would give us heat in winter—the new barracks at Dix and Lee had automatic oil heat. One large bathhouse with rows of showers, wash basins and toilets served the four barracks that were in use. I calculated that our unit would have about 160 men and used about one third of the original camp buildings.

The large mess hall standing on a little hill was clearly the center of the compound and was designed to serve not just this small unit but all of the buildings, if they would ever be occupied. On the steps to the mess hall was a bulletin board on which I saw for the first time the names of some of my new companions: Spitzer, Watanabe, Paulinetto, Schmidt, Rykowsky, De Santo, Davidson, Gato, Reuter. The commanding officer, Captain Bailey, and the First Sergeant Kramer, I heard, were regular army. Perhaps one third of the listed names had the rank of corporal or sergeant, which surprised me. It explained why the arrival of a private was welcome, because it added to the pool of men who would do KP. Suddenly I understood a remark from one of the men in my barrack who on seeing me had said: "It's nice to get another KP."

The Special Announcement on the bulletin board: **THREE DAY PASSES** caught my eye.

> **Three Day Passes** will be issued only after a soldier has been on the post for at least one month and has a perfect performance record. Passes, when available, will be issued for three days from Friday after work to Monday night (12 P.M.). Applications for the pass must be made one week prior to the date of the pass. Special forms are to be obtained at the

orderly room. The application must show the exact address where the soldier expects to spend the pass, must give the names of all persons with whom he will stay and associate during the time of the pass, and the telephone number where he can be reached at all times. Any false information in making the application will result in the permanent loss of pass privileges.

I did not recall that I had ever seen such restrictive terms for a pass before. This was considerably more confining than even my parole after my trial as an enemy alien. When I had made an application for a pass at Camp Lee, I had just signed my name. I had had only one pass during basic training, so maybe this was the real army. I began to calculate when would be the first day when I would be able to see Marion. I would write her that I was now much closer to New York—about four hours—and that we should certainly be able to work out a plan that the army could accept.

When the breakfast bell rang, I was the first to enter the mess hall. It was different from Camp Lee. There were tables set for eight men, with china and utensils. The table was loaded with scrambled eggs, bacon, and fruit. A pitcher with coffee and cream gave the mess hall an almost restaurant like flavor. The two men from my barracks arrived a moment later and took seats at my table as far away from me as possible—they treated me as if I had leprosy. Except for saying: "Pass the coffee, please," not a word was spoken at breakfast. When I left the mess hall I saw the company commander approach. I saluted and was surprised when he said "Good morning, Von Rosenstiel." Later on I was told that this was the way in which he surprised every new man in camp. But despite that greeting I never had a chance to talk to that man.

As I wandered around the area, I heard music coming from the day room and found Reuter, the corporal who had checked me in the night before, playing the piano. It was a familiar church hymn, and he finished it before talking to me. I asked him what kind of an outfit this really was. Were we all confined in this place like a glorified concentration camp? His was a sad story. Born in Germany he had come to America with his parents in 1911 at the age of four. He had gone to school here and was back in Germany once in 1937 for a short visit. People in Germany had been very nice to him and had obviously been interested in showing him the great life they were living under Hitler. His grandparents still lived in Germany and he had corresponded with them until Pearl Harbor. His father was a typical German who never really learned English well and loved his beer.

He had been 34 when he was drafted and had found the basic infantry training tough, because he had to compete with boys of 18. But he had managed and had even gotten into Officer Candidate School (OCS). When he was accepted they had asked him if he hated the Germans. He had answered that he disapproved of the Nazi system, but that he could hardly bring himself to hate every German. Then they had asked him if he would fight them in this order: Nazis first, Italians next and then the Germans. Apparently the answers satisfied them and he was accepted and started in OCS. On the day before graduation, when he had already bought his lieutenant's bars, the school commander called him to his office and told him: "Sorry, Reuter, we cannot graduate you. Here are your orders. You are transferred at once to the 1576th Service Unit. Don't take it too hard, we all liked you, it's orders from above; everything will turn out alright." It was the saddest day of his life when he had to tell his wife that she should not come to Virginia because he would not graduate. "What could I tell my wife as the reason?" he asked me. How could he explain this to his friends? Could they believe that this was really a true story? He had arrived about a month ago just as depressed and confused as most of the people who come here. He could not explain why he was here. Except for the captain nobody knows anything, and he is polite, friendly and silent as a tomb about the reasons for all of this.

Since nobody will give you an answer, he told me, we have tried to dope out a solution of our own. We think it must have something to do with your background that they want to clear up. Except for a few non-coms who were specially shipped in to operate the place, most of us are foreign born or have shown some interest in activities that are undesirable. There is also a fellow who believes in some form of socialism (maybe communism?), another one does not want to fight with offensive weapons, but the majority are foreign born or have spent time abroad. He looked depressed when he said: "I feel like an American and it hurts my pride to be put into a class with people who have been associated with the Bund or have refused to fight. But there is nothing I can do about it. This place is a cleaning station where they filter out all people who are dangerous to our war, and they have good methods for that work. There are stool pigeons around and they open your mail and go through your footlocker—that's just a tip off. Perhaps they use this camp as a training center for men they want to send behind the German lines. Aside from that, you don't have to worry. The officers are nice, the treatment is very good, and the food is better than any place I have been. Don't get scared, there is one good feature about this place, you can get home in 4 1/2 hours. And then there is one main thing that keeps me going: There have been some pretty bad guys in the army and perhaps by locking us up they will find some who would do harm to this country. If that were the case, it would be worth having us here."

Reuter took me to the supply room where he issued two blankets and sheets, and the special fatigues for our service unit. Unlike the other soldiers in camp we would not wear the regular olive drab fatigues or the camouflage work clothes of the armored troops, but blue denim fatigues and an Eleanor hat. That was a wide brimmed suntan hat, which Eleanor Roosevelt had seen on soldiers during a state visit to Brazil. Rumor had it that she had been so impressed with this wonderful headgear that would protect soldiers against the brutal heat of the equatorial sun, that she had persuaded Franklin to make it available for American soldiers. The army had jumped at the opportunity to please Eleanor and bought a large supply that had been sitting around in some army warehouse with no takers for years. Now the army was glad to match it with the blue denims to identify us to the whole camp as "The Foreign Legion." It was not a badge of honor. The soldiers we met in the PX disclosed their disdain for us by briskly turning away, and some of the younger men reported that if they were identified as members of the 1576th Service Unit at USO dances, the girls refused to dance with them.

I kept my Eleanor hat when I left the unit and gave it to Marion to save for me. After the war I used it when I went fishing with my children. When a gust of wind blew it away into Barnegat Bay one day I felt I had lost an old friend, who had shared with me an experience that had taught me patience in what I had thought was adversity.

I took my blankets and sheets and went to my barracks made the bed, and organized the footlocker. On Saturdays there would be the standard inspection. Since no one was issued a rifle, there would be one thing less to worry about.

The dayroom in one of the empty barracks had a few tables, which were used for playing cards, and a few books—gifts or duplicates from some other day room. There was the *Guide to the Perfect Marriage,* obviously often consulted despite the publication date of 1892; the *Handbook for Garden Owners* (1907); *The Education of Our Baby* (No date of publication). There were six copies of *Anthony Adverse,* a few classics and three books on the war.

That night at the PX I had picked up a newspaper that discussed John L. Lewis and the 1943 coal strike. I found it difficult to understand that these men could strike for money while most of us had to make do with $50 per month and could get court- martialed if we were late returning from a pass.

About midnight I was awakened by some of my new buddies who, totally drunk and uninhibited, were singing: Drei Lilien, drei Lilien die pflanzt ich auf ein Grab (Three lilies, three lilies I planted on a grave . . .). It was an old German soldiers' marching song that had been revived by the Nazis and was very popular when I served in the German Army only five years ago. For a moment the barrack was in a big uproar, when the high pitched voice from one corner screamed: "Stop that racket you bastards, we want to sleep." It was the voice of the platoon sergeant Dening, a slender youngster disliked by everybody. But he exerted some authority because he was one of the original strictly American non-coms. The fact that he had served before in a Military Police outfit was known and everybody suspected that he was there for a purpose but no one knew what that was. The noise stopped. I heard two of the singers whisper that they had been in a German beer hall not far from the camp where they had gotten free beer and had been invited to sing German songs.

At five the CQ (Charge of Quarters) came with a flashlight and woke Barbeck and Angelo, a tall Italian with a heavy lower lip and a nervous facial twitch, and me. I got dressed, washed, and walked over to the mess hall. It was still dark outside, and a little chilly; a thin strip of light toward the east and the clear sky promised a nice day.

The mess hall was still dark, but I could see that all tables had been set by yesterday's crew. In the kitchen a few lights were on. Barbeck and Angelo came a moment later. The mess sergeant was already in the kitchen drinking coffee from a saucer. He smelled of liquor and was unsteady on his feet. Years of army life and drinking had left their marks—his eyes were bloodshot and his hands were shaky. He was foul mouthed and ordered us "to get the hell going and be done with breakfast before the men come." The cook, who had started at 3:30 to mix the wheat cake dough, gave each of us a good helping with bacon and syrup which we ate standing at a counter while the mess sergeant nervously walked back and forth, burping and urging us to hurry. The moment we were finished, we put the milk, the big plates loaded with wheat cakes, bacon, and the syrup pitchers on the tables. Shortly afterwards the mess bell rang and within minutes the mess hall began to fill with sleepy, disgruntled looking men, who would never accept rising early and eating what the army thought was good for them.

The mess sergeant assigned me to washing dishes. Barbeck was to scrub pots and pans, and Angelo was to wait at the tables. With each meal we moved to the next station so that by the evening meal each of us had been at all three. It was to be an unvarying routine, one I had already learned at the preceding camps. There was one even more disagreeable task and that was to clean the grease trap, which was located under the big sinks. That job was always the job the mess sergeants reserved for their special hatreds.

I started washing dishes. To get the dishes clean the water must be very hot, and it is laced with strong soap. As soon as the men were finished with their meal they took their dirty dishes and stacked them on the counter next to the sink. The speed with which the dishes arrived and had to be cleaned and then washed in the hot soapy water always made me feel like a rat in a treadmill cage that is speeding up to test the poor animal's limits. Having been on KP before, I knew what to anticipate and had stripped to the waist. By the time I had reduced the gigantic mountain of dirty dishes to manageable proportions, I was dripping with sweat. Now I had to arrange them on large towels for drying and then get them ready for redeployment on the tables.

I knew that the next station would be worse, and was prepared for it. Pots and pans, which I had to do at noon were much worse, because the water is even hotter and the soap attacks not just the grease on the pots but the skin of your hands. To handle dozens of heavy 20 gallon pots, greasy frying pans, and giant ladles and serving spoons made me think of what purgatory must be like. In all of these demanding physical jobs, I often thought back to the times when I shoveled coal on that tramp steamer between Singapore and Marseilles—how nice that I at least had an experience, which enabled me to count my blessings. Compared to dishes and pots and pans, the job of waiting at the tables was a sinecure.

While we peeled potatoes Angelo told me that he had been drafted in Italy and had served for three years in the Italian army. After that he had met his wife, a native-born American from Staten Island, who was visiting relatives in Sicily where he had worked. They fell in love, married, and he had come to America on a preferred visa just like mine and had found work as a laborer in a junk yard on Staten Island. After he had picked up enough knowledge he had started his own little junk business, which a relative of his wife was now running for him since he had been drafted. He was proud to tell me that his wife was having a bambino. His enthusiasm was genuine and I felt that he could not possibly be one of the stool pigeons.

By about eight we were done and on the way back to our barracks. Barbeck mumbled with real bitterness, "I volunteered to fight the Nazis in 1939 and fought in the French Foreign Legion over there, and what do they do to me here? They put me in a camp of Bund members, fascists and conscientious objectors! I'm fed up." Angelo chimed in "I would be glad to give up my citizenship if I could only get out of the army." All of us were weary and dead tired. A hot shower revived me and as I was lying on my bunk, I tried to sort out my thoughts. The work was not worse than it had been at Camp Lee. Sure the mess sergeant was a drunk and a bully and the cooks had been nasty, but that was not a reason to feel so totally drained.

I realized that the problem was the company in which I found myself. Barbeck had worked hard but not once had he relaxed or cracked a joke—off and on he had mumbled about injustice. Angelo wanted to go back to Italy. Once I had been drafted, I had felt that I had a job to do, and as yet I had not sunk as deep as those two. And then I remembered that while I was working near the kitchen, two of the cooks had hummed a Hitler Youth song, which I had heard many times while in Germany: Es zittern die morschen Knochen der Welt vor dem grossen Krieg (The world's decaying bones they tremble at the thought of the great war). The tune was catching. As I was lying there mulling and sorting out my feelings, I was aware that Barbeck was staring at me. When he saw me noticing it, he crushed his cigarette and went to sleep.

Lights went on at 5:30 for reveille the next morning. It was chilly. We lined up for roll call and were promptly dismissed. After breakfast a sergeant took me to "my beat," a section of the camp where I would from now on pick up papers, trash and matchsticks every morning. After that we were lined up for the assignment of details. I heard job descriptions that meant nothing to me but which in time I recognized:

Dam detail—Farmers—Cowboys—Movie actors
Rack Engineers—Sidewalk Gang—Janitors

After each of the first five details had been called there were still 10 men left who were now assigned to the Sidewalk Detail. The first sergeant, heartily detested by everyone, was creative in inventing jobs. Barbeck, Angelo, and I were to be members of the Sidewalk Detail, a job that required ten men. Our task was to build sidewalks connecting the various buildings in our area of the camp. On a piece of brown wrapping paper the first sergeant had prepared a sketch which indicated what he had in mind. A sergeant with a marked Harvard accent was designated as our leader. He indicated full comprehension of the task to be accomplished and collected us, string for measuring, a tape measure, a saw and some scrap lumber, a hand drill, a bag of screws, a screw driver, a mallet and two wheelbarrows. For the next week I built sidewalks. We speculated that there were three possible purposes: (1) The barracks would remain empty and the construction was ordered to keep us busy (2) The Service Unit was to be enlarged—need for a larger foreign legion, and (3) Improvement of the camp would meet the needs of the Pennsylvania National Guard.

The sergeant in charge picked one of the detail to assist him in the construction of the frames. These would hold the crushed stone, which another man and I would bring from a pile that had been dropped near the orderly room. At the beginning I showed moderate enthusiasm for getting on with the job, but I was quickly wised up by my co-workers who said that such attitude was neither needed nor welcome. Eager beavers were making life difficult for everybody. So it was that a job that could easily have been done in two days took about a week and a half and I was reminded of the early pictures of PWA workers who were always photographed leaning on their shovels. It would not be long before I too acquired the proper work ethic.

The other wheelbarrow operator was Watanabe, a tall Japanese American who spoke with an Alabama drawl and was about as Southern in manner and outlook as any soldier I had met. When I asked him how long he had been here, he shrugged his shoulders, "Maybe three or four months" he said, "I really don't care. This is easy." He was born on his father's farm in Alabama where they had raised vegetables and chickens. Maybe the Alabama air or the hominy grits had done wonders for his physical development, because he was about six feet tall with broad shoulders. In 1936 he had been in Japan for four months to visit relatives of his father. The visit was a strange experience he told me, because he was never really comfortable there. He felt like a giant among dwarfs and had difficulty with the language. His Japanese, which he had practiced only with his parents, was good enough for talk about chickens and vegetables, but his relatives were working in factories or trades and he could not keep up with them. The treatment of women in his uncle's family struck him as unfair and preposterous. One day while he was riding in a streetcar with his uncle, he wanted to offer his seat to a tired looking pregnant woman. His uncle had held him back and later lectured him on the position of women in Japan. He was totally upset when his old aunt knelt before him and his uncle to serve them food. Having grown up on hominy grits, vegetables and fried chicken he did not enjoy the steady diet of rice, pickled vegetables and the raw fish. But what he found most difficult to cope with was the feeling of being shadowed. Every day a man with thick glasses came and spoke to his uncle. Sometimes he thought the man was trying to follow him. After four months in Japan he was glad to get back to the States. His name was in the first draft. He got into the army and had been in 18 camps since 1940, and had run a big mess hall before he came here. He had kept his rank as a sergeant and would not have to do KP. The question of why he was sent here did not seem to concern him. There were several other Japanese in the unit but he did not associate with them any more than with the others. He was unconcerned and taught me how to be very slow with my work.

Barbeck and Angelo, my KP associates, were also on the Sidewalk Detail. Angelo spent most of the time speaking Italian with Paulinetto, an unpleasant shifty Italian—a man whom I had seen in my barracks on the day of my arrival and instantly disliked. Most of Paulinetto's conversation concentrated on Mussolini, women, and dice. Because of my lack of Italian I was never sure how profound his discussions on Mussolini or women were, but there was no doubt that on the subject of dice he always had an attentive audience. He carried a pair of dice in his pocket and produced them instantly for needed demonstration of his dice rolling technique. Several weeks later he showed clear signs of having been beaten up during a payday crap game. He had substituted loaded dice for his demonstration models and had been found out.

Another man on our Sidewalk Detail was Lichterman, a refugee from Czechoslovakia and trained chemist, who bitterly resented being assigned to do manual work. Considered this below his dignity, he practiced passive resistance by not working. Since none of us really worked, we hardly noticed that he did nothing, and we certainly did not object to his attitude. None of us ever saw Lichterman lift a finger; he had developed a technique of sleeping propped up by his shovel. In time his passive resistance brought him to the psychiatric ward of the camp hospital from where he hoped to obtain a medical discharge.

Our Harvard accented detail sergeant was difficult to fathom. Born in Germany, he had come to America with his parents when he was two months old and had spent all of his life in America. He had graduated from Harvard, studied a semester at Heidelberg in 1937, and attended a conference at which Alfred Rosenberg, the Nazi Party philosopher had spoken. Whether he was one of the stool pigeons that I had been warned about, or whether he was merely an odd duck, I never found out. But he had the strangest habit of never discussing anything political without prefacing every statement by citing a reference. When I asked him why he was always beating around the bush, he explained by saying: "Look here, it is really a matter of self defense. If you say that you think that socialism has some merit, you are immediately reported as a dangerous man—possibly a Communist. But when you say: *Time Magazine* reports that leading Englishmen consider socialism worthy of investigation and re-examination, nobody will object. This example you can apply to every situation. I figure that it is safest to be cautious." When I asked him why he was in the Foreign Legion he smiled and mentioned his birth in Germany and his studies at Heidelberg, and slyly added: "I am a member of the Republican Party which wants to overthrow the Democratic administration."

In the morning we had managed to finish about 10 yards of sidewalk. In the afternoon we went back. Paulinetto spoke about Mussolini, women, and dice; Watanabe discovered a spider that had caught a big fly and watched their struggle for hours. Occasionally the sergeant said "Let's go" which led to a brief readjustment of our resting positions. The landscape was idyllic, the weather pleasant and warm and if it had not been for the uncertainty, I could have liked the place. At 4:30, the end of our work day, we had constructed about 17 yards of sidewalk. We were dismissed to clean up for retreat and inspection dressed in khaki at 5:00 P.M.

Sergeant Bloom, the bugler, stood halfway between the orderly room and the barracks waiting to perform. Blowing six signals a day and shining his bugle did not really wear him out. He never lifted a finger and could always be seen reading mystery stories on his bunk. Now he was waiting for the signal to sound retreat. As always his signals sounded strained. All of us felt a little tense, doubting that he would make it, but he always managed somehow.

On the bulletin board at the mess hall that evening, I noticed that I and five others were listed to report to the camp photographer the next morning. Corporal Reuter, who stood near me kiddingly said, "Don't worry, we all have been there. They are looking for movie stars and this is their screen test. Hollywood is just crazy about those pictures." I was not particularly upset by being photographed—the FBI had done it before several times. After all, I was still an enemy alien, and the remarks of an older legionary in our group who considered it an invasion of privacy, did not really upset me. I always had to think how someone in a similar situation would fare in 1943 Germany.

A truck took the six of us, properly clothed in khakis, to the headquarters building where each of us had to pick letters from a print box to put together a strip showing our name and army serial number. With that identifying label placed in front of us, a photographer made the necessary photos (front and side) and then sent us back to our quarters. I was surprised that they did not fingerprint us.

What the pictures were used for was a matter of much conjecture. The most frequently heard hypothesis was that they wanted to compare the pictures with films that the FBI had taken at the German Bund rallies. Between the outbreak of war in August 1939 and before the United States entered the war, Germany had created a strong Nazi presence in America. Organized to resemble the Nazi storm troopers, the word, "Bund" (a synonym for association) had been chosen to give it an innocuous name. The Bund spread Nazi propaganda and preached racial superiority and isolationism to encourage resistance to America's growing support to the allies. Several months later, when I was made a citizen, I discovered the photo gracing my naturalization certificate.

After I returned to camp and had changed into my legionary's uniform, I found that my absence had retarded progress on the sidewalk job. It took another ten days to complete the assignment, giving me an opportunity to form a pleasant and unusual relationship with Angelo. Suspicion was a curious by-product of the assignment to the service unit and it made us cautious with each other. Who were the stool pigeons that were collecting information about us? There were several men who were obviously interested in befriending some of us. It was best to talk to them only about the chow. Angelo was not bright enough to be a stool pigeon and he had a problem which he confided to me. I knew from his many comments that he was deadly afraid of being shipped overseas and of being separated from his wife. From his earlier comments I knew that his wife was pregnant and that he had already obtained advance permission for a pass at the time of the anticipated delivery. His was a genuine problem of communication. He and his wife spoke Italian and English as the circumstances required, but she could neither read nor write Italian and Angelo could write Italian but could not read or write English. So, he asked me to become his secretary. Every evening we found a quiet corner where I wrote down for him the English letters that he dictated, and when the mail from his wife arrived, I read her replies for him. It was a wonderful experience to see him trying to put tenderness into English where Italian would undoubtedly have been much more persuasive. I was glad when I could help him find some way of saying what I suspected might be in his heart. He got his pass when the delivery was due and we all were waiting for him to bring the box of cigars that he had promised.

He did not show up when his pass expired and there was talk that he might have gone AWOL. Two or three days later I woke in the middle of the night because I had heard him come in and go to his bunk. I got up and looked at him in the semi-darkness and saw that he looked terrible. He was unshaved, his eyes were bloodshot and as I whispered inquiring about the bambino he merely said: "Bambino dead—beautiful boy, ten pounds, born dead." I asked about his wife: "She okay, we will try again she says." Even though he had been AWOL nobody made an issue over it, and that evening he dictated to me this letter of consolation to his wife.

"My beloved wife:

My trip back to camp was ok. I was sorry, but I could not stay with you. God will give us another boy. Don't worry and get better soon. All will be taken care of, and the doctor said the next baby will be much easier. Don't worry and forget this bad luck. There is nothing that is important, but get better and don't worry. I will write you. I cannot say all

that I want to say, but I think of you very much. I send you
my affectionate kisses and don't worry.

Your affectionate husband

Angelo."

After he finished dictating the letter he walked to the PX. When
I turned in later that night, I found a candy bar on my bunk and
Angelo nodded when I picked it up.

In the evening Angelo played in the crap game, was lucky and
won $40. He gave me all of the money and asked me to buy a postal
money order for his wife at the post office. In the morning he
changed his mind, or perhaps more accurately his luck had changed.
He had lost $20 and had borrowed that from one of the cooks. Now
he was sending only $15 home and keeping $5 in reserve until
payday, when he had to pay back the cook.

It was obvious that our mail was of interest to someone. Letters
from New York took five to six days and I soon found that they had
been pre-opened because when I received them they were almost
open. The glue had been steamed and they opened without the least
effort. Marion's letters were always typed so I did not see any evidence of the steaming technique, but one of the men showed me a
letter where the ink had spread due to the steaming and it was
almost impossible to read. There were many complaints but nobody
dared do anything about it for fear of punishment. In a way it felt a
little like being back in Germany, where one was always worried of
being under surveillance and in fear of the unknown.

Among my companions was an older lawyer, who had been just
as bewildered about coming to Indiantown Gap as the rest of us. He
had been in the first draft and must have been in his early forties.
He never mentioned why he had been sent to this outfit. When he
discovered that his mail was steamed open, he became agitated and
upset. Unlike the rest of us, he decided to see the captain to complain, even though we told him that it was a hopeless cause. We
stood around him to hear what he had done and how the captain
had reacted. He had first seen the First Sergeant to comply with all

army formalities and had obtained his permission to see the Company Commander. The captain had been smiling and very polite and had invited him to state his case. He had told the captain that his mail was not only delayed but had been steamed open. He had then pointed out that he was a native born American, that he had an unblemished record and that he was an attorney who knew that even the army must respect his rights and stay away from his mail. If the army thought it necessary to open and read the soldiers' mail in this unit there might be valid reasons to do so and he was not challenging that. But if he was not transferred immediately, he would have to raise the issue with his senator, pointing out that the practices in this unit were a violation of his rights, which had not been abrogated by the draft. The captain had listened politely. When he had finished his statement there were a few moments of silence and then the captain had quietly indicated that he would arrange for a transfer. He had thanked the captain, saluted and left the room.

This was certainly different from the way it would have been done in Germany. I could not possibly argue my case with the captain as I was still an enemy alien without any rights. But it crossed my mind: Would I be better off when I was finally naturalized? Could it be that only native born citizens enjoy all the rights granted by the Constitution? Would naturalization do little for me and would I have to be satisfied to remain a second class citizen because I was not born here? My course in Constitutional Law had not provided me with a ready answer.

After having proved myself at the Sidewalk Detail I was assigned to the Dam Detail. The pace of work was even slower than on my first job. Four sergeants and eight privates were assigned to build a path and a stairway across a little mountain that started at a tiny dam that regulated the overflow from a mountain stream. It was an ideal job to keep soldiers occupied and away from the barracks so that our possessions could be inspected leisurely by whoever wanted to learn more about us. The path that we so thoughtfully constructed led nowhere and was not used by anyone. It certainly looked like a well-planned army recreational project.

We used the same sidewalk building technique that I had been taught, but from time to time there was an elevation and we had to build stairs, which required cement reinforcement. It was my job to bring sand and an occasional bag of cement to Gato, a tall powerfully built Japanese who had developed a particularly effective technique of covering stairs with an absolutely perfect, smooth surface that was admired by one and all, even though it was produced at a snail's pace. Since he always was sitting in a deep crouch and held a smoothing tool in his hand, nobody could ever accuse him of loafing on the job. Like several of the other Japanese in the unit he had been born in the States and had returned to Japan as an adult after he had finished high school here. His father had been a laborer and his mother had worked in a laundry in Los Angeles. When his father died, his mother had returned to Japan and taken him with her so that he could get a college education. While living in Kyoto, it did not take him long to discover that he could never be satisfied living in Japan, where his mother had very quickly reverted to the culture she had left shortly after she had been married. Gato had attended an agricultural college in Kyoto and become interested in poultry farming. He had been taught to determine the sex of newly hatched chicks and he became an expert with this skill. When his Japanese family tried to select a wife for him he returned to Los Angeles and quickly found employment in one of the large chicken farms, where his skills were in demand and he was extremely well paid.

On my return from my first day on the Dam Detail, I saw my name on the bulletin for guard duty. Guard duty in our section of the camp was a charade. At 6 P.M. we had to report to the corporal of the guard, who equipped us with our guard weapons: a webbed cartridge belt without shells and a sawed-off billiards stick. We were given a route to walk and told to report back at the post every hour. Once at Camp Lee during my basic training I had been assigned to guard duty. The army wanted to teach us that guard duty was an important task. We were told that we had to protect our fellow soldiers so that they could rest. It was something I better know well if I ever would meet the real enemy. Then I had been handed a rifle and live shells and given a password that anyone approaching me better know if he was not to be shot. I had been ordered to demand the password when I saw anyone on my beat. Fortunately at Camp Lee nobody had approached me that night. Here at Indiantown Gap, nobody had given us weapons, a password or ordered us to challenge. Here the guard duty was akin to occupational therapy— keep the boys busy, make them do something—just anything. They did not trust us with a gun.

The night was clear with the moon up and it was chilly. In the distance I could hear the rumble of the heavy tank engines that rattled day and night along the mountain roads. From time to time Sally, the company dog came by to see that all was in order. My beat took me to the day room where a crap game was in progress.

From the outside I could hear Paulinetto's high- pitched voice calling "Seven may be." This was the night when Paulinetto was winning. The moment any of the other participants had the dice he bit his nails in an undisguised sign of nervousness. Among the men at the table was Rykowski, the crazy, mad Russian, who claimed to have fought as a youngster with the White Russians. His English communication was still difficult. But it was good enough for the essential exchanges during the crap game. He was a giant of a man and cursed everyone with his loud bellowing voice. Stripped to the waist he displayed blond fur that covered his chest, back and both arms like an animal pelt. The excitement of the game had made him break out in sweat all over. He was on the losing side and had just pulled a twenty dollar bill from a crumpled wallet before he resumed his combat with Paulinetto, who seemed to be invincible that night. When his twenty was gone he tried to borrow but no one was willing to give him a loan, so he grunted, cursed and left. At midnight my shift was over and I had four hours off.

KP was one of the curses of the army that I endured for almost a year. On my next stint, where Gato was also assigned I met a new arrival in camp. It was known that the first sergeant had developed the routine of a very early KP assignment for every newly arriving private. The new victim for the first sergeant's sadistic assignments was Spitzer. Uncombed and unshaved with a cigarette dangling from one corner of his mouth, he walked into the kitchen with a gait that reminded me of an Orangutan, his head moving with every step. He passed Gato and me to get to the counter and demanded a cup of coffee. Then he bellowed: "This is the goddamnest outfit I have ever been in. Everybody around here is a fake. Maybe it's a concentration camp and they have the nerve to throw you in the kitchen before you even have a chance to unpack your barracks bags." The cook gave him a cup of coffee and said, "Take it easy, bud, we don't like the place either. It is not a concentration camp and you better keep your damn mouth shut." After finishing work on the dishes and pots and pans we had a break and Spitzer told us that he had been with an artillery outfit that was getting "hot," meaning ready for shipment overseas. A few days before their shipment he had been pulled out and shipped here. His mother was Jewish and he had left Germany with her in 1937 because he was not an "aryan" and had no future in Germany. Now he was eager to get even with the Nazis and here he was at this lousy camp hearing German and Italian and sensing a strongly subversive atmosphere. Although Spitzer had worked well on KP on his first day in the unit I had the feeling that he was putting on a show. I never trusted him.

Was he perhaps one of the stool pigeons that I had heard about?

For only brief moments the curious tension that always hung over all of us would lift. One morning there was great excitement in the latrine. Sally, the company dog, had given birth to a litter of eight pups. They were in a margarine cardboard box, which the latrine orderly had stuffed with used dishrags in anticipation of the blessed event. A cheerful soul had made a sign **MATERNITY WARD—SILENCE.** Sally stood next to the box watching the crowd of curious soldiers coming to see her offspring.

The dam project proceeded at a snail's pace and since all of us realized that the road we were building led no where, it did not make any difference. I recall one afternoon a group of black soldiers came to swim in the small lake where we were upgrading the surroundings. It was obvious that they enjoyed being away from whatever they were doing. Suddenly one of my co-workers said aloud, "It's a shame that they permit those niggers to bathe where white soldiers swim. In Virginia, where I come from, they keep the niggers in their place." One of the men added, "In Texas they treat niggers just the same, but I wonder if it's right. They are drafted and they might get killed". Aaron, one of the refugees from Germany, who had thrown pebbles into the water, joined the discussion. "I agree, it's certainly wrong to have white and colored soldiers use the same beach. I wouldn't have colored men look at my wife when I go swimming". At that moment Mueller, the conscientious objector from Ohio, who rarely took part in any discussion, dropped his saw and said, "Aaron, I'm surprised to hear you say that. You were chased out of Austria by the Nazis because you were Jewish. I'm glad you came here to be safe, but a man with your sad experience should think twice before he makes such a remark. Those Nazis were very mean to you and your people in Europe because you were Jewish and instead of learning how hard that is, you are doing the same thing to others now." He picked up his saw, moved to the next pole to cut it and started working. Aaron's face was very red. For a few minutes everybody worked silently. Then the tension eased, Gato smoothed the steps, most of us leaned on our shovels and from below we heard the black soldiers splashing in the pond and enjoying themselves.

From our lookout man we heard that Gaertner, the CQ, was approaching from the Orderly Room. He walked up the stairs, crossed the road and climbed up the hill to where we were resting on our tools. He came to get Berger, a cheerful Hungarian who had been in the army since 1940 and had been in this unit for about 4 months. Two months after he landed in the U.S. he had been drafted. When he arrived he did not speak a word of English and what he had acquired in the two and a half years since joining the army was a mixture of technical words, ungrammatical chit chat, and a complete vocabulary of army slang and vulgarity. He dropped his shovel on which he had been leaning, took his Eleanor hat off, and while scratching his head said: "Well, them. . . . shipping orders must be there. Hell, now they will make me soldier again, goddammit, me lucky. . . ." With that he walked off to the orderly room. When we returned at 4:30, he was dressed in his khakis with his grip packed to go on a three-day pass before leaving for his new assignment. We all crowded around him trying to find out where he was going, but he did not know. The captain had not mentioned it and he had been too shy to ask. So, when he came back into the orderly room, the first sergeant had smiled at him and said: "Can you keep a secret?" Berger had eagerly replied, "Sure!" and the first sergeant had replied, "I can keep it too." Berger was livid with rage, but there was no way of getting back at the first sergeant.

I had been at Indiantown Gap for about three weeks when the orderly clerk told me to put on khakis and report at 3:30 to the intelligence officer at post headquarters. Army intelligence had interviewed me at Dix and Camp Lee, and I assumed that they would probably have some new questions to ask.

The interview at post headquarters was conducted by a young and very superior lieutenant. The questions were precisely those I had been asked at Dix and at Camp Lee, and when I mentioned that these identical questions and more had been answered before and were available from the Enemy Alien Hearing Board in New York and the FBI, he seemed annoyed, and told me to stick to his questions. The inquisition followed a pattern that I knew well. Since it followed a standard form, I had to be careful not to answer questions before they had been asked. After about 45 minutes I was dismissed and ordered to return to my unit. As time went on I began to understand that intelligence officers found it fascinating to interview a man who had seen Hitler.

Upon my return to camp my buddies who had been at the camp for a long time and knew how to assess the signs, assured me I would remain for at least ten weeks before the higher ups would make up their mind what to do with me—or it could be longer. Nobody, they assured me, with an accent like mine could hope to get through in a shorter time.

For some reason there had been no parades during my first three weeks in camp, but this Thursday, a murderously hot day, we were to participate in the post parade. It was held only for the units that administered the camp, not for the combat units that received their field training. At 3:45 the company assembled and stood at attention awaiting the arrival of the captain and the officers who would lead us. The captain gave a little speech in which he stressed that proper discipline was demanded and there would be no talking and particularly no German or Italian songs and no cracks at women, whom we might pass on the way to the parade ground.

We were the last unit to arrive at the assembly point before the movie theater. The clerical unit for the post and the two station complements were already lined up. A colored band was tuning their instruments—sort of like a jam session. Upon a signal, the band struck up a tune and moved onto the parade field followed by the post units with the 1576th Service Unit bringing up the rear. All units that preceded us had some sort of a banner, but we had nothing to display but ourselves. As soon as the post commander had received the reports from the various company commanders, the band passed the reviewing stand in rag time, with a display of uninhibited enthusiasm and a total suppression of military convention. I could not trust my eyes or ears! The only time that I had heard a colored band before was at the Savoy Ballroom in Harlem in 1935. I had been impressed particularly when I had seen the abandon with which the dancers on the floor had translated the music into an unbridled swirl of enthusiasm. But it had never occurred to me that such music could be adapted to military parades and could replace the Prussian type fierce music with which General Steuben had instilled martial spirit even into American revolutionary soldiers. My mind went back to the time only five years ago when I had paraded in Hitler's army, concerned with marching to the beat of the music and determined to conform every muscle to the perfect goose step. I was shocked by my first parade and felt a little ashamed. When we returned to camp, one of the men said: "Now you can see why we don't like to march at those parades." In time I became fatalistic about the parades and learned to endure them like KP, sidewalk building and other activities that superiors deemed necessary for my advancement. Compared to shoveling coal and serving in the German Army it was an easy way to spend time.

My correspondence with Marion had continued but the frequency of our letters had declined once we realized that her letters were opened before they reached me. She confided to me that she felt embarrassed to know that some sinister guy, probably with a green eye shade was "evaluating" her letters.

Whether my letters to her were similarly censored, I was never able to determine. I always took them to a mail box near the PX to avoid immediate identification with the Foreign Legion detachment. But despite these interferences with our correspondence two important messages reached me: (1) There was no question, Marion wrote, that she was pregnant with prospects of the arrival of the child which she had instantly named "Pee Wee" early in 1944, and (2) She did not think that my coming to New York with all the ridiculous restrictions that were imposed upon me made sense. Instead, being an experienced travel agent, she had researched the neighborhood of Harrisburg for a suitable motel and had found one overlooking the Susquehanna River a few miles above Harrisburg and easily reached by a local bus. So, she suggested that when time for my first pass was at hand, she would meet me on Friday evening in Harrisburg and we would take up weekend residence at the motel.

The prospect of being a father in the near future reminded me immediately of Wilhelm Busch's famous quotation: "Vater werden ist nicht schwer, Vater sein dagegen sehr (To become a father is very easy; however, to be a father is very difficult)." But with it came of course the instant question: What does a private in the United States Army with a cash income of about $13 per month give to his wife as a baby present? I had to come up with something spectacular. Whether this requirement was a flashback to my youth, when only something produced under sweat and tears would do, or whether it was something romantic that I had read since, I do not recall. But I was determined, despite my financial doldrums, to produce something outstanding. Always prepared to aim high, I called my friend Bill Froehlich in New York, a man of impeccable taste and excellent access to art treasures to disclose to him my problem. I suggested that a small original Duerer print of a Madonna and Child would undoubtedly fill the bill. He cautiously mentioned that even small Duerers were expensive—they rarely got on the market for less that $500 and more often reached $1,000 or more. At $5 a month, even taking into account possible advancements beyond private, it would require four or five years, perhaps longer to pay for my foible, but he would be glad to extend the credit. My weekly, furtive calls (Marion was not to know of this dream-project) gave me no encouragement, and as Marion grew in size, my nervousness increased and occasionally I urged my friend to exert himself more—a service that he could really perform as he, despite good health, had been spared the draft. About December 15th he told me that my problem was solved. He had located a Madonna and Child that most people who did not know much about art could well take for a Duerer print. The picture was small, about 3" x 5," and he would have it suitably framed. The price—complete—an unbelievable $75. How was this miracle possible? Who was the artist? The artist was Ludwig Krug of Nuernberg, the man who was reputed to have taught Albrecht Duerer the art of copper etching and in addition had so impressed Duerer with the necessity of creating an identification mark that would forever tie his name to that mark. That mark is, of course, the famous two letters AD, always placed into a tablet. And, to make the point on the Krug print there is the Duerer touch, a little table with the letters LK. When Helene was born and I saw her for the first time in Cincinnati I presented the Madonna and Child to Marion with a feeling of great pride. The picture that accompanied us every place we lived, now belongs to Lena.

There is one additional fact about that picture that merits telling. In September 1945, when I arrived in Nuernberg, and walked through the ruins of this historic city that I had seen in all of its glory before the war, my eye was arrested by a small plaque attached to a door entrance. The entrance was all that was left of the house. It read: "In this house lived LUDWIG KRUG - . . . . - . . . . a master engraver, whose most famous apprentice was Albrecht Duerer."

When my first pass came, I submitted my detailed weekend plan; it was approved without comment. As expected, I was rewarded with KP on the day following my pass. But the weekend was a refreshing change from the glum atmosphere of the camp. Suddenly our perspectives had changed. We could now, for the first time since we were married, think in terms of a family, something that we had not dared contemplate while the possibility of my confinement behind barbed wire as an enemy alien hung over us. To Marion my worries about my future in the army were of only secondary importance. "Relax. You are serving your adopted country," she assured me, "and ultimately they will find out that they can make better use of you than doing KP or peeling potatoes." It was the best advice that I could have gotten anywhere.

Our little motel with its moderate dining room housed us comfortably during my two-day pass. It sat on the bluffs of the Susquehanna, where I discovered the hunger stones, which in most years were covered by the river and could be seen only during drought years. Their location was known to the Indians as I had learned from Cooper's Leatherstocking Tales. Marion and I swam in the river, crossed it carefully stepping from stone to stone, and realized how life would be for me now, if I had not managed to get out of Germany.

My Monday morning's KP assignment brought no variations of the familiar pattern, except that the first sergeant informed us at dinner the captain would make an important announcement at 1:OO P.M. The company was lined up, awaiting the earthshaking news. We stood at attention, when the captain emerged from his office near the orderly room to give us "at ease" and deliver the following speech: "Men, for many of you this will be bad news—I must cancel all passes and furloughs. There is a serious emergency and we have to enlist your help in meeting it." A long pause. Could it be that we would be asked to do something worthwhile? Then the captain continued with a smile, so obviously it was not too serious: "The post has several hay fields and the post commander has chosen this unit to harvest the hay. Hay is a valuable commodity, the amount of hay involved is worth between $500 and $1,000 and we must do everything to bring it in. The first sergeant will read the names of those men who will work in the hay fields. They will work in two shifts six days a week and won't have to do KP or guard duty. I'm sure that every one of you will agree that this is an emergency and will not mind, if under the circumstances all passes must be withdrawn." With the command "Dismissed" he returned to his office and we stood there wondering what they would invent next as entertainment for us. With our work ethic, harvesting hay would not be a new test—but to cut our passes . . .

I was among the lucky ones selected for this emergency job. The first sergeant divided us into two groups. Group one would work from 7 to 12 and 5 to 9 on even days and from 12 to 5 on odd days. The thoughtfulness of this arrangement impressed us. Perhaps the first sergeant had in his youth worked full days on a farm and sweated? In my group was Rykowski, the mad Russian. After an early breakfast a large army truck brought us to a farm at the other end of the camp. The first thing we noted was that the stables were empty. There was not a single animal on the farm. We were handed brand new pitchforks and then moved to a field of fresh cut grass. It was still early, the hay was heavy with dew and it was cool. All of us sat under a big tree waiting for the sun to dry the hay before we could start turning it. Rykowski had taken his shoes off and was enjoying wiggling his toes and scratching his soles by moving them over the bark of one of the tree's roots. I had heard snitches of what Rykowski had done before he came to America, but now I could piece together a story similar to those of other Russians I had met who had managed to escape from the Bolsheviks.

At eleven, already large for his age, he fled the farm where he had lived with his family, and with his brother joined the White Russian partisan forces that resisted the Bolsheviks. His brother was killed and he lost track of his family. Despite his huge size he was a coward and could be intimidated by men half his size. His massive body needed much food and he bragged about getting it regardless of the needs of others. He would take two or three pieces of meat even if it meant that his comrades would starve. Somehow he had managed to get to a Black Sea port where he had joined a Spanish ship. For several years he worked on Spanish ships that took him all over the world. By that time he had grown into his enormous dimensions. His voice was a booming bass and his blue eyes under heavy brows gave an impression of fierceness that completely betrayed his cowardice. Soon he discovered that women were attracted to him. He exploited them as a pimp. Working for him they provided the money which he usually gambled away. Lazy, he moved from port to port and country to country staying only until the police caught up with him. He had acquired fluency in Spanish, spoke a fair English and had acquired a smattering of German, French and Italian, so that at the camp he would astonish newcomers from those countries when he butted in on their conversations in their native tongues.

When war broke out in 1939 ships were no longer safe. He decided on the United States as the safest place in the world. How he had managed to get admitted to the United States as an immigrant he never disclosed, but for a few weeks he had worked as a window washer at a hotel in New York. There he had met a chambermaid who liked him and for months provided him with bed and board. The few dollars that he earned in his job as window washer, gave him a start as a gambler along Broadway, where he picked up greenhorns and fleeced them with loaded dice. Once he found that skinning people along Broadway was much easier than window washing and less strenuous, he converted to full time con man operations on Broadway, until the draft caught him and exposed him to the dangers of war.

His attempts to avoid the army by mentioning his age were to no avail. He was careful not to resist the army too much for fear that they might release him and authorize his deportation to Russia. This he considered the ultimate fiasco, because the Russians might send him to fight the Germans or find out that he had served with the White Russians and either shoot him on the spot or send him to Siberia. So, reluctantly he had made peace with the American army, which fed him well and even gave him a small stipend sufficient to participate in occasional crap games. His main problem, however, was that the crap games usually cleaned him out. His main companions were Angelo and Paulinetto, who educated him on the theoretical aspects of these games and also taught him how to "correct misfortune" in other words taught him how to cheat without being caught. Among the men in the camp he was not popular because of his terrible table manners and the known fact of his cheating. However, since he told of his adventures with women realistic frankness that covered the most intimate details, he always had a group of listeners who were either attracted by his lurid tales or found his stories a welcome interruption of the utterly boring daily routine.

Rykowski was lying under the big tree and telling how he was arrested in Rotterdam when he had beaten up two sailors, who tried to take money from him. At the moment when he described the arrival of the police, the lieutenant showed up and made us start turning the hay. We worked slowly and it got warmer and warmer. After an hour we got a ten minute break. Most of us had taken off the fatigue jackets and were working in our undershirts. All of us were soaking wet.

Once we had turned the hay, the trucks came and we began loading. When the trucks were fully loaded I went with the first truck to the barn and helped unload. The truck entered a long passageway through an enormous Pennsylvania barn still half full with hay from last year. A big electrically operated claw that moved on a rail system suspended from the roof rafters, grabbed a load of hay, lifted it from the truck and dropped it where the lieutenant indicated. Two of our crew spread the hay in the semi-darkness of the barn. After loading and unloading about four or five of the trucks I felt that the work was about as difficult as shoveling coal in the tropics. If we had been assigned to fill the barns to maintain livestock it would have been a reasonable activity, but as it was it was just like building roads that led nowhere.

That evening the bunk next to mine had a new occupant. He had come from an air corps unit. Dave Lott was just as depressed as everybody who came to this camp. Like everybody else he asked: "Why did they send me here into this camp of foreigners?" I could not answer him and after he had calmed down a little I asked him what he did in civilian life. He had been working in the garment industry in Manhattan and in the last years before he was drafted he had organized garment workers to join the local union for better wages. Well that fit the pattern. He would find among the inmates several men who were union organizers—obviously the army considered them revolutionaries, on the same level as Communists or Nazis.

After a week on the hay detail I reported that I was sick from the dust, and I was assigned to build an enormous cement and steel structure that was to serve as a grease rack for vehicles. Before this project had been dreamt up, there had been a wooden platform of about 15 x 20 feet on which the garbage cans were lined up and could be hosed down with a stream of water from a nearby faucet. Someone had obviously determined that a grease rack was needed in the middle of this idyllic rest camp, while there were grease racks galore in the main camp where tanks and heavy trucks could be serviced with ease. The new design showed specifications for steel reinforcements, cement thickness, etc., and it was designed to withstand air attacks. Gradually, day by day we could see the monster rack growing in size. Finally after about two weeks of mixing tons and tons of cement our task was completed. The company commander came to inspect the job, praised our work, and returned to his office after he had picked up some ice for drinks at the kitchen. Whenever I think about Indiantown Gap, I am sure that the grease rack is probably the only thing still standing. I never saw a car being greased, but before long we were instructed to store the garbage cans in the rack. They were now more difficult to reach and we could not hose them down as easily as before. But the army in its infinite wisdom had discovered a method to protect the garbage cans from rain.

It must have been on a Sunday when five or six of us went to the little lake to swim. We were united by the realization that we were trapped in a camp that in some way would sort us out before we could be used, and we had accepted this as a necessary evil. Pat had just received orders for a new assignment and we wanted to say goodbye to him and tell him that we would miss him. We had found a shady place and Pat, a charming man from New England who had been sent here because he had advocated that all public utilities should be state-controlled and other "revolutionary" ideas like shortening the time for patent protection, had now been cleared and was about to ship out. We all had liked him and were sorry to see him go. The atmosphere was relaxed. Our discussions moved to whether our paths would ever cross again and then we wondered what the war would ultimately achieve. Most of us were convinced that little would change in America, except that women who now worked in factories and proved their equality would demand more rights. Reuter, one of the regulars, agreed with Pat, who, as always had come back to his pet peeve about privately owned utility companies, which he thought should be operated by the state, but he thought that the main change would be the end of the supremacy of the white race. The Chinese and Filipinos who had helped in the war would demand recognition and equality. As we were just moving into the discussion of racial prejudice, Sgt. Patterson, one of the original cadre non-coms, came walking over from the camp to join us. Nobody trusted him. The conversation did not stop at all, but with a subtle wink in his eyes, Reuter kept the conversation going as if we were still on the subject we had been discussing when Patterson joined us—"Pat you are right, education is an important aspect of public policy and it will be broadened after the war is *won*."

It must have been at the end of July or the beginning of August when Bauer, a new arrival, was shipped in and assigned the bunk next to mine. He was about my age, of medium height, lean and with a dark tan that one often sees on people who have done a lot of skiing. It was obvious from the moment he set foot in the camp that he was a stool pigeon. Actually what gave him away was the astonishing amount of information that he already had about many of us. On the first evening he accompanied me to the PX to buy a piece of soap and to tell me, in his accented English, of his miraculous escape from Nazi capture in Austria in 1938, just after Hitler had taken over. He then casually mentioned his service in the French Foreign Legion. He claimed to have fought with the Legion against the Germans in France, which I felt was unlikely but which I praised as virtuous. He somehow knew that I was from New York and expressed interest when I mentioned that Marion was working in the publishing business. He suggested that we could visit New York together and that he would love to meet Marion. He mentioned that he had interesting material that he was attempting to place.

A few days later he came back to the topic of a visit to New York. He also talked about the stuff from the Foreign Legion that he wanted to place. I told him that I would not get a pass to go to New York but if he got there he should call Marion at Gramercy 5-1336. She worked as a secretary to the editor-in-chief and she could give him the address of Lurton Blessinggame, an agent who could help him with his material. Bauer was delighted. I wanted to be helpful, and it had not occurred to me that I had sent my friendly stool pigeon inadvertently on a wild chase

Marion told me on her next visit to Harrisburg that Bauer had called her and asked for Lurton's telephone number. Bauer continued his interest in me, but like most, I felt uncomfortable with him. Contacts dwindled and then ceased. I had classified him in my mind as a stool pigeon and when I left Indiantown Gap, I was glad to forget him. But the army having engaged his services wanted to get more mileage out of him and possibly out of me.

Bauer would re-enter my life four or five months later, after I had been liberated from Indiantown Gap and ended up in the XIII Corps Headquarters in Fort DuPont, Delaware. At the corps headquarters I was often interrogated by intelligence specialists, always in the precise manner in which I had been questioned at all the preceding army stations. I gained the impression that when new officers were assigned to the section, they were given the job of interviewing me as a training exercise. It became a never varying activity that was repeated about every two or three weeks. I would report, as ordered, be questioned and answer the inquisition with precision. After about 45 minutes I would be released to continue with my work.

I had again been summoned to report and instantly noticed that the interrogation would follow a different pattern. This time it was the colonel in charge, accompanied by several of his subordinates, who would hold the interrogation. Clearly the colonel was up to something special. He had my file before him. I noticed that it was more massive than before, and there was a marker in the file, where he occasionally took a quick glance. The interview followed the conventional pattern with the same routine answers. And then came the great moment, where the colonel was going to show how to catch the Nazi Spy. Clearing his throat and lowering his voice he said, "And now, Private Von Rosenstiel—who is Lurton Blessinggame?" I almost fell off the chair, laughing out loud—an unpardonable sin in the army and particularly in the presence of officers of high rank. I realized that this was a serious matter to the colonel and suddenly I saw Bauer, that funny Austrian stool pigeon before me. I turned serious and explained patiently that during my confinement with the 1576th Service Unit at Indiantown Gap Military Reservation, one Corporal Bauer had asked me if I could give him the name of an agent to place material on the French Foreign Legion for publication with a publisher in America. I had given him the telephone number of my wife, who was employed by the Doubleday Publishing house in New York and knew Lurton Blessinggame as a reliable and competent literary agent. Apparently Bauer was not familiar with the book publishing business and assumed that Lurton Blessinggame was a "foreign agent," engaged in sinister and dangerous activities. I would have thought that a glance at the Yellow Pages of Manhattan could easily have answered most questions about Lurton Blessinggame. The colonel was clearly an-noyed and I was sent back to my work.

After this brief diversion we are back at Indiantown Gap. The irritation in camp was noticeable. The Hay Detail had been at it for almost three weeks and had filled barn after barn with no sign of animals to use the hay. What took the cake was an article from a local paper that was pinned up on the bulletin board:

AT INDIANTOWN GAP PATRIOTIC SOLDIERS
HELP FARMERS BRING IN THEIR HAY CROP

The soldiers are all volunteers, who work after they are through their day's training. For the last few weeks they have brought in hundreds of loads of hay which otherwise would have rotted in the fields and which now will feed many heads of livestock and will materially help in the war effort. The Post Commander and the Governor of the State have repeatedly visited the unit and have expressed their appreciation for the magnificent spirit shown by our men in uniform.

There was a throng of men around the bulletin board who read it in silence. When the captain passed on his way to the mess hall, a clear voice said: "Fine stuff these bastards write—it's just crap."

It was now nearing the end of August. The company was at lunch when the company commander got up and spoke. As usual he was polite and suave but there was something in his voice that made it clear he wanted to be understood without fail. The room turned very still. The cooks were leaning against the counters, the KPs had stopped clattering with dishes and pans, only the big ventilator over the stove could be heard, sounding like a distant waterfall. Then the captain spoke:

"Men, you have heard that the Pennsylvania National Guard Division will be assigned to this camp for their fall training begin-ning next week. Some workers will come into our area to make some changes in the buildings that have not been used for some time. During the time when the home guards are here I do not want you to talk or sing in any language except English. That means there will be no German or Italian spoken in this camp. Nobody from this unit will talk to members of the home guard or visit their tents. I do not want to see anyone play dice or drink beer with any of those people. There will be a special PX in the camp area for the convenience of the home guards; no member of this outfit will use their PX or any facility made for them. Is that clear?" After a pause of silence he said: "Any questions?" Rykowski, the mad Russian, got up and said: "May I talk Russian to myself?" Everybody was just about to burst out into a storm of laughter when we saw the captain's face turning red, the veins on his neck getting thick. All faces turned into tense silence. Then the captain said: "Rykowski, you know what I mean, Russian will not be spoken." The captain dismissed us and walked back to his office. We were wondering if he, too, lost his temper from time to time.

For the next week scrubbing and clean-up converted the area into a model camp. A construction company came for major repairs and additional construction. And then the Pennsylvania National Guard arrived. They were all volunteers and they would have a leisurely two week training course after which they would go back to their families and jobs until they were mobilized and sent to the front—which to most of us meant never—by 1943 few National Guard units had been sent.

And then they came, led by a band that played "The old gray mare, she ain't what she used to be." The drummers beat the skins like crazy and the brass instruments showed that their players were not short of breath. Suddenly the whole camp was transformed into a big county fair. The Home Guards had new uniforms and gleaming new rifles with bayonets. We stood in silence watching this display of military might. In our blue denims and Eleanor hats, we looked like prisoners and we were frankly envious.

At supper the captain again called the company to attention. It would be necessary to have table waiters for the Guard officers' mess and some extra KPs. They would be paid $1 extra per day—and it was all voluntary. There was no showing of hands, just silence. The captain waited for a few moments and when nobody came forward he said: "Well, then I will have to select the people who will do this work. You all know that I have the records of all of you and will very quickly determine those who have the necessary experience." That remark helped. The men assigned to this job worked seven days a week from 5:30 A.M. to 9:00 P.M. for four long weeks while the National Guard gave two training courses of two weeks each to ready their officers and men for war. At the end of those weeks we hated hearing their battle hymn, "The old grey mare . . ."

On August 23, 1943, Marion had taken the Pennsylvania railroad to New York after a wonderful weekend at our little motel on the Susquehanna and I had returned to my post. To my surprise I did not find myself on KP, the usual reward that the first sergeant had reserved for privates who had been on pass. I merely found myself on the roster for guard duty. So, August 24 started at midnight, when I began my beat armed with the rifle belt and the sawed off billiard stick, fearful that a soldier from the National Guard would accidentally challenge and shoot me with his beautiful new rifle.

The following is from the letter that I wrote to Marion on the evening of August 24. Marion had typed my handwritten letter and mailed it to her friend Marvin Felheim, who was then a captain in the air force in England. He returned it to us with Marion's note still clipped to it with a safety pin:

> I'm sure this will interest you greatly. But keep it just for the family. It all happened so fast that it's still unbelievable. Incidentally Werner's furlough request has been refused.
>
> M.

> This is not an ordinary communication but the first letter of a brand new U. S. citizen. To give a blow by blow account I shall start at 12:20 A.M. when I returned to camp. To my surprise my name was not included in the group of KPs but

I found myself on the guard roster for that night. This letter is, therefore, written while I am off the beat around my territory. I fell asleep after a shower and rose rather bright and still enchanted by the wonderful weekend to have breakfast, calisthenics and "short order drill." After that I found myself on a detail which had to remove the mattresses on which the Home Guard had nursed their tired bones. We were bringing the mattresses to a depot where the WACs will get them after they have been sterilized.

I was just bending low under a load of two mattresses when a truck came screaming around a corner and yelled for me. I was pulled out from under the mattresses and the boys waved me a sad farewell (because they realized the impending loss of a KP). The truck rushed me to the barracks and the driver told me that I had to get quickly dressed in khaki and report to the orderly room. When I reached the barracks the captain admonished me to hurry, because my naturalization was up. Sweating from the mattresses, panting from the rush and slightly smelly from the nervousness, I threw myself into my uniform, rushed to the orderly room, jumped a truck and was off to the appointed building. The room was so bare of furniture that it almost looked like a frontier lawyer's office. The room, maybe 25 x 20, was filled with about 20 soldiers and three civilians. The most important person was the clerk, who interviewed each and every soldier and wrote brief notes on the final application. He wore a jacket despite the heat, apparently in an attempt to give some dignity to the occasion. He was quite industrious and a rapid worker, who smoked with the kind of abandon which one often sees in very nervous persons. The deputy clerk, not responsible for any dignified appearance had taken off his green jacket. The interviews proceeded very rapidly until the man came to me. I do not know what it is, when I have to explain my immigration into this country with all the preceding complications, most people get more than somewhat interested and this fellow was no exception. The fact that I have a quite complete family over there caused him to write many more lines than most of the other fellows were awarded.

We were released for lunch and then loaded on a truck that took us in about 45 minutes to the courthouse in Lebanon for the naturalization ceremony. While sitting on the truck I saw myself at the threshold of the new land and although I had thought so much about it, I was emotionally quite unprepared. I felt that I should have about a day or two of contemplation so that I might clearly and concisely realize all the implications of this tremendous change. The time was too short for me to get any order into the mass of thoughts, feelings, hopes and expectations. Jefferson was in my thoughts and you were and somehow I thought of John F. X. Finn, and for a moment Mother's face was there, trying to understand my decision. The truck slowed down and rumbled into Lebanon to unload us in front of a gray painted brick building with a New England belfry on top.

We were herded toward the courtroom through a long corridor, which smelled like all older government buildings. It is a conglomerate of scents from cold cigar butts, brass polish, disinfectant from toilets to just regular human stink. A few signs informed us that the rooms belonged to clerks selling dog and hunting licences, and accepting fines and filing wills. We arrived at a large courtroom and sat down. A door opened and an exceptionally fine looking man in the judicial robe appeared. We got up while he assumed his seat on the bench. The court crier made us form a half circle in front of the judge. Once we were lined up, the judge looked at us silently for quite some time perhaps because he was aware that this was a farce of what should be done in an instance of such importance. His face was sad and his eyes seemed to say—what is it that I could give you? Perhaps if I knew you or could talk to you for some time, I might make you understand that this is perhaps the greatest moment of your life—but you men are in a hurry; you are not prepared to listen to a civilian—you listen to orders only. So instead of giving us anything like a talk, he only said: "Your uniform alone gives evidence that you are willing to make this country your home and defend it. When you now receive your citizenship remember that it is conferred upon you by a civil court; that by itself is something very significant, because there are few countries left in this world where a civil court can still function and command the attention of even the military authorities. To preserve this status is fighting for democracy." That was a fine thought and perhaps in a nutshell meant as much as he could give us, but I am afraid few of the boys understood what he was talking about. Standing in the middle of the half circle I noticed blank faces right and left. "What is a civil court? What does it have to do with democracy? What is democracy?" their faces seemed to say.

Then he turned the proceedings over to a major, a chubby fellow who gave us the cheery, cliche stuff with "The most liberty loving country " and its achievements in the line of dams and railroads, of factories and electricity. It was like selling a customer on taking a sightseeing trip through the U. S. with a pep talk, given by a proud agent of Thomas Cook, Ltd. There was not a word about our obligations of citizenship—he did not mention the right to worship freely and to read books we like, to educate our children at home. His America and the rights of citizenship seemed to consist in a rightful share in bigger and better automobiles, trout fishing on Sundays and the conviction that progress cannot fail in a land that is richer than any country in the world. His speech came to an end when he had reached the bottom of the page on which he had written his theme: "On the thoughts worthy to be conveyed to soldiers upon the occasion of their becoming citizens." He handed us our certificates. We saluted, returned our alien cards and for a few moments could physically convince ourselves that we were actually fully qualified members of the community of America. Then they took away the certificates and told us that they would be made part of our service records.

America is losing an opportunity by giving away the greatest right and privilege like handing out a set of uniforms. It may be that I am too sensitive and perhaps romantic, but still how can a poor immigrant be blamed for disgracing his rights and privileges if he is never really told. The church makes every child remember their communion; even as sober a church as the Lutherans; can't the democracies see that they have a mission too?

Tomorrow I shall write of a few business matters, but today I just want to think about you and the tremendously important fact that I am now a citizen of the United States of America, something really great in these sad times.

"With all my love—I sign the letter your Citizen Werner"

Judging from the experiences of the many foreign legionaries who had been made citizens before me, I knew that my orders for transfer would come soon and it was only a question of whether the first sergeant would select me for one more KP session. Instead, the next morning the first sergeant ordered me to report at once to the intelligence officer at the Post Headquarters. With his gritty smile he added: "You probably caused some trouble." A jeep took me there and I reported to the G-2 section where the young officer, who had quizzed me several months ago, sat at his desk waiting for me, looking very stern. In his hands he held a Western Union telegram. I came to attention, saluted and stated: "Private Von Rosenstiel, reporting as ordered" in my most military fashion. With a grim stare, disclosing utter disapproval, he said: "Soldier, you know that it is forbidden for a soldier to send coded messages and you are not authorized to receive them!" I meekly replied that I had not sent any coded messages and that I was not aware that anyone had sent me such messages. With that he handed me the Western Union telegram, addressed to me with Army serial number and unit designation, with the following text:

"Luke 2, 14

John McCaffery"

I was about to break into a quick laugh, but suppressed it realizing that to the lieutenant this was a major issue. I pointed out that this must be a congratulatory message sent by a friend on the occasion of my having been made a citizen yesterday. By way of explanation I suggested that it looked to me like a biblical citation and offered to go to the chaplain's office to procure a New Testament. Greatly annoyed the officer permitted me to go next door and borrow the New Testament from which I read:

Gospel of St. Luke, Chapter 2, Verse 14
Glory to God in the Highest,
Peace on Earth,
Good Will toward Men.

He now recognized the passage, but perhaps felt that in August it was out of season and inappropriate. He handed me the telegram and instructed me to advise Mr. McCaffery not ever to send coded telegrams to any soldier as it was forbidden in war times. I saluted and left his office to return to camp.

The next day my orders came and took me to the 67th Quartermaster Laundry battalion at the Elkins West Virginia Mountain Training Area. I had finally joined the United States Army. Now I began to realize that my time in Indiantown was in fact a probationary period during which the army wanted to have an undisturbed opportunity to observe me and perhaps even use me in the training of intelligence personnel stationed not far from Indiantown Gap at Fort Ritchey, Maryland—the army's intelligence training center. It also would give them time to decide what to do with me and to select a job where I could do no harm.

Had I been a little bit more perceptive, I might have realized that the army's decision to send me to a Quartermaster Laundry Battalion was a brilliant solution. Here was an elegant way to neutralize this newly created citizen who only recently had been labeled an enemy alien. Permanent assignment to marking dirty laundry, or keeping inventories of shoes, field jackets and handkerchiefs would keep me safely occupied for the duration. The army had pegged me for safe, uneventful activities—it was a perfect solution, EXCEPT that the Army had not taken into account the ambitions of Captain Scoggins of the 49th Machine Record Unit at the XIII Corps at Fort DuPont Delaware.

CHAPTER 4

THE DREAM OF CAPTAIN SCOGGINS

MY COMRADES AT the Quartermaster Laundry Battalion in Elkins, West Virginia were wonderful. The battalion's first sergeant and his assistants had studied my service record. There was nothing about me that they did not know and they were delighted to have somebody in their midst who had been in Germany and Japan in those fateful years before the war and could tell them about it. My having seen Hitler and most of the notorious men of the Nazi era made me a mixture of a peeping Tom and a war reporter. Lt. Col. Cooper, the battalion commander, gave his non-coms a free hand to run the place and did not care about trivia. He was glad that his people were happy to have me. In his office hung the unit's flag embroidered in gold thread on light blue silk with the assuring motto: **We Wash'm Out !!**

This group of non-coms could not hear enough about what I

had seen. Although I was considerably older than any of them they soon found an apartment in town where I was invited to join them. We could live in comfort and would not have to face the cold winter in the six man squad tents with Franklin type stoves and the nightly crayfish visitors that were native to the area. They assured me that KP was something for which they had lots of better qualified privates and I immediately accepted the wisdom of their planning. During the day I took inventory, learned how the army coped with dirty laundry and was happy to serve my country. In the evenings I socialized with my newfound buddies and went to a nice YMCA in town, where I jotted down my impressions of Indiantown Gap.

The future looked wonderful, the only problem was the distance to New York—about 550 miles. Marion was not enthusiastic about my assignment to the mountains of West Virginia. We knew West Virginia was one of the states that we crossed on Route 22, when we drove to Cincinnati, but we were blissfully ignorant of the mountainous location of Elkins. Marion researched rail connections and cities with hotels for an early reunion, and selected Clarksburg, which she could reach in about seven hours by train and I in about two hours using Greyhound. The chances of getting a pass for such an extravaganza were excellent with all my new friends rooting for me.

And then, only four weeks after my arrival, a teletype arrived from XIII Corps Headquarters ordering me to report at once to the commanding officer of the 23rd Machine Records Unit at Fort DuPont, Delaware, a mere 120 miles from New York.

My newly acquired buddies, although depressed about losing an accredited entertainer, gave me a great farewell party, pressed my tickets, travel orders, and the famous brown envelope into my hands and loaded me with my barracks bags on the train to Wilmington. I had just accepted a life of service in the army cleaning department as my contribution to the war effort and now what? In Wilmington I boarded a bus for Fort DuPont. As I am trying to trace my steps more than fifty years later, I find that Fort DuPont, like so many places that I have known, has vanished from this earth and can no longer be located on today's maps. Probably the army sold the area to a developer to reduce the Federal debt—but to me Fort DuPont remains forever the launching platform for an astonishing army career.

At that time Fort DuPont, about 15 miles South of Wilmington, had been a typical army post for many years, with the standard red brick office buildings, officers' quarters and barracks. In 1941 wooden buildings had enlarged the capacity of the post. A stockade at the edge of the area had been converted in 1943 into a prisoner-of-war camp to house the first German soldiers of Rommel's Africa Corps taken in North Africa.

I reported to the post headquarters where the CQ had an orderly take me to the 23rd Machine Record unit. The administrative office was in one of the new wooden buildings. With my brown envelope in hand I reported to the desk sergeant and was told that Captain Scoggins, the unit's commander, was still there and wanted to see me. Entering his office, I gave him my very best salute and handed him the brown envelope with my service record.

Captain Scoggins was in his middle thirties, about 5'6", and a little overweight. It was obvious that he was not a regular army officer but rather a businessman hastily put into an officer's uniform, one of the thousands of business executives who had been drafted and commissioned because his business skills were suddenly needed. He had the friendly attitude of a man in middle management, and he was eager to spot good recruits for the business, which he was now running for the army. And here I stood before him—identified by the infallible IBM card as a very bright prospect—a really perfect match for his outfit.

With his strong Southern drawl he explained to me that machine record units were the most advanced technical units in the army. The complex IBM equipment, managed by him and his men, provided the fighting men much needed vital statistical information through the use of specially designed IBM machines—the word computer had not yet been invented. With glowing pride he mentioned that his unit was composed of the brightest men that could be found in the army and that he was determined ultimately to command the unit with the highest AGCT score in the whole United States Army. And, with a friendly wink he added, "Your high score of 147 is just what we need here, and since you have worked with IBM equipment in your civilian job, I just decided that I had to bring you in here as a perfect addition to our crew."

After this delightful sales pitch, worthy of Thomas Watson, the legendary chairman of IBM, he opened the brown envelope. When he saw the service restrictions in my service record that made me useful only in lowly quartermaster assignments, he saw that his great coup was beyond his reach. He looked like a little kid who had just seen his balloon take off. I felt sorry for him, but probably more sorry for myself, worrying where I would be shipped next.

But Captain Scoggins was a decent man. Sadly he looked at me and said: "Once the G-2 guys find out about all those restrictions they have written into your service record, they'll yank you out from my outfit. After all, we handle very confidential material. But that may be two or three months away, and I'll keep you for that time and give you jobs where I can tell G-2 that you never laid eyes on restricted or confidential material. And, when they start pressing me to get rid of you I'll see if I can't get you some assignment in corps headquarters, where I have many friends. I know that you studied law and I am sure that they can use your legal training. Let's wait and see."

And so I had graduated from laundry to IBM. The man who actually ran the outfit for the captain was Charley Kurek, a charming bachelor about 38 years old, who had been one of the first to computerize a railroad—the Central Railroad of New Jersey. And now he lorded over about fifty men who worked in half a dozen big trailer trucks loaded with the newest IBM equipment and the necessary generators that made the unit completely independent of locally supplied electricity. They could operate in the Sahara or in Siberia, as long as the army provided gasoline. Today all the work that could be squeezed out of those six big monsters would probably be produced in minutes from a lap top computer and laser printer.

I went back on frequent KP but it did not really matter, because all weekends were automatically off-duty and the round trip to New York by Pennsylvania Railroad was only $5.20. Marion, about five months pregnant, was delighted to see me cheerful and now close by.

My new work was simple—equipped with brown paper and string, I became an expert at bundling IBM cards and reports and mailing them to the Pentagon, confident that they would never be opened or read. Only one event of my work has remained vividly with me. Captain Scoggins suddenly called the whole unit to the administrative office. It was very urgent and he was furious. He sat at his desk, his face bright red, and we realized that something terrible must have occurred. Every morning Charley would place before him one of those endless, gigantic reports that the machine had printed during the night. The captain would examine the first few pages, the proud evidence of his crew's competence, sign it, and turn it over to me for wrapping and shipment to Washington. This time curiosity had gotten the better of him and he had turned perhaps 200 pages and discovered that hundred of pages had been imprinted with the most popular army term:

F . . . you, f . . . you, f . . . you, f . . . you, f . . . you f . . .
you, f . . . you, f . . . you, f . . . you, f . . . you

Endlessly it went on for page after page repeating this simple, popular phrase. Nobody had noticed it. How could this have happened? It remained a mystery that was never solved. All the men were questioned individually and intensively and swore that they had no knowledge and would never have done such a disgraceful, filthy thing. I certainly had nothing to fear because all of it was confidential information, which was barred from my eyes. Whether some of the men had perhaps perjured themselves was a question of interpretation. Ultimately Captain Scoggins accepted Charley's clever explanation. Obviously, Charley argued, some practical joker at the IBM factory must have programmed this as a test sentence onto some of the spare parts and forgotten to remove it, before turning it over to the army. I was very relieved that I was clearly innocent since I had not been exposed to genuine confidential information.

On one of my visits to New York I managed to get myself admitted to the bar. Again my tendency to romanticize events in advance played tricks. Marion and her parents were present and all of us, I in particular, expected something impressive. I imagined myself standing before a judge listening to lofty declarations about equal justice for all and then swearing to uphold the Constitution in a crowded courtroom with an American flag. Instead, a clerk at the New York Supreme Court office on Madison Avenue led us into a small, dirty room filled with big books. He took one of the books down, imprinted **Attorneys Register,** placed it on the table and said: "Sign your name here and hurry—I have to get to the courtroom— and don't forget to pay the $20 at the cashier. We'll send you the certificate in about two months." With that he ran off and I was an attorney of the State of New York. Marion laughed and called me esquire. My father-in-law took us to a restaurant for a sandwich and a cup of coffee. The certificate arrived in a short time and is still in the cardboard shipping roll.

Captain Scoggins was right. After about two months the intelligence crew got hold of me, studied my service record, gave me the routine going over, but did not return me to Elkins. Upon the captain's urging they let me work for Lt. Col. Decker, the Corps Judge Advocate, a West Point graduate who at the outbreak of war in Europe had providently switched from the infantry and weapons to the law and paragraphs. Impressed with my legal credentials he instructed me to provide him daily with an ample supply of superbly sharpened pencils for his desk. My industriousness in meeting his pencil requirements persuaded him to test my other skills and soon I found myself writing briefs and court martial opinions in officer cases. Strictly speaking they were considered confidential, and thus were in an area where I was not permitted to operate. But by not stamping them "Confidential" they allowed me do the work unchallenged. Once I had drafted the opinion, the chief clerk marked it "CONFI-

DENTIAL" and thereby removed it from being again seen by me. I was happy to see somebody use his head and am proud to report that Col. Decker's acuity was ultimately recognized and rewarded when he became Judge Advocate General of the Army.

In December of 1943 during a weekend visit to New York I was hospitalized with the flu. When I returned to my post in January I was told that my sickness report contained instructions that for the next two weeks I should play basketball every day for one hour to build my strength after a severe case of flu. My basketball instructor was Lt. Peter Flanagan, a young lawyer from Brooklyn who had obtained an officer's commission in the Judge Advocate's Department and had been assigned to Colonel Decker's section. Since his officer's record showed that he had been a prominent college basketball star he had been given the job of developing a basketball team for the post in addition to his duties at the judge advocate's office. Being still in fairly good physical shape I found playing basketball a challenging sport. I had never played it before and it was not likely that in those two weeks I would develop any skills or even any comprehension of the finer points of this sport. But it was fun and Lt. Flanagan and I became friends. He taught me a tiny dose of basketball and entertained me with tales of the glamour of being a basketball star. In exchange I told him about the inner workings of Col. Decker's office and helped him write opinions for the colonel, whose legal idiosyncrasies I had by that time completely analyzed.

On January 14, 1944 while I was reviewing court martial cases, I received a telegram with the news of Helene's birth. Marion had gone to Cincinnati, where her family lived, to have the baby. Col. Decker graciously gave me the day off. Dressed in my parade uniform I decided to go to Wilmington and see if I could con Willard Crane, a cousin of Paul Geier's who was then the director of research for DuPont, to take me to lunch. A milk truck gave me a ride into town and Willard bought me a fine lunch where we toasted Marion and Helene. After I bought some Phillies for distribution among my friends at the post I returned—proud and happy. Marion, whom I telephoned in the evening at the hospital, sounded pleased and was working on plans for when I could come to Cincinnati. She sounded particularly pleased when I reported to her the next day, January 15th 1944, that I had been promoted to PFC—private first class. It did not exempt me from KP but it increased my monthly pay by $8—about one and a half fare to New York.

At the beginning of February I received my first one-week leave to go to Cincinnati. It was a wonderful visit. Marion was home from the hospital and was being trained by her three maiden aunts to take care of Helene. Except for the nursing activities, where Marion was better qualified although not very efficient, all of them had practiced their nursing skills on Marion, and her brothers and were delighted to assume responsibility for the first product of the new generation. I was carefully instructed on bottle warming techniques, diaper changes and all the endless procedures that until then I had successfully avoided. But it was fun, and I very quickly found that Helene was not nearly as fragile as I thought she was. The time in Cincinnati was gone in a hurry, but Marion had arranged for a permanent nursemaid in New York so that she could resume her work at Doubleday in February. When I visited our apartment in February 1944, now occupied by Marion and Helene, she had already made the necessary changes to house Helene, who did not require a great deal of space.

Again I resumed my weekly runs to New York and became a weekend father, who woke at the slightest sound from the crib, ready to feed, re-diaper or perform any function of a devoted father. The army was looking with greater favor upon me and on February 18, 1944, made me a corporal, a promotion that I valued more highly than any other I received in the army, because it removed me from KP.

The war in Europe came closer. With Allied troops fighting their way up the Italian peninsula, and Stalin's clamoring for a Second Front becoming louder every day, we knew things were heating up. In the middle of May the XIII Corps was suddenly alerted for shipment abroad and three weeks later, about the week of D-DAY they were on their way to England. From the West Coast the XVIII Corps—primarily tank and artillery divisions—took over at Fort DuPont. Lt. Flanagan and I, the leftovers from the previous corps were transferred to the judge advocate section of the new outfit. For us the most important change was that we now had to sew onto our uniforms the XVIII Corps patch. The war had been a bonanza for the design of patches. For our new unit some commercial artist had created a fierce fire spitting blue dragon in a white diamond, bordered by a blue line. I never gave up the sewing kit a well wisher had given me when I was drafted, and now I could immediately identify myself with this strikingly aggressive unit by changing my identification patches.

For a few days life with the newly arrived XVIII Corps seemed to be the same. I reported to the new Judge Advocate, Lt. Colonel Haines, and his assistant Major Moroney. I met the two enlisted men—the chief clerk Ethan A. Ristow, who had been a salesman for a coffin manufacturer in Columbus, Ohio and the clerk-typist Harry Leykauf, a salesman for an oxygen manufacturer whose wife was the district manager for a large cosmetic firm in New York. They seemed to be nice people and it looked as if nothing had really changed.

In the middle of June, Col. Haines called me to his office and told me that I would be transferred to the Airborne Training Center at Camp Mackall, N. C. They had a rash of jump refusals by paratroop soldiers, which required prosecution and involved sentencing to the disciplinary barracks (jail). It sounded fishy to me, and depressing because I would again be far away from New York and my little family. Marion was furious but sure that we would manage.

Camp Mackall was one of those training areas that WWII had stamped out of scrub pine lands. Temporary roads and wooden barracks had appeared overnight, and now this miserable stretch of land had become an airborne training center. There were 150-foot high jump towers where young men were taught the secrets of landing from the sky. All of the men were converted into tough long distance runners—one rarely saw soldiers walking—and overhead day and night was the never ending roar of airplanes dropping parachutists from the skies. In about two months a slogging infantry soldier could be converted into a swift, rakish paratrooper. The extra pay and the glamour that come with danger had brought what seemed an endless supply of the best soldiers—all of them volunteers. To earn the coveted parachute badge, the soldier had to display uncommon courage and macho. He had to complete an arduous eight-week training course, which ended with five jumps under battle conditions—fully armed and loaded down with all gear and ammunition needed for immediate action. After the fifth successful jump, one of them a night jump, this macho status was affirmed by the paratrooper badge and a pay increase of $50, but also by the army rule: Any qualified paratrooper who refuses to jump will be court-martialed and sent to the disciplinary barracks (jail) for punishment.

When I arrived at my new station a large batch of jump refusal cases was waiting for me. Jump refusals were endemic when a unit lost men because the chutes did not open. It was simple legal work that could have been done by anybody. Clearly my assignment was an oblique way of neutralizing me again. My letters to Marion sounded depressed, and even the large quantities of reading material, which Marion supplied regularly, did not console me.

On June 29, 1944, I was just returning from lunch to my dreary jump refusal cases, when I was told that three people from Corps Headquarters at Fort DuPont were there to see me. I was directed to an interrogation room similar to those that army intelligence had provided for the usual investigations that I had undergone before. The room had the barest furnishings: wooden chairs and tables and strong overhead lights that would facilitate observation of the candidate selected for interrogation.

The men from Fort DuPont were all non-coms, but clearly experienced investigators, who told me that they wanted to question me and that they had brought a court reporter to take my testimony. To impress me with the importance of their mission they read me Article 24 of the Articles of War, which explained my right to refuse to testify. After this formal initiation they asked me if I had something to say before they would start questioning me, assuming, of course, that I would have no objection to their starting with the questions. They were slightly taken aback, when I told them that I had no objection to being questioned again, but that I suggested that they obtain transcripts of the numerous investigations and interrogations that I had already behind me. By assembling all those data in one place they might save themselves some work. They did not go for it. They followed the same pattern that I had gone through before, but having done considerably more homework they went into greater detail. I remember that despite a fan going full blast we were all sweating and from time to time an orderly came to bring us a fresh pitcher of ice water.

They were at it from about one to six thirty, when they finally said that they had asked all the questions they needed to have answered and that they would take the early night train back to Wilmington. I was dismissed, went to the mess hall for a delayed supper, and was in bed by eight and asleep, when an orderly came and woke me with orders to report to the office. The three men from DuPont were still there and they looked embarrassed. On the way to the train the court stenographer had made a confession to them, which had caused them to come back to the post: he could not read his short-hand notes because he was out of practice and had been too embarrassed to admit it. So, they asked if we could do the whole thing over with me being the typist. They would dictate to me their questions as they had formulated them and I would then type my answer and read it back to them. In this way we would have an absolutely perfect transcript and record of all the material that we had covered in the afternoon. I readily agreed, but mentioned that they were in for a long session, because I was a very slow typist. By one in the morning we had a report of 11 pages single spaced of which I was allowed (as a special concession) to keep one carbon copy. The men left on an early train, and I went back to bed, convinced that I had done the best I could under the circumstances. As I reread the transcript I was surprised by the patience I had developed. Even my typing seemed congenial.

Two days later on July 2, a teletype message arrived transferring me back to Fort DuPont and my old job. Lt. Flanagan, who welcomed me back, told me what had happened. When he heard that I had been sent into exile in Camp Mackall, he had gone to the G-2 people in the XVIII Corps headquarters and raised hell. He had told them more about me than they had in their files and suggested that they should either clear me or discharge me for the convenience of the government and let me go back to my wife and child. What they had been doing to me was, he claimed, utterly unfair and indecent. He must have been very persuasive because in July, the XVIII Corps filed a report in my behalf with the Second Service Command in New York, which was later entered on my service record, to avoid repetition and duplication of the original investigations. Although nobody told me about that at the time it had converted me into a real American. When I returned to Fort DuPont I felt very pleased with myself and with the army. It looked as if I had finally made it—and in fact I had. For the next year and half—my remaining time in the army—I was treated like any other American soldier. To top it off I was a promoted to the rank of T-4 technical sergeant, with a monthly salary of $78.

I resumed my weekend runs to New York, but when I came back around the end of July there was great excitement at the post. We had been alerted for shipment to Europe by the end of the month. Rumors were flying about when we would leave for the Port of Embarkation (New York), who would be included, etc. About five or six selected non-coms and two officers left immediately by air—in those days transatlantic flights were matters worth bragging about—to assist a British liaison group with preparing for the arrival of the corps in England. This was conclusive proof that this was not a false alarm. The war was now upon me.

CHAPTER 5

ENGLAND EXPECTS EVERY AMERICAN TO DO HIS DUTY TOO

SECRECY WAS THE key word. We heard it all day long when the XIII Corps was alerted about shipment to Europe in June. It was part of American planning that the enemy must not know about the arrival of American units in England. The depressing fact was, however, that despite the greatest precautions to keep such movements a secret, it never worked. Frankly, that system never had a chance while relatives were encouraged to say good-bye to their soldiers before they embarked. Invariably Hitler's intelligence people found out who was coming, and on the day when troops landed in England, Lord Haw Haw, the infamous British renegade broadcasting from Berlin, would welcome the arrival of the unit, citing its size, naming the commanding officer, and wishing them well.

Now that shipment to Europe was almost upon us, one of the most secret procedures was imposed. We were immediately admonished not to disclose where we were going and when. But to avoid mutiny we were also allowed to have one last fling with our families. We all had been instructed that we could invite parents, wives, mothers, or girlfriends to the camp area for a few days using the following pre-arranged code approach: "I would love to have you come to camp because they have restricted our passes, and, please, **do not forget to bring me a pack of razor blades.**" This last sentence was the secret code. I had told Marion casually about this secrecy racket when the XIII Corps had left and both of us had been amused by it, and I had hoped that she would remember it. Since the idea of my being shipped was not very high on the list of worries on our minds, she had probably failed to recognize the importance of remembering this sentence. Immediately after I realized that I was on my way to Europe, I called her and invited her to come to Fort DuPont because the army had cut our passes, and when I concluded my invitation by asking her not to forget to bring me a pack of razor blades, she replied, "Why don't you buy them at the PX? I really don't know which you like best." I had to beat around the bush for some time before she got the message.

For about a week we remained at the post, watching movies and hearing lectures from people who had fought the Germans and could tell us what to expect. The greatest emphasis was on booby traps. We were led through specially prepared mine fields and our memories were refreshed by filmstrips about these dangers. For the first time we heard that under no circumstances must we fraternize with the enemy. There were several lectures on mail. We still had and would continue to have the free mailing privilege but every letter written by an enlisted man from now on must be censored by an officer. In our case Maj. Moroney would be the man who would read our mail once we had arrived at our new post. He would be the judge of what we could say and he would cross out everything that gave away secrets. It was strictly forbidden to disclose our location and what we were doing. Suddenly I realized that the opening of my mail at Indiantown Gap had hardened me for this new constriction of my civil rights.

Marion arrived and I helped her finish the translation of a book from German into English that she had undertaken, confident that she had in the wings the man who would always be available to clarify any linguistic mysteries. With my foot almost on the boat to Europe, both of us slaved over the translation and got it done.

One morning we were surprised by a special army carpenter unit that had moved to the post with a portable buzz saw and an ample supply of pre-cut lumber. They showed us how to nail together pre-cut boards and convert them into wooden boxes. We would line them with water repellent paper and then fasten typewriters—our instruments of war—securely to the boxes for the long journey to England. It was the kind of job that I enjoyed. However, there were two things that the army in its wisdom had failed to take into account, namely (1) the destructive talents of stevedores, and (2) the need to attach visible stickers saying: **EXTREMELY FRAGILE—HANDLE WITH UTMOST CARE.** Later we found that the boxes had been turned over to enthusiastic stevedores who had treated them worse than airline baggage is treated today. The ship that carried us also brought the boxes. While we managed to survive the transatlantic crossing, the boxes did not; when we opened them there was not one workable typewriter in the lot. We were delighted. An army without typewriters was unthinkable, so we were certain that some solution would be found soon. After about three or four days we were re-equipped with brand new manual British typewriters, which had only one, slight shortcoming, they had a pound sign where we expected the $. We were instructed to use a capital S with a slash through it, and before long we became experts at the job.

Back to the last night in Delaware. Officers and enlisted men were treated alike. All of us received a generous pass—we did not have to report back to the post until 10 A.M. the next morning and a bus was waiting in Wilmington to be sure we returned. Marion had reserved a room at the Hotel DuPont and at dinner we were wondering if I might get another pass from the New York Port of

Embarkation. I was ready to go to Europe, but Marion was in the dumps—she knew that my fighting the Germans in Europe brought with it the possibility of capture and being shot as a deserter. To her the future looked very bleak.

There was a lot of scuttlebutt because the section chiefs of all the sections had been transferred out of Fort DuPont to new positions. We speculated that when we arrived in England the corps would receive a new commanding general, who would bring with him his own staff. For the Judge Advocate section, Major Moroney would be the officer to remain with us.

On August 12th, a Saturday, we left Fort DuPont. Of the train ride to New York I remember only that it was very hot and that we still wore khaki. At some pier on Staten Island we boarded a ferry that took us up the East River to the Port of Embarkation, where we would be refurbished with appropriate clothing, receive final physical examinations and the necessary booster shots, and instructions on how to behave if our ship were torpedoed.

The place (the name has escaped me) was like any major induction center with barracks and large warehouses that disgorged all the paraphernalia that we would need in Europe, including steel helmets, but no arms—those we would receive in England. Our khakis were replaced by woolen shirts and pants. Long underwear and wool socks showed up and every piece of clothing was dyed olive drab.

I had with me a little 1944 pocket calendar in which I recorded an amazing amount of details of those days. It was then that I began to write my daily letters to Marion, numbering them serially for her so that she would know that she was kept fully informed. Marion in turn followed the same pattern.

The next day on the Port was a Sunday. Even in war times the army is not eager to work on that day, and so they were generous and gave passes to those who wanted to go to New York City. I managed to see Marion and Helene that afternoon. We played with Helene and were depressed. My diary shows for Sunday the 13th a sad face with tears running. The war was moving ahead with ever

WERNER H. VON ROSENSTIEL

increasing momentum, but the future looked dark. From our apartment we heard the deep sonorous horns of the big ocean liners, now troop transports that ceaselessly moved in and out of the harbor accompanied by the short barks of ferries and tugboats. In a day or so one of those liners would have me on board.

Back at the port impressive preparations had been made to show us how to abandon ship, a matter to which I had not given serious thought. On a hill the army had erected a wooden wall about 25 feet high and perhaps 150 feet long, slightly tilted, simulating a sinking ship. Hanging down from the top was gigantic rope netting that we could reach from a catwalk attached to the top of the wall. Equipped with life vests we were herded to the top and then virtually pushed over the edge and made to clamber down this obstacle without killing each other. To give the whole training exercise additional realism, there was a lot of noise, bellowed commands, bullhorns etc. The exercise was repeated several times. It was comforting to see that the army had thought of preparing us for something that might well happen.

We spent the better part of a week getting ready. The censorship regulations had already been put into effect and Captain Sanders, the commander of the headquarters company, had announced that he would censor all mail. I felt lonesome after the last day with Marion and had used the endless periods of waiting to write my first letter, subject to censorship, and had deposited it in the mailbox in the company commander's office.

Rumor had it that the army was giving all of us one last final going over to see if there might be some reason why we should not be sent to Europe. The army had asked me repeatedly whether I objected to serving in Europe, but I had always replied that I would serve any place where they decided to send me and that this was a decision that they would have to make. They had drafted me, I always told them, and it was their responsibility to use me where they thought I would be most useful. But with all the trying investigations that I had behind me I was still nervous and sort of gun shy, never feeling secure that I might not be yanked. After all that I had been through, I was determined to get to Europe.

My fear increased when a nice young private, a driver in the motor pool and the son of German immigrants was yanked at the last moment. Jubilantly he walked out of Captain Sanders office to the ferry slip and waved us "good-bye" saying: "No Europe for me— bye bye!" I almost went into shock when a few moments later an orderly from Capt. Sanders came over to me and said, "Captain wants to see you." I walked to the orderly room, almost sick to my stomach from fear that now I might be yanked. I came to attention, saluted and stated: "Sergeant Von Rosenstiel, reporting to the company commander, as ordered." He looked up from his desk took my letter to Marion from the box of letters that he had to censor and in a gruff and unfriendly voice said: "Listen sergeant, I have more important things to do than to decipher your goddammned letter. Here, take it back and copy it in nice block letters, and if you want to do me a favor keep it short. Dismissed." I came to attention and gave him the most heartfelt salute: "Thank you, Sir," marching away as if I had won the lottery, which in a way I had. I re-wrote an abbreviated version of my letter to Marion and recorded it as #1 on the 14th—beginning a series of probably well over 500 letters.

One of the important civic activities that was sandwiched into our final preparation for overseas service was the filing of absentee ballots, so that we could participate in the impending presidential election. Franklin D. Roosevelt in 1944 sought his fourth term and there was much talk that even in war times a fourth term was a little more than the founders had planned. So it was anticipated that some of the soldiers might not vote for their Commander-in- Chief. To be sure that the millions of soldiers who were away from America could exercise their vote, extensive plans for giving us this right had been made. When I signed my papers, proudly identifying myself as a citizen of the state of New York and applied for my first ballot as an American citizen, I had no idea what a powerful weapon the ballot really was. Later during my service in England I remembered that I could demand this right to vote.

On August 17, we embarked on the Isle de France, one of the luxury liners that had been converted to a troop transport to deliver 10,000 men to England every 14 days. It was murderously hot and steamy as we were loaded at about 6 P.M. on the dinky ferry that would take us along the East River and then to one of the big Hudson River piers. Dressed in our woolen uniforms, each loaded down with two heavy barracks bags we slowly entered the stream of traffic on the East River. All of us were soaking wet from a slight steamy rain and sweat. Even the chronic jokers had nothing further to offer, as we slowly and silently made our way along Manhattan, turned into the Hudson River at the Battery and then tied up on a slip next to the pier where the Isle de France was waiting for us. On the other side of the slip loomed the gigantic Queen Mary, almost twice the size of our ship, taking on a whole tank division of 16,000 and their equipment.

We had to climb a narrow stair for about thirty feet to reach a deck from which we could gain access to the transport. Getting up the stairs in the darkness, loaded down with bags was more than some of the smaller men could do, and it was nice to see that there was always a willingness to help. On the deck American Red Cross girls were handing out coffee and doughnuts—they were the first Red Cross girls that I had encountered.

As soon as we entered the ship we heard the clipped English announcements and realized that the ship, despite its French registry, was run by a British crew. We were herded to our deck, a large room covering the whole width of the ship, fifty feet long and perhaps ten feet high. Crammed into this space were double rows of four deck bunks with room under the lowest bunk for the storage of eight barracks bags. There was a space of about two and a half feet to provide access to our assigned bunks. They were high enough so that we could turn over, but we could not sit up. From one hour before darkness until an hour after sunrise we were confined to this room in which about four hundred men slept with very little ventilation. Air conditioning had not as yet made its appearance. Smoking was forbidden and the light was minimal—not enough for reading. As soon as we were settled, we heard a crisp British voice announce over the loudspeaker: "**Now hear this:** For the next seven days we shall travel through sub infested waters without escort. Surveillance planes will advise us of subs in the area and assist us in avoiding them. During darkness ONLY crew members of this ship are allowed on deck. I repeat ONLY crew members. No matter what happens below deck you will not be permitted to come on deck during darkness. One hour before darkness all doors from rooms occupied by soldiers leading to the decks will be locked. There will be only two meals every day, breakfast and dinner. There will be lifeboat drills and you are required to know at all times where your life vest is. Your accommodations are crowded and will not permit you to unpack your barracks bags. For the next few days you will need only your toilet kits and a towel. Remember toilet and washing facilities are limited. Be considerate. Cheerio."

By the time they unlocked the doors next morning the air in our quarters was terrible and we hoped for a smooth crossing without seasickness. As we came on deck we were steaming at full speed on a totally deserted ocean with hardly a ripple. It was fortunate that Marion had provided me with ample reading material for my "sojourn to England." She had obtained most of Somerset Maugham's writing that had been reproduced in pocket book form. I remember reading "Of Human Bondage" in a quiet corner on deck and thinking what Mildred might have looked like and then my thoughts got lost and I wondered what would be left of my German family. The tide of war was clearly turning. The trip is a blur from which I remember distinctly that Bing Crosby was one of the passengers, headed for some USO shows in Europe. From time to time he would be called on the PA system and we all chuckled when the British announcer with his clipped accent said, " Will Mr. Harry B. Crosby kindly report to the purser's office." The British Navy certainly knew when they had a VIP on board.

In a letter to Marion written on ship board on August 20th, I reported: "I have finished what A. J. Liebling so fittingly describes as a "Whore's Bath." It consists of a complete (?) washing—head to toe—with the amount of water that fits into one steel helmet.

"The sea is calm and there is little news. I watched a cherubic looking, young British sailor do his job of paint scraping. He discovered an officer right under his working place—one deck below. A couple of GIs were ready to seize the golden opportunity. By subdued winking they encouraged him and after a few moments water and paint chips fell on the poor officer. Properly directed by the GIs the sailor remained invisible, except for the hand that pushed the water and the paint dust down. The GIs and I enjoyed ourselves immensely.

"I finished Maugham's *Cake and Ale* and I am really astonished to see Willie write such perfect love scenes and such surprisingly lush descriptions of Rosie's naked body. It really reads as if he'd slept with her, as the book expressly states. Since he is gay, I'm a little confused. Are Rosie and Mildred the same person after all? Or was Willie in his youth a regular? "

As we approached Grennock, our port for disembarkation, some destroyers raced back and forth like shepherd dogs to protect us from sneak attacks by lurking subs, while two large tug boats carefully moved giant submarine nets studded with contact mines to let us reach the area of the harbor where we would be unloaded in secluded safety. To our surprise the Queen Mary had been there for over a day and was on her way back to New York as we entered.

Lighters came as soon as we were anchored and took us to a railhead perhaps two miles away. As I boarded the lighter I remember seeing in the distance low warehouse sheds with open doors and an endless stream of people moving goods with wheelbarrows. As we got closer I realized that all of the people manning those wheelbarrows were women. I came to the shocking realization that the British had sent their men to fight and had the women replace them to make this possible. Compared to their human sacrifices our American efforts appeared suddenly very small.

When our lighter tied up at the railhead, our advance detachment was there to welcome us and we could hardly believe what we saw. The five enlisted men and two officers wore shining new para-troop boots with the pants stuck into the tops of the boots. The famous blue and white "Reluctant Dragon Patch," the XVIII Corps identification, had been given a 45 degree tilt and the message: XVIII Corps **AIRBORNE** had been added.

The new corps commander, we were told, was Major General Matthew B. Ridgway, who until recently had commanded the 82nd Airborne Division that had fought in North Africa, Sicily, Salerno and most recently in the invasion in Normandy. Mitch, one of the enlisted men of the advance detachment, who had been a ballet dancer with the Follies Bergere in Paris before the draft had con-verted him into a typist, could not hide his professional dance train-ing as he floated from group to group and gave us a briefing on our new commander: "Let me tell you, he is tough as nails. He never went to jump school and has only five jumps to his credit!!! All of them were combat jumps and he was the first one out of the plane every time! Let me warn you he is spit and polish! Get close to the razor, fellows, polish those boots and never walk around with a jacket unbuttoned! And that's not all: He brought his staff with him. You are all going to have new section chiefs and they are as tough as he is. He runs them personally every morning at 6 A.M. for 6 miles!!" Then, on he danced to the next group with the same mes-sage, received with a mixture of admiration, fright, and disbelief.

A train was waiting for us at the railhead. I recall an announce-ment on the loudspeaker reporting the Liberation of Paris by the Allied High Command. Red Cross girls—this time the English vari-ety—handed us cups of tea and kidney pie. Most of my comrades, accustomed to steak and hamburgers courteously declined, but I was delighted to receive this British delicacy.

It was a long train ride to Swindon, a main railway center in the south of England. The train was very different from the American trains in which we had been transported. A narrow passageway on one side of the car left room for compartments that seated eight passengers in two rows of four facing each other. From Swindon, which was the nearest rail station, buses took us to Ogbourne St.

George, a British airborne training center that had been vacated for American troops. For the next three and a half months it became our training and staging area. Surrounded by airfields and staging areas for the 82nd and 101st airborne division, we underwent a very rapid transformation into the new tasks that were waiting for us.

Waiting for us were carbines, a much lighter weapon than the M-1, which was the standard weapon of combat troops, and the famous "jump boots." We were assigned huts that housed about twenty men. The barracks were primitive by the standards of our American training. Double deck bunks with straw sacks as mattresses were embellished by two wool blankets, two bed sheets, and a pillow. A brown coal-fed potbelly stove would keep us warm. We learned very soon that the latrine was called *WC* and the wash room was christened *ablution* room.

In our barracks we now met T-4 Maurice E. Lerch, Jr., 19 year old clerk typist and battle hardened veteran of the 82nd Airborne Division, who would bring our section up to full strength. He was a good looking, slender youngster about 5'6" tall with dark hair and an engaging smile. Waiting for us in the barracks he welcomed us and when he saw me, his first words were, "Werner, call me Junior, I'll call you 'gramps' and to get you into shape for airborne duty, we are going to have a wrestling match *every* night." That was to be my assignment. Every night without fail Junior would challenge me and I had to accept this ordeal. Our barracks waited for this evening entertainment with the other soldiers vying for good seats. The outcome was always the same: After inordinate and often heroic efforts on my part, I always managed to pin him. But the price was high. The moment I had accomplished my victory, I staggered to my bed and needed about half an hour before I could again engage in further activities of any kind. Junior, in no way exhausted by his defeat, would review my performance and usually come to my bunk to observe my revitalization. This, plus the prescribed physical exercises and touch football games hardened me for the things to come.

Junior had graduated from high school in Pittsburgh and had

started to work for the Heinz Company, where he maintained that he had to count the bumps on the pickles. His devotion to Heinz was so strong that he returned to Heinz after the war and worked his way up to become one of their accounting officials. Once toward the end of the war, when we were stopped by a mass of surrendering German soldiers, he suddenly jumped off our truck, raced toward a German soldier, ripped off his shoulder epaulette and returned triumphantly climbing back on our truck. In his hand he held an epaulette with the number 57—"This is the finest **57th variety** for my boss in Pittsburgh," he proclaimed as we moved on. He was in the early draft and came to the 82nd airborne division as a clerk-typist and was qualified as glider infantryman. From the beginning he served under Lt. Colonel Casimir D. Moss, the Judge Advocate of the 82nd under General Ridgway and now our new commanding officer and section chief, whom we met later that day.

Lt. Col. Moss was a lawyer from Louisiana, where as a student he had worked as a secretary for Huey P. Long, the famous kingfish Governor of Louisiana. Athletic, tall, about 6'4", and lean with a nose that obviously had been broken and poorly set, he told us that he expected us to quickly learn our new duties as airborne troops. Since Major Moroney had worked with us for some time, he expected that work would be produced promptly and in good order. For the next four months we saw little of our chief, who was one of General Ridgway's closest advisors—few generals had the luck to find a man among their staff who was trained by Huey P. Long.

Below, my grandmother's house, the paradise of my youth

The author as a lowly private in the Wehrmacht, 1938

Ready for the next move by C 47 transport plane

Return to Germany over a re-built bridge

Always on the move in Germany

V-E Day: Victory in Europe Day. Clean clothes

Residents of Hagenow digging graves for victims of
Wobbelin Concentration Camp

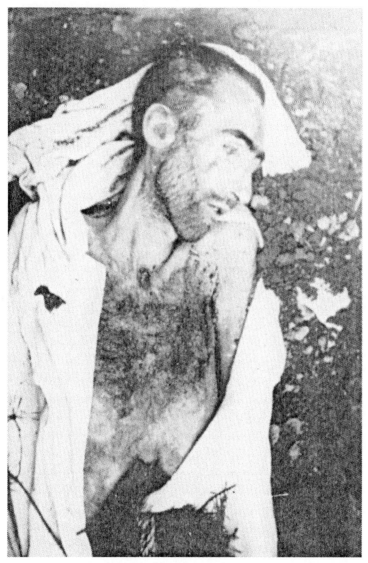

A victim of the concentration camp

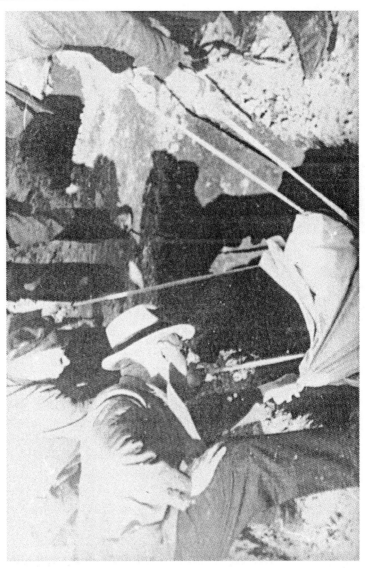

Lowering a victim into his grave

Maurice E. Lerch, 18 years old, "Junior"
with the author, 34 years old, "Gramps"

Finding my sister, Ilse and her children

Hitler's mountain retreat, Adlerhorst,
"The Eagle's Nest" in Berchtesgaden

Visiting Rothenberg. Col. Fairman, Peggy Brown,
and Col. Behle, November 1945

CHAPTER 6

ENGLAND

WE HAD BARELY gotten our fancy paratroop boots and shined them to the high gloss, which from now on was demanded, when we were herded to a small training field where I saw the first gliders used for transporting soldiers. Today, fifty years later, we know that gliders are certified deathtraps, but at that time the Allies were enamored of this newly invented mass transportation device for soldiers. After all, the Germans had demonstrated at Crete that gliders were a superb invasion tool. However, to them soldiers had always been expendable, so nobody asked how many men they lost with those great gliders. Now, the British had built an enormous glider to carry fifty men and the United States had opted for a smaller type, a glider that could carry 13 fully armed men or a jeep and five soldiers.

We were intrigued by these contraptions that we eyed with a mixture of awe and trepidation. Our comfort level was not raised when we discovered that these gliders did not have metal wings but rather a frame of wooden spars that were covered with a densely woven, silky fabric that had been made impervious to rain by a water-repellent, lacquer-like varnish. When I touched the wing, it reminded me of a similar wing that I had found in an abandoned WW I airplane manufacturing plant near Stralsund in 1929. That wing had been designed for and was left over from the WW I Flying Machines. Now I would be privileged to test a like wing for its air worthiness.

Our enthusiasm was not increased when we found that each of the three gliders had a small plaque affixed to its undercarriage, which disclosed that the manufacturers included two of America's famous beer brewers, Anhauser Busch and Budweiser, and the Steinway piano company.

Before we could engage in any further exploration of our new transportation equipment, a bullhorn announcement told us to observe a show that Ridgeway's defense platoon would put on for us. When Ridgway assumed command of the XVIII Airborne Corps, he had personally selected 12 of the most highly decorated enlisted men from the 82nd Airborne and 12 from the 101st Airborne Division to serve as his personal bodyguard. These 24 men, all battle hardened veterans, armed to the teeth, accompanied him in six jeeps, ready to defend him against all enemies. Now this bunch of certified heroes was going to give us a demonstration of how paratroopers were used in war. Within a few minutes a single C-47 appeared, circled the area where we were standing and then disgorged the 24 men whose camouflage colored parachutes blossomed out as they floated toward the earth and then disappeared in the underbrush about a mile away from where we stood.

We waited in excited silence when suddenly we saw our selves attacked from several sides by our just landed friends, who had stealthily reached our area and were entertaining us with bursts of blank ammunition fusillades fired from their light machine guns.

After this demonstration we were told that those who wanted to join the paratroopers should sign up for training that would start the next day. There were no volunteers and all of us were now classified as "glider infantry" and given additional instruction which consisted essentially in teaching us how to load gliders and particularly how to tie the jeeps that would ride with us. Our instructors had no difficulty persuading us that proper loading and lashing of the jeeps was in our own interest. Their friendly comment that gliders in which jeeps had gotten loose during flight had never made a successful and safe landing was received with concern, and we used every moment to perfect our technique of tying secure knots.

Two weeks of intensive instruction in loading and lashing were considered sufficient to prepare us. We were now taken to an airfield where a number of gliders were waiting to take us for our first ride. The instructor explained to us that we would take off and land on the same field. Specially designed training gliders were used for this purpose. They had wheels so that they could be used over and over again. Under combat conditions, we were told, the gliders had ski-like undercarriages so that they could land almost anywhere. Most gliders used in actual combat would be written off, because of the structural damages that they usually suffered in landing. Each of the tow planes, the trustworthy C-47s, pulled two gliders which reduced their speed from about 160 to 120 miles per hour. Experience had shown that best results were achieved if one of the gliders rode on a short tow rope and the other on a longer one. The only disadvantage of this system was that occasionally the tow ropes would damage the wings of the glider on the short rope.

Equipped with this information and praying that the glider pilots would be attentive we boarded our gliders for the first of our four qualifying rides. There exists one picture of me in steel helmet with a very tense expression, taken inside a glider. The small smile that can be discerned looks forced. The sound of air rushing past rattling the wings and making the wooden members of the wing creak and groan was frightening as we were lifted into the air. It was both exciting and nerve wracking as we could look past the jeep and our pilot to see how the longer rope of the second glider came closer and then moved away as the laboring C-47 dragged us for about 45 minutes over the peaceful English countryside. At a command: **Prepare for Landing,** we all tensed. When the airfield and the runway came into sight, the glider pilot pulled a lever that released the tow rope and suddenly the glider seemed to stand absolutely still. For a period of perhaps two or three seconds there was total silence. The glider then began to tremble as it began its floating descent to the airfield where the plane touched down, having been slowed to perhaps 40 miles per hour. Our jeep had been properly tied. The moment we touched ground and came to a stop, we released the jeep. The driver started it, and with a cable attached to his trailer hitch lifted the whole front of the glider and raced the jeep onto the airfield. Our next ride was with 13 men in the glider and another crew of five men took the jeep up for a spin.

The whole proceeding was repeated the next day, and it was surprising to see how the anxieties and tension had re ceded giving way for confidence and hope. It was Junior, our veteran, who assured us that the "Legal Eagles" would rarely be landed in combat behind enemy lines. That was a comforting piece of information. And most importantly we learned, with our having qualified as glider infantry we were now not only entitled to wear the glider badge on our uniform but would receive extra pay of $50 a month as "risk premium," as long as we were exposed to the prescribed risk. It is curious how risk and money are related. Every month, no matter where we were, we insisted on being taken up for our required glider ride so that we could honestly collect our $50 risk money.

V-Mail and Sightseeing

Within about three weeks at Ogbourne St. George life had settled down to a routine, very similar to the one that I had experienced in Fort DuPont. The main difference was that the only recreational facility on the post was Sally's (The Salvation Army's) Canteen, where we could sit, buy tea and crumpets and read *Stars and Stripes*. The surrounding village inns had liquor and beer allocations that were consumed long before we could get there. Every evening we would congregate at Sally's and read about the war. It was a curiously peaceful environment for us. We were training for war, we heard from our friends in the defense platoon what war was like, and yet during those early days of September 1944 war was very distant.

I recall our excitement on the early morning of September 18, 1944 when we heard the roar of swarms of C-47 planes overhead. They were carrying paratroopers or drawing gliders full of infantry soldiers circling endlessly overhead until all the fighting men of our two airborne divisions loaded into about 750 transport planes were assembled in the air and could begin their flight to Holland. There they and a British airborne division would land to capture the Rhine bridges at Arnhem, Eindhoven and Nijmegen. One of the surgeons from our headquarters medical unit had been lifted from his job and put unto one of the surgical teams that accompanied the troopers—later that month we would hear that he had been taken prisoner. About six or seven hours later we saw the planes return to base. Some had big holes in the wings and parts of their rudders shot away.

The grandiose plan, I believe inspired by Field Marshal Montgomery, to cross the Rhine in Holland and open the flat area of North Germany to the vast allied tank armies, had been foiled by the Germans. With heavy losses, the 82nd and 101st divisions returned to England for training of replacements from the replacement depots. Our buddies from the Defense Platoon had kept up with their friends in both of those divisions and so we got first hand stories about the campaign. Suddenly it brought home to us that we actually lived in total ignorance of what war was really like and that the war was still to be won.

It was amazing how quickly the army managed to provide us with mail. One of the great inventions of WW II was the V-Letter. On a preprinted white sheet 8 1/2" x 11" with specific instructions printed in red ink and available free of charge at every post office, soldiers could write—postage free—letters and receive letters in the same format from home. Postage for civilians was 3 cents per letter anywhere in the world where American soldiers were stationed. The army collected these letters, photographed them onto microfilm and flew the developed film to and from the war fronts. Processing machines on both sides of the ocean printed the film on photographic paper in a reduced size of 4 1/4" x 5 1/2" and delivered them to the addressee. Months later the originals would be sent to the addressee, when there was space on shipboard. With most of us equipped with 20/20 eyesight reading those miniatures was a cinch. Today trying to decipher them—even with a magnifying glass—is a chore.

Proof of the efficiency of the Army Postal Service is the fact that already in early September 1944, I received my first V-letters and there has survived an almost complete set of my letters to Marion from August 1944 until my return from Europe in January of 1946. But even "non V-letters" made good time and one of the first book shipments from Marion was a Baedeker of England published in 1897, the only guidebook for England she had managed to dig up. She encouraged me not to laugh at it, but to use it, assuring me that nothing had really changed in England. The first opportunity to verify Marion's hunch came when I had a chance to go with an army truck to a place near the Salisbury Plain, where our unit had made arrangements with a local laundry to care for our needs. A review of Baedeker's recommendations for sights in the neighborhood had alerted me to the astonishing nearness of Stonehenge, a site I remembered from my geography school book about England. So I volunteered to help with the laundry—there was no important legal work—and now I spent an unforgettable afternoon with my truck driver friend, wandering over the totally deserted Stonehenge area, wondering how men without hydraulic equipment could have moved those giant lintels to the top of the bearing stones. Weeks later while in London I bought a little print of Stonehenge which from time to time surfaces among my unsorted mementos and reminds me of that day.

In September Harry Leykauf and I managed to get a day off to go to Oxford, only an hour and a half by train from Swindon. We were impressed with what we saw and chuckled when we learned that at Oxford the new buildings were those that were constructed in 1730. As casual visitors we received from university guides only the conventional welcome, and lacking specific information on the English educational system we were not well prepared to gain the full impact of that university. But I recall how surprised I was when I went to the Chapel and saw a plaque for the students of Oxford University who had been killed in WW I. Among them I discovered the name of my cousin von Sell, who had been a Rhodes scholar from Germany before the war and had been killed in 1915 in Flanders.

Harry Leykauf and I shared many of our war experiences. Both of us were older than most of our buddies; booze and women were not high on our list; and we both liked to read, if there was nothing else to do. Harry was always first on the waiting list for books that I regularly received from Marion. Our wives—both in New York— met frequently and exchanged information that they had received from us. One of the riddles that continuously perplexed them was the question of exactly where we were. The army did not permit us to tell them and unless the newspapers made reference to a unit in the field at a particular battle, we could not really tell -but when I told her about Stonehenge and Oxford, Marion correctly placed me into Wiltshire.

Meeting the British

The opportunity to establish any kind of social contact with English people was extremely difficult and often almost impossible. British civilians essentially lived on mere survival rations, while American troops with PX facilities never had the feeling of being away from America. Our headquarters had made efforts to arrange for visits with local people and, to eliminate the embarrassment of the two different styles of living had provided "Special Host food packages" a well meaning effort which never really overcame the embarrassment. Unless we ourselves could somehow manage on a person to person basis to establish some kind of communication, the chances of learning anything about the British did not exist.

During a few visits to Swindon—the army provided buses—we

were able to buy fish and chips from a street vendor, which he wrapped in a newspaper. We could also purchase a bottle of luke-warm beer from a nearby bar and drink it while leaning against a wall, but that was about the extent of making contact with our allies.

It was Marion who had laid the groundwork for my first suc-cessful contact with native English people. Winifred Nerney was the Doubleday representative in London, with an elegant office at Great Russell Street. For many years she had worked closely with Nelson Doubleday and had personally cultivated contacts with numerous famous authors among them Joseph Conrad, and during the last twenty years Somerset Maugham, for whom Marion now worked as a private secretary in New York. From time to time—even dur-ing the war—Winifred had visited New York and she and Marion had struck up a delightful friendship, of which I now became the beneficiary. Marion had also alerted a close friend from our univer-sity days in Cincinnati, Marvin Felheim, to my presence in En-gland. Marvin, now an air force captain, had established contact with Erna, a charming Viennese woman, who worked as a bar maid at the White Room Club for officers near Trafalgar Square and the famous Rainbow Corner. Arrangements had been made for me to visit that exclusive club—even though I was a lowly sergeant.

Fortified by those two letters of introduction to Winifred and Marvin I set out for London. I had obtained my first of four passes to London on September 20th. The pass system was relatively easy and usually allowed one day and night in London, with sleeping and eating facilities for enlisted men in some YMCA like facilities. Bomber raids over London had been replaced by V-1 and V-2 bomb attacks and we were cautioned to follow all precautions. Destruc-tion by these infernal weapons was substantial. From camp I took a musette bag with a few supplies to facilitate contact, like chocolate, cigarettes, and six oranges that had just arrived that day in camp. An early afternoon bus took me to Swindon, where I caught a train that would get me to Paddington Station early enough so that I could see for the first time what war had done to London.

Just before leaving camp I received a letter from Marion which told me of all the preparations she had made for my amusement in London and also that she was pregnant.

During the two and half hour train ride from Swindon to London, I had made plans of what I wanted to accomplish during my visit. My faith in Winifred's ability to help me accomplish all my dreams was unlimited.

With Marion pregnant again the problem of producing a suitable baby present had achieved top priority. I knew precisely what it should be, but was fearful that I could neither find nor afford it. It was to be a French carriage clock, one of those brass clocks popular during the first part of the 19th century with a simple white face, usually with Roman numerals, with the works of the clock visible through glass windows on the remaining three sides. Just before leaving New York I had spotted one at an antique store on University Place for $125, which was then way beyond my reach, but now with my "risk money" income it looked like a distinct possibility. The reason I wanted to acquire it was that when I was a small child my mother had taught me to tell time with a French carriage clock.

The war news in the *Stars and Stripes* left no doubt that the end of the war would see my family stripped of everything. I felt certain that none of us would ever see Below again—the place where all of us had grown up. So, I wanted to be sure that at some future time, if I ever saw my brother Gerd again, I could give him a picture that would remind him of that place. The picture that I had in mind had hung in the entrance hall in Below and I had admired it from the time I was a small boy. It had an English caption, but at that time I knew no English. But it did not really matter, because it showed a dramatic confrontation between two men both backed by large groups of armed partisans. It was a picture one could never forget. I was determined to find it in London.

And finally there was the desire to see if I could reestablish contact with Roderick Bashford, the British Vice Consul in Breslau, who had made possible my escape from Germany in 1939 by talking the American Vice Consul into granting me a visitor's visa to the States.

As I rode on a bus to my billet in London, I saw for the first time what Ed Murrow had described in his broadcasts from London during the Blitz. I was shocked by the devastation that had ripped whole blocks and often single houses and churches—random destruction that still showed the blackening of the ruins and no effort to repair. The random occurrence of devastation always raised the question: Why this house and not that? Months later, when I saw the destruction that had been wrought upon German cities like Hamburg, Aachen and Wesel I realized that in the area of destructiveness there is no limit to escalation. When I returned to London in November of 1945 the city with its war damage looked like a place that had only been dusted with war compared to what I had seen in Germany.

I found the quarters and the mess hall and after supper had enough time to make my way to the Rainbow Corner, where American soldiers met at night. Knowing how important my musette bag was and aware that its contents represented value, I had kept it with me the whole time. There were taxis and buses, all meeting the very strict black-out orders, creeping along the streets, and my bus finally brought me to Trafalgar Square and the Rainbow Corner. The place was packed with GIs and girls. Having the address of Marvin Felheim's Officers Club—the White Room Club at 14 Denman Street—I groped my way in total darkness to the address and found #14. I pressed the bell and noticed how someone looked at me through a peephole very similar to those shown in the Hollywood version of speakeasies during prohibition. A very British voice said: "Are you an American Officer?" When I replied: "I have a letter of introduction from Captain Felheim to Erna" there was a moment of silence and then the door opened. I entered a dark black vestibule and then came into a fairly large brightly lighted room, filled with American air force officers. At the entrance was a well stocked bar with six bar stools and behind the bar two attractive girls who looked up with surprise when they saw me, an enlisted airborne soldier, approach the bar. The moment I said: "Marvin Felheim sent me here to see Erna," the younger one said, "Oh—I know, you are

Werner, I am so glad to see you." With that she reached for a bottle and poured me a scotch and soda and inquired about my association with Marvin, who was a well known visitor of the club. When I attempted to pay for my drink, Erna refused to accept any money but she was not averse to taking two of the six oranges that were in my musette bag. I noticed that near the bar was a sign "To the Toilets" directing people to the basement. Erna saw me look at the sign and said: "You know, we still have a lot of alarms with those V-bombs and when the alarm goes on we have to rush down to the basement—it's unpleasant but it's safer down there." I remember from a later visit how we raced down those stairs and heard glasses and chandeliers rattle above us as bombs exploded in the neighborhood.

Our conversation was going just fine. Occasionally Erna would get up to take drinks to some of the officers who occupied several of the tables that were spread around a small empty dance floor. Frequently I heard the buzzer and officers entered, greeted the bar maids, ordered drinks and joined some of the men already seated. Suddenly the place took on the excitement that comes with the entry of a celebrity. I saw a petite woman of perhaps 60 with fine features, dressed in a superbly fitted Red Cross uniform enter the room, wave at the barmaids and proceed to a table next to the dance floor where she was instantly surrounded by eager, young American officers. When Erna whispered to me, "That's Lady Cavendish," and noticed the blank expression on my face, she explained, "Lady Cavendish was Adele Astaire, the sister of Fred Astaire. She used to dance with him until she married Lord Cavendish, and then Fred made Ginger Rogers his partner." I was impressed although I was a little embarrassed because I was not really up-to-date on Lady Cavendish's fame. As we were happily gabbing at the bar, Erna got up, grabbed me by the arm and said, "I'll introduce you to her," and with that we were halfway across the room. She maneuvered me into the circle of admiring officers, introducing me as: "Sergeant Von Rosenstiel, a friend of mine and Captain Felheim." Lady Cavendish eyed me with amusement as I bowed politely from the hip and refrained from kissing her hand. She thanked Erna for bringing me over and asked her to bring us both a scotch and soda. When Erna delivered the drinks, I protested and said that I thought it was really my duty to provide the drinks for this occasion, because where I came from a man who accepted drinks from a lady would be ostracized. She smiled, but she stoutly refused. The officers next to me enjoyed my defeat and snickered. When I said, "Lady Cavendish, it is obvious that I cannot win in this contest, but I would like to show my appreciation in a small and modest way," she smiled and said, "And what could that be?" I replied, "Lady Cavendish, I happen to have four fresh oranges in my musette bag, and I would like to present them to you so that tomorrow morning you can have orange juice for breakfast." Whether it was just perfect acting or real delight she said that it was the best gift she'd had in a long time, because oranges were not in the British diet these days.

In 1955 I returned to London and for old times sake went back to the White Room bar, which I found almost unchanged, except that there were no American officers and the place was not very active. When I sat on the same bar stool that I had used 11 years ago, I inquired whether either of the two ladies working there knew Erna. To my surprise, I learned that she had worked there until about six months before, when she had gotten married and moved to the country. When I told them about my wonderful visit with Lady Cavendish, the bar maid told me one to top all. There was again the entry of Lady Cavendish and she was instantly surrounded by those young, eager American fly boys. One of them—probably the youngest—just could not suppress his curiosity at seeing this charming, delicate woman and asked her: "Lady Cavendish, how old are you?" There was an embarrassed silence—the young man's co-officers were ready to murder him for this dreadful breach of etiquette—but Lady Cavendish was up to the question. Holding her hand to her throat she said: "Above my hand it is 62, below it is 18." The young officer blushed and Lady Cavendish smiled.

And next morning I was ready to meet Winifred at nine. Her

office was on the second floor in a converted elegant residence at Great Russell Street. She was a trim woman in her early 60s and she spoke with that enviable British inflection. Maybe the climate and the smog from all the chimneys that spewed forth smoke from brown coal heaters had given her a real whisky voice and a frequent cough. But it did not interfere with our conversation, which proceeded as if we had known each other for years. My question about a place where I could find the clock was instantly answered: "Jacobson, a few blocks from here—totally reliable, has wonderful silver goods too, with reasonable prices." Finding the print of the Below picture: "McMasters near Foyles bookstore can help you if any one can. From your description he will be able to tell you what it is." And now there remained one thing left for her to solve: "Where can I find Bashford?" She was not stumped for long. She said: "You know, my brother works for the Air Ministry and they have lots of leads to many people. Why don't I give him a ring?" She dialed his number and explained that she was looking for a man by the name of Roderick Bashford who until the beginning of the war had been the British Vice Consul in Breslau. She handed me the receiver and at the other end I heard the familiar voice saying "Bashford, who is this?" The recognition was instant and we made an immediate date for tea and crumpets before my train left from Paddington. It was another stroke of luck that happened so often in my life. Bashford had a desk next to Winifred's brother and they shared the same telephone.

At the clock maker I bought the clock for the baby present, with Winifred loaning me ten pounds and agreeing to deliver the present in person on her next visit to New York, which was scheduled for February. The price seemed most reasonable and made both the clock maker and me extremely happy. I was the first American soldier to find his way into the shop and he confessed that business was very slow. I promised to be back and drum up customers for him.

A charming old man at McMasters Print Shop at Charing Cross Roads inquired of my wishes with the courtesy of a man who had served lords and the like his whole life. When I confessed to him what I wanted to achieve and gave him a demonstration of what the picture looked like, he smiled, and said: "No doubt, it is *Oliver Cromwell Dissolving the Long Parliament* by Benjamin West. I know the picture is in every school book on English history and I am sure we have several small prints." He disappeared and in a few minutes returned with a small reproduction of the etching that had been made of Benjamin West's monumental oil painting. He did not have the size I wanted, but he directed me to a competitor who specialized in those prints. He gave me the page from the school book and it finally came to rest in the home of Gerd's widow. The print, which I bought that same day and mailed to Marion, was lost along with other treasures when we moved.

After the war I came to roost in Cedar Grove, New Jersey a few miles north of Montclair. One day I saw in *Time* magazine a double spread, four color reproduction of the famous painting and discovered that it belonged to the art museum in Montclair, where some generous benefactor had dedicated it many years ago.

Bashy had rounded up his wife for a quick bite before I had to leave from Paddington. The visit was wonderful. I felt so much in his debt for having maneuvered that visitors visa for me in 1939 that I wanted to do something special for him. It was difficult to get him to say what he could use, even though I explained to him that he had saved my life. Finally I wore him down and he asked for a few pairs of long underwear, because winters in England were very cold and long underwear heavily rationed. My connections with our supply sergeant were always the best and so I was able to meet my promise on my next visit to London.

Before I boarded the train at Paddington Station I had bought a copy of *Punch* hoping to read it on the two and a half hour ride to Swindon. All of my seven travel companions were English and none of them had invested in this expensive luxury magazine. I realized that they all knew what was in the magazine and that stealthily they were observing me to find out how I reacted to British humor. It turned out to be the key to one of the great discoveries I made while I was stationed in England. Soon after the train had gotten underway I'd opened *Punch* and begun to examine it slowly page after page. There were several pages with the most wonderful cartoons that would have had most readers rolling on the floor. But I examined each without showing the slightest bit of amusement or comprehension. All the while, I noticed from the corner of my eye that my fellow travelers were giving up on me and finally one of them said, "Sir, don't you think that *Punch* is funny?" When I replied that I thought it was hilarious and I had hoped they would ask me because it was the only way I knew to break up their reserve and involve them in conversation, they opened up. The scheme never failed and, in fact, brought me one of the most wonderful moments of my whole time in England.

Again as on the previous trip, I had bought a *Punch* and was using it as bait. On my knees was a beautifully drawn cartoon showing a medieval knight, weary and worn out from the wars arriving on his skinny horse at the moat of his castle. The drawbridge is drawn and his wife stands near one of the big towers and says "George, I'm glad you came back alive. The portcullis needs painting very badly." Again my reaction of boredom or inability to comprehend. This time my audience included a young RAF officer. Within minutes after I had confessed that the whole gambit was an attempt to engage them in conversation, the whole compartment was involved in a discussion about the English and the American languages. My friends gently got across to me that Americans were mistreating Shakespeare's grand language and had no feeling for language. I conceded that we often did injustices to fine English, but I proposed that when we really looked at all the bad things that we had done to their language, we had still retained the ability to communicate with Englishmen. And, when the need for **understanding** was really at issue, I thought I could prove my point to them with two poems, which I carried in my wallet. Both poems spoke about love, and the loneliness that comes with separation. And, I thought they might concede that despite BAD grammar and TERRIBLE word choice the real message would come through. With that I whipped out my wallet and first read them my all-time favorite, which I had clipped from an English magazine on December 5, 1936, the day on which King Edward VIII had abdicated, and then the version of a Black American girl lamenting the loneliness with her man gone. Here they are:

The Return (by H.M.)

You are not gone as yet,
But still I dream of that far
distant day
When I will nigh forget
The desolate year you will
have been away.
All will be as before
When once I pass the door
Into your room, that warm and
friendly place
and see the smile of welcome
on your face.
We'll have no need for speech;
The subtler language of our
eyes will bleach
The memory of that faded year
apart,
For each will see the other's
naked heart.

Since You Have Went

Since you have went,
The hours have drug an'
slowly passed away.
Since you have went,
The night is long; there
never seems no day.
The sun is dark an' never
shines no more,
The moon's done quit, the
stars is mighty poor;
Their glimmer's glum, the
worst that I have saw,
Since you have went.

Since you have went,
I seen no birds, or saw
no purty flowers.
Since you have went,
There ain't no joy, jes'
weary, dreary hours.
I listen clost; I thought
I heered you call
"Tain't nothin'! wind
a-whispring
like it's fall.
Aw! What's the use?
There's nothing doin' a-tall,
Since you have went.

It was an electrifying discussion and there was the atmosphere of a dinner table with all of us enjoying the opportunity to talk openly about something that most of us tuck away for fear of someone touching a sensitive nerve. We had forgotten time and place and were disappointed when the train stopped in Swindon and I had to get off. They all shook my hand as I got off the train. As I walked down the platform to the exit, someone touched my shoulder. It was the RAF officer who said: "Sergeant, here is my card. It would be great if we could meet again." I took the card, thanked him and boarded the bus for Ogbourne St. George feeling that I had met for the first time real Englishmen—who, after all, if they did not speak like us they at least felt just like Americans.

Fighting the U. S. Army to Get Mail

Toward the end of September all of us were getting edgy because mail had ceased to arrive. Every evening we went to Sally's Salvation Army Canteen and bitched about "NO MAIL," but we also knew there was furious fighting going on on the continent and we felt uneasy taking such a little matter as our mail problem to our company commander, who would have laughed at us. It was early in October with NO MAIL being the daily all consuming topic, when I was reading in Sally's Canteen an article on War Ballots in *Stars & Stripes*. The article dwelt on constitutional rights and the fact that there were 4,800,000 American soldiers overseas who were entitled to participate in the issues for which they were fighting.

It dawned upon me that in those ballots might be the hook to bring the army around to get us our mail. When I screwed up my courage and asked briskly: "Who wants some mail?" the hoots were deafening and I was kind of amazed that those born-in-America guys did not get it immediately. In fact, it took a lot of one-syllable explaining to make them recognize the blessings of being in an army, a democratic army, where even in wartime *civilian* authority—we, as citizens, not as soldiers—were still supreme. It was certainly worth a couple of shillings to cable our senator that we were being deprived of our constitutional right. We needed to impress the United States Army that not getting the war ballots to us was violating the Constitution and might sic a Senate investigation on the army.

> "So we get our ballots! So what?"
> "A lot the army will care!"
> "The army will care plenty. Just you watch."

I got the price of the cable, but they all trooped along to be sure it was properly invested. On the way to the APO the discussion still raged. When one of the disbelievers said, "So, we get our ballots! So what?" one of the new converts to my cause blurted out, "The ballots are in the mail, stupid!" A bored APO clerk counted the message.

> SENATOR ROBERT F. WAGNER
> SENATE BUILDING
> WASHINGTON, D.C.
> MAIL CONTAINING SOLDIERS' BALLOTS WITH-
> HELD FROM UNIT DUE TO UNEXPLAINED CIR-
> CUMSTANCES. LETTER FOLLOWS. PLEASE INVES-
> TIGATE.
> T/4 VON ROSENSTIEL ASN 32826569

"Ten and six"—the clerk tossed the message into a large basket marked BASE CENSOR.

If he had thrown the ten and six out of the window, the boys wouldn't have been more incensed. They thought the cable would go through the unit. Base censor, they were positive, would never pass it; their shillings would have been better spent on beer. I was pretty sure base censor would pass it, since it contained no military information, and even surer that for our purposes it wouldn't matter much one way or the other. The important thing was that it was sent.

"And who is going to impress the army?"

"Me," I said miserably, sick at the thought of the maze of army brass I was leading myself into.

I was hardly a distinguished spokesman. For, appreciative as I was of my life as an American soldier, I was scared stiff of army authority. Whether it was the indelible mark left by six weeks in the German Army during the Czech crisis, or whether Germans are just born with it along with eyes and ears, I don't know. But instinctively my inside froze and my body tensed at the sight of anybody of a higher rank, which for a sergeant, was just about everybody. It was no joke. I hated it; I knew it wasn't warranted, but I just couldn't help it.

And I had been brash enough to promise to leach the mail out of the army. But I had taken their money, so that night I sat down to write the "letter follows" to my senator.

It was a real tearjerker, but I meant every word of it. I mentioned that I had left Germany because I hated Hitler, who had made such farce of elections; and how proud I would be to vote for the first time, not only as a new citizen but as a soldier serving my admired new homeland; and how impressed I had been that filling out the absentee-ballot forms had been part of the processing at the port of embarkation. I knew firsthand, I said, how important the vote is to maintaining democracy, and now it seemed the ballots were being withheld from us—a matter possibly of 4,800,000 votes and certainly a violation or our constitutional right.

The next morning the letter had to be censored by the Inspector General, a nice man whose section, located in the same hut as mine cleared all complaints. But to get to him, I had to get permission of the first sergeant (three stripes and three rockers) to see the company commander (two bars) for permission to see the Inspector General (eagle) Oh, Lord!

I took a deep breath and reported with my very best salute and a wave of nausea. The captain looked up from his desk and asked me what I wanted.

"I'm concerned about the mail, sir."

He cut me short. "You don't want me, sergeant. You want the chaplain. Maybe he can help you. I certainly can't!"

But, sir, this isn't quite the usual," I hurdled on. "It's our ballots."

"Ballots ? Oh, the absentee ballots. Um-m-m. Afraid I can't do much about them, either, son. Um-m-m. No." He looked slightly uneasy.

"No, sir. I just want your permission to see the Inspector General, sir."

"Oh sure!" He laughed good-naturedly. "By all means, sergeant. Go right ahead."

Letter rattling in my hand, and walking like a stork to keep my knees from banging, I saluted stiffly and reported that I had the permission of the company commander to see the Inspector General. He offered me a seat. I sat on the edge of it ramrod-stiff, befitting the presence of a colonel and told him about my concern about the lack of mail.

He smiled kindly. "I know sergeant. My mail isn't coming through either. "Yes, sir," I said, "I understand that, sir. But it isn't just the ordinary mail I'm worried about"—a lie, of course; a terrible offense in the presence of an officer—"but the soldiers' ballots are supposed to be in the mail, sir. It doesn't seem right that all these soldiers are being denied their right to vote and Election Day is coming very close."

"That's right. It is, isn't it? " he mused. "You've got a point there, sergeant." He smiled sympathetically. "But there isn't a thing that I can do about it."

I half rose as if to leave and there was nothing I wanted to do more. But my hands very politely pushed the letter across his desk.

"I understand, sir," I said meekly, "So, if you'll just censor this letter so that I can mail it. . . ."

He glanced casually at the letter. The smile faded from his face. "Sergeant, I can't let that letter go through. I—No. No, indeed I certainly can't pass this. It's—, " he glanced at the letter again, "It's against all regulations." He almost shouted the word with relief, and my stomach dropped at the sound of it.

Then it dawned on the colonel that the telegram was already on the way. "You've sent the cable?" The voice was small for a man of his size.

"Yes, sir," I smiled bravely. "You see, sir, for me the first vote—"

He didn't hear me. He sighed heavily, and suddenly I was sorry for him. He was just as frightened of civilians as I was of him—the higher authority. He was probably imagining, as he stared out of the window, my letter still in his hand, a big army limousine speeding up the road. A big army limousine full of a couple of generals escorting lots of senators, stopping right at his office door. They made a difference, those senators. In Germany, nobody had them.

"Sit down, sergeant." I jumped. "Perhaps we should talk . . . No!" Suddenly he lifted the telephone, cranked the handle and said, "Get me ETOUSA . . . No. ETOUSA, dammit! European Theater of Operations United States Army! Inspector General Haines at Headquarters! Right away!" There was a pause.

I sat there, very still, very stiff, my hands laid correctly on my knees, elbows in, fingers neatly side by side, trying to look as though I weren't listening.

The colonel started talking very slowly, very deliberately and in a wide circle. Gingerly he edged himself to the point of saying: "Well, sir, it's not really just the mail. It's the war ballots, sir. The sergeant has cabled his senator to investigate the delay, sir. Yes, sir, his senator." There was a long pause. "Yes, sir," and the colonel put down the receiver. He looked at me and said, "They'll call back in a few minutes. Stay right here."

It was very quiet. The letter was still lying on the table, but the colonel silently ignored it and me. The fire crackled in the little potbelly stove, and at the far end of the corridor a typewriter rattled urgently. I sat still and stiff, looking respectfully mournful, as I felt a proper sergeant should.

It seemed an eternity until the telephone rang again. The colonel snatched it and snapped to attention. "Colonel Smith speaking. . . . Yes, sir. . . . Yes, sir. . . . Yes, sir." He put the receiver down and said with true conviction, "Well, sergeant, we surely fixed that one in a hurry!" He smiled broadly. "General Haines just advised me that instructions have been issued to all ports to ship every sack of mail immediately, regardless of any other priority. If there is a sack of mail not shipped within the next 24 hours, there'll be hell to pay!" He casually handed me my letter. Uncensored. "Thank you, sir!" I saluted, turned and walked out.

The hullabaloo at Sally's Salvation Army Canteen was tremendous. Twelve hours later the mail trucks came. The postal boys worked around the clock, and for a couple of days I was pushed to the front of the line every time I went to chow. I got over forty letters in that mail. The ballots weren't there, of course. They came around Christmas, instead of greetings from home, and it was 1948 before I got to exercise my constitutional right as a citizen to vote in a national election.

But the army had tried and I appreciated it. I was always sorry I didn't get a chance to do something big in return. I kept trying, but the best I could manage was saving them the embarrassment of shooting me during the heavy infiltration of the Bulge, when I pronounced all the passwords just like a spy. Except for the small group of fellow citizens in Sally's, I was nobody's hero. But among my buddies in our headquarters I had gained a lot of friends.

The House of Commons with Churchill at the Helm

Army life comprises an almost unbelievable amount of boredom and waste of time. If it had not been for the never ending supply of books with which Marion entertained and educated me, I would probably have taken to drink or found some other form of misery. But on the horizon was always London and the adventures that could be found there.

My next trip to London was with Harry Leykauf. We had both studied the Baedeker and had singled out everything that a good tourist would see on a one day tour of London. The whole area from which the government operated was protected by sandbags but despite these impediments we could see #10 Downing Street, and of course Westminster Abbey, the Tower of London, and Parliament. King James Palace and Buckingham Palace were there, and in fact the Guards were changing but Alice was not there. We saw all of it, and had even obtained tickets for a show that was then very popular, "The Hasty Heart."

On this visit, when I delivered the long underwear to Bashford, I had hoped to see Parliament in session. When I got there I learned from a big bobby that the house was not sitting and that there was nothing going on. I was a little more persistent and inquired if there was not something that could entertain an American lawyer? He said: "I don't think that you can get even a glimpse of the British government, but go to that building," pointing to one perhaps 100 yards away. "That's where the House of Lords meets and right now the Law Lords—they are our highest court—are sitting. But I don't think that you'll have much luck, because the sessions are not public. It's just the Law Lords and the Barristers." I thanked him and trotted over there. A tall, impressive bobby at the entrance let me into the building. I told him that I was an American soldier, and that I was in civilian life an attorney. A colleague of his at the House of Commons had told me that the session was not public, but I would really appreciate it if he could let me have a peek at the Law Lords. He cautioned me not to cause him trouble and allowed me to stand inside a dark gallery within sight and hearing of the court. When I was tired, he told me, come out and he would let me out of the building.

And now I saw the Highest British Court, with Lord Simon, the former Secretary of the Exchequer, presiding and running a very tight ship. Normally when one goes into court and hears a legal discussion it really does not matter whether it is in a language that one understands or not because the discussion is so technical that one might just as well attend a Kabuki Theater. But I was in luck. The court was hearing a problem on the frustration of contracts, an issue that at that time was discussed with considerable eagerness in England and America. It dealt with a contractual business problem created by war. For example, a man rents a big showroom for the specific purpose of using it to show new automobiles. A month after the first automobiles are shown, war breaks out and the manufacture of pleasure cars is discontinued. Can the tenant be allowed to withdraw from his lease? I had written an article on the subject for the Fordham Law Review and had cited all the British cases that I now heard the judges and attorneys cite and debate. I stood there for well over an hour soaking in the elegant formality of the judges and barristers, all operating in wigs and displaying a courtesy that seemed to go back hundreds of years.

When that case was finished and the next one started, I realized that I was lost. So, I slipped out, thanked the Bobby and asked him to give me his name and address, because I wanted to thank him for his kindness. He wrote onto a small slip of paper with the Seal of the House of Commons, taken from a pad that he had in his pocket: PC (Police Constable) **162A Robert Gordon, Police Room, House of Commons London SW 1.** He let me out of the building, and smiled with the kind and slightly condescending expression that officials everywhere, who constantly deal with all sorts of strangers often display. I walked away on wings. That evening in camp, I wrote him a little note thanking him for the great treat he had given me, and I sent him a package with some of the things that were rationed in England: cigars, pipe tobacco, and a few Hershey bars. The package went off and I felt really good about my adventure.

Never could I have imagined what that little slip of paper with PC Gordon's name could accomplish. On my next visit to London, the first item on my list was "Parliament -House of Commons." When I arrived on the morning of November 29, 1944, I could not believe my eyes. There must have been more than a thousand GIs lined up in single file reaching around Westminster Abbey. I walked to the front of the line, where one of those familiar gigantic bobbies was standing and smiling benignly at the endless line of GIs. From time to time he would count off groups of 20 that would be escorted by a guide into the House of Commons. There they would be walked around the ground floor, and would be allowed to peek through a small window into the chamber where they would see the Speaker of the House in his ornate uniform. As they left the building, they received a little printed pamphlet, which explained that these were temporary quarters for the House, because the "real chambers" had been destroyed in an air raid during the 1940 Blitz.

When I walked up to that big bobby, I could already see how he was readying for me that conventional smile with which he would explain that there was still room at the end of that long line behind Westminster Abbey. He was completely perplexed when I said: "Officer, I have no intention of seeing the House of Commons. I would just like to see a friend of mine on your staff." With that I presented him with the small slip that PC Gordon had given me and asked if it might be possible for me to see him. He blew a whistle, a runner from the entrance of the building appeared, and he handed him the slip. It was not more than perhaps five minutes when PC Gordon appeared—not with his official high bobby hat, but bare-headed. He recognized me instantly, pumped my hand and walked me into the building leaving behind a totally bewildered bobby and a long line of GIs.

Inside the building I asked PC Gordon if there was a chance to see the House in action. There was not a moment's hesitation. He led me up a stairs, opened a door, directed me to an empty seat, and there I sat in the special diplomatic visitors' box looking down and seeing the whole English government in all its glory perform for me.

A long table divided the room. At the very end of the table, on an ornate, decorated chair with a high back, elevated by a platform was the Speaker in his ornate uniform. The Speaker was the personification of British Pomp and Circumstance. Almost below me was a banister with a swinging door through which every member who wanted to enter the Commons had to pass. But before he could proceed to his seat he had to attract the Speaker's attention, who would acknowledge his desire to get to his seat and wave him on by a mere nod. If there were no nod he would have to wait.

The row to the left of the table was occupied by the government, which entered by a side door. And there, surrounded by Attlee, Eden, Bevan, Beaverbrook and his whole war cabinet, was Churchill, totally relaxed with his feet on the Dispatch Box, the symbol of governmental power. I watched the proceedings as members entered and left, invariably greeted and released by the Speaker. To the right of the table was the opposition.

Luck was with me in another way. I had picked the one day in the month when the government had to answer questions from the floor—questions that had not been sent up before. They were fresh and often unexpected and totally unpredictable. I recall seeing Lady Astor, one of the perhaps two or three women sitting in the house.

Uninformed as I was about British parliamentary customs, I was a little disappointed that the great man down there, who had rallied the nation by promising them "Blood, Sweat and Tears," and who had praised his gallant air force by proclaiming "that never have so many owed so much to so few," did not say a single word during the more than two hours that I was there. And yet, his mere presence added a curious tension to the proceedings, where the government was asked to provide answers to questions that may have been bandied around and were often asked to embarrass the government.

Winifred Nerney later obtained for me a transcript of the proceedings of that great day, which I saved. There are a few questions that I marked at the time, because they illustrate so nicely that in war and peace fools insist upon being heard.

> Question to the Minister of Information: Whether he will arrange to offer the bound volumes of Hansard to the State Libraries of the 48 States of the U.S.A. as a contribution by His Majesty's Government to the increase of knowledge in the U.S.A. about Great Britain and the Colonies.
> Question to the Parliamentary Secretary of the Ministry of War Transport: If the ancient milestone that was removed in 1940 for reasons of security from the place where the old packhorse track from Horston and Ling Ghyll Bridge met the Roman Road from Bainbridge on the buttress of Cam Fell near Settle has been replaced, or if he can state the whereabouts of this stone.
> Question to the Minister of Agriculture: Whether he will

consider establishing within 10 miles of London 10,000 goats, in view of the fact that they could supplement the milk supply and relieve the milk shortage.

And, inquiries about Yugoslavia were high on the list in 1944 as they are today: Question to the Parliamentary Secretary of the Minister of Economic Warfare: Whether he is aware that voluntary organizations in this country and the U.S.A. have large quantities of medical supplies, clothing and other much needed goods ready for shipment to Yugoslavia, but are finding great difficulty in getting transport facilities; what prospects there are of some shipping being made available for these much- needed supplies; and when the last shipment of those supplies to Yugoslavia took place.

All of these questions were quickly disposed of—usually by the responsible minister saying that he would look into the matter and that he would inform the Honorable Member by letter. It was amazing how civilized and courteous the interchanges were. I recall one member accusing a member of the government of "taking unusual liberties with the truth," a phrase that had been passed by the Speaker as acceptable if someone wanted to assert that someone had lied.

But the most fascinating episode I observed dealt with a very pointed question of whether the government had taken action to construct needed housing for a project that had been discussed before. The questioner, who obviously wanted to goad the government into action, used in his question the flowery phrase "the government after an elephantine period of gestation has produced no visible results—My question is: Can we have an answer from the government whether the government is prepared to build this needed housing?"

Perhaps it was the unusual phrasing. Perhaps Churchill was tired of hearing it. He merely pointed to Eden as the one who would deal with the question. Eden now rose very slowly. Before uttering the first word he had handed a slip of paper to a runner who disappeared through a back door, apparently to produce the pertinent file. Very slowly to gain time Eden now began to paraphrase the question, using long winded mellifluous language and regurgitating it several times. He spoke with amazing skill saying nothing. After about 10 minutes of this dilatory exercise the runner returned with the file. Eden glanced at it and merely stated: "The government's answer is NO" and sat down.

When the Commons adjourned, I found P C Gordon and thanked him. The next time I saw him was in October of 1945, when I again came to visit at the House of Commons. He gave me a collection of 12 Postcards of the Houses of Parliament, inscribed: Just a little token of friendship—Bob Gordon—October 1945.

We kept in touch with him and saw him several times in London and for the last time in 1976 a few months before he died. His daughter wrote me after he had passed away that he had retained all my letters and Christmas cards covering almost 25 years.

Toward the end of December it was obvious that the war was gaining momentum. On December 16, news came over the radio that the Germans had mounted a gigantic surprise attack in the Ardennes, the same area where in 1940 they had surprised the French and British armies and ultimately knocked France out of the war. The 101st Airborne Division had holed up in Bastogne, controlling a large traffic net, surrounded completely by a sea of advancing German troops. General McAuliffe's cocky message: "Situation normal, completely surrounded" was reported as a sign of utter confidence.

General Ridgway immediately transferred most of his staff and support troops to Reims. Planes were coming and going day and night. As place on transport planes became available, our section moved to the continent.

Col. Moss, Junior, and Leykauf were the first to go, Major Moroney, Ristow and I followed on December 28. Now the real excitement would start.

CHAPTER 7

FRANCE

ON THE MORNING of December 28, 1944, still in England, I was sitting in the office in Ogbourne St. George, anticipating orders to get ready for a flight to Reims at any moment. The telephone rang. I answered, recognizing Col. Moss's voice at the other end. The connection was terrible. To make me understand better he increased the volume of his voice and now the buzzing in the line was comparable to a truck stuck in mud unsuccessfully racing its wheels. Although I could not understand a single word of what he was saying, I replied with an enthusiastic "Yes sir—Yes sir—Yes sir," hoping that when I saw him in France I would make some sense out of our strange conversation. Finally I heard him say: "See you tomorrow" and hang up. Within minutes Maj. Moroney came and said, "We are leaving in an hour. Pack all the stuff that's left and get going—we can't miss that plane.

Traveling as a soldier was simple. Our worldly possessions fit into two bags, both marked with our name and serial number stenciled large on the outside to avoid mix- up. We had been issued one blanket and a shelter half at the Port of Embarkation in New York. Shelter halves were the equipment of the infantry soldier. Two of them could be joined to provide a pup tent and very primitive lodging for two soldiers. We discarded those halves when we discovered that this was equipment for real hardened fighting men, not for us, the softer more refined men in corps headquarters. As the campaign in Europe went on, we added sleeping bags and a pillow to our possessions. It is amazing how much comfort even a small pillow will deliver.

Except for my qualifying glider rides, I had no experience with flying. The flight from Ogbourne St. George to Reims—a distance of about 300 miles—was, in fact, my second flight. The first had been a Lufthansa flight from Berlin to Nuremberg in 1934. Now I was climbing into a C-47 transport war plane with 26 bucket seats for paratroopers. It was a wartime workhorse model. Above the metal bucket seats with seat belts was a strong cable where the troopers would hook their chutes upon the command of "Stand-up and hook-up" before they were pushed out of the door by the jump master. There were not even buckets for those of us who would experience air sickness. But the sergeant in charge of the load cheered us with the information that our steel helmets were designed to serve as wash basins and to accept airsickness deposits. The plane was full. I was lucky to have a seat near a window and could follow our flight.

It was a smooth but cold ride—C-47 planes had no heating equipment. After a short time we reached the channel with the white cliffs of Dover visible in the distance. There was heavy shipping traffic and then the coast of France appeared. I remember noticing a number of shot down American and British bomber planes lying clearly visible in the fields. There was no other destruction that I could see. At the airport in Reims a jeep was waiting to deliver us to our official quarters, the famous **Red School House** in which four and half months later, on May 8th 1945, the Germans accepted the terms of unconditional surrender. It was wonderful to be re-united with my buddies, but we were very happy to move out three days later and turn this place over to General Eisenhower, who was moving his headquarters closer to the fighting. Before the Germans had yielded Reims to the Allies they had done a mean trick. They had poured cement into every toilet in that big building and all of us had to use emergency latrines that had been dug by German prisoners- of-war in the court yard.

Colonel Moss met us there and the first thing that he asked me was: "Did you get me the eagles?" Now, it dawned upon me what all his talk, of which I had not understood one word, had been about. He had been promoted from lieutenant colonel to the full rank of a colonel and wanted to display his new eagles. I confessed that I had failed to understand, but that I would produce a set of embroidered eagles for his field jacket and his lined raincoat in a couple of days. He looked dubious, but merely said, "Let's see what you can come up with."

I remembered that one of the full colonels in Ogbourne St. George wore on his field jacket not the conventional metal eagles with a safety pin fastener, but an eagle stitched with yellow thread on a ribbon. So, I spent the next morning walking through Reims in search of a notion store to find some bright yellow thread, a pack of needles and some greenish-grey ribbon about 1 1/4 inch wide. Triumphantly I returned to the office, found the model that I remembered, made a sketch and set out to produce four embroidered eagles that I had promised Colonel Moss. Both of us were proud when he walked out of the office to parade his new eagles. Some time later, when he had to make an evaluation of me, he commented on my resourcefulness and perhaps he was thinking of the eagles as he wrote that word of praise.

How I got all the film for the pictures that I now began to take, I cannot remember. But I recall that we were allowed to have cameras and take "approved pictures." The only complication was that nobody knew or would tell us what "approved pictures" were. The PX, which handled this problem, always returned the exposed film completely black with a note: "Did not pass censor." This alerted us to be creative about developing film. As I found out later my creativity in this area almost got me court-martialed and sent to jail.

After only three days in Reims, we moved with all of our paraphernalia, which included our typewriters and books to Epernay, where we were billeted in the champagne factory of **Moet et Chandon,** today the largest of the French champagne manufacturers. An imposing administration building and a smaller office building had been set aside for our headquarters. The place was well chosen, because in vast caverns underground there were endless fields of bottled champagne. In time we discovered approaches to those treasures. We stayed for about three or four days and then started out for Belgium, where after initial setbacks, the **Battle of the Bulge** was gradually turning into a giant trap for the German elite forces that had hoped to reach Antwerp and cut the American supply lines.

The Battle of the Bulge

For the next five months our mode of transportation was a large 2 1/2 ton truck from the headquarters motor pool, which carried six enlisted men and the typewriters and other equipment for the Judge Advocate's and Inspector General's sections. I still have a picture of that truck and most of the regular crew. With our barracks bags, sleeping bags, and the bed rolls of the officers for which we were responsible, it was crowded. The truck was equipped with some bows to which a tarpaulin was fastened to keep us protected from the rain and snow that we now encountered, but most of the time we rode in the open to have better visibility. It was very cold and we huddled together for warmth. We always had a small supply of hard liquor—not authorized for enlisted men—to restore us to health after those icy rides. The officers were transported in jeeps that usually led the pack.

Banneux-Notre-Dame

From the first day we were sent into battle there was never a moment of panic or question that the Germans would be beaten no matter what they threw at us. Every morning General Ridgway was out running with some of his closest advisors. After breakfast, armed with a Springfield rifle with scope he led his caravan of staff officers, all armed to the teeth, into battle. The convoy of jeeps, with the six jeeps of the defense platoon taking off at break-neck speed for the front, is one of the memorable pictures that I never managed to snap. We did not have to wait for *Stars & Stripes* to hear what had happened at the front. Every evening the defense platoon provided us with on-the-spot commentary of what they had seen at the front that day.

Our first stop was Banneux-Notre-Dame, a small town with a convent and a school for girls not far from Liege, which I think with Antwerp was one of the main targets of Hitler's attack. I always wondered how our headquarters staff had predetermined the places where we would be located. There were always cleverly requisitioned buildings with ample office space—cleared of their normal inhabitants for our convenience. Within hours of our arrival field telephone service would be installed and in the evening there would invariably be hot chow—i.e., hot C-rations. I still have a little booklet about that convent, but what fascinated us more than anything else was that we were billeted right next to what was known as **"Buzz Bomb Alley."** The Germans were plastering Antwerp, the big Belgian harbor that brought vast military supplies to the Western front, with Buzz Bombs hoping to interrupt the stream of supplies that was overwhelming them. These bombs were in effect a heavy load of explosives fitted into a rudimentary airplane body with two short, stubby wings and a motor that had the harsh sound of a two cycle engine. We stood in awe, as these monsters flew clearly visible in an endless chain on their course to Antwerp, and we prayed that they had enough fuel to get away from us. One of them must have read our minds. It stopped right next to where we stood and exploded upon hitting a farm building, less than a quarter of a mile distant. We ran over to have a look. Where moments ago a solid farm building had stood there was now a deep crater with twisted beams and the remnants of the bomb. Fortunately there were no casualties but the war was getting closer. We withdrew to our convent, hoping that the divine protection that the convent had enjoyed thus far would extend to us as well.

War has many faces. We had not anticipated that diarrhea could be a formidable enemy too—not as deadly as the Germans but unpleasant just the same. Whatever the cause, all of us, officers as well as enlisted men, were touched by it and the dispensary was fortunately equipped with vast supplies of bismuth and paregoric that kept us working. The moment the plague hit, the medical unit realized that the indoor toilets in the convent would never be sufficient to stem the rush, so an enormous trench was dug in the convent's court, 2 x 4 beams were erected for our sitting comfort, and a giant tarpaulin protected us from the heavy snow that had started to fall. During that night as one after the other from my section made a run for this battlefield, we fortunately remembered that General Ridgway had issued orders about conduct in enemy territory. We all reached the 2 x 4's in our long underwear but fully armed and with steel helmet, securely strapped. The MPs who were waiting to collect fines for disobeying standing orders were thwarted.

Among the mountains of military communications that flooded all headquarters was a December 1944 directive from Eisenhower's headquarters that airborne units should look for competent enlisted lawyers in their ranks to be commissioned as officers to fill vacancies for which there were no suitable replacements. Col. Moss saw the report, and told me to file the application so that I could be made a lieutenant and assigned to him. Clearly I had arrived. For the next week I used every spare moment to bring together the facts that I needed for filing that application. I found it very encouraging that everybody in headquarters went out of their way to help me assemble all the essential facts—there was not the slightest bit of that suspicion which had pursued me for such a long time.

Since I was by far the least competent typist of the four enlisted men in our section, I was constantly used as messenger between the widely dispersed judge advocate units that were part of our command. I was on the road almost every day. Traveling at that time in Belgium was not safe, because the Germans had infiltrated the American held territory, equipping their English speaking soldiers with American uniforms and weapons that they had taken off dead Americans or prisoners. These saboteurs shot up random single vehicles and occasionally misdirected American convoy forces at road crossings. This caused some damage but above all created apprehension and confusion and made many Americans trigger-happy for anyone who spoke with an accent. I was clearly an endangered species, fully aware of the unhealthy climate in which I was a potential target not only for German infiltrators but also for trigger-happy, nervous Americans. My rifle became my beloved companion, and I never left without discussing my predicament with my driver. Before I took off we both rehearsed the passwords for the day and hoped that we would not be confronted with unaudited but difficult challenges like: "Who is the King of Swat?" a question that only a person steeped in American baseball lore could answer correctly with "Babe Ruth." I was fortunate that every driver I had was a native born American and we had agreed that if we were ever challenged, he would be the one to say the password, particularly if it contained a "th."

Much later I learned that Germans posing as American officers were easily spotted and invariably shot. The real American officers carried an identification card that had a deliberate typo. It read: **Indentification Card.** The German craftsmen who reproduced the identification cards for the fake American infiltrators spelled it correctly—**Identification Card**—and enabled American MPs to shoot those with correct spelling on the spot.

The roads in Belgium were icy and covered with snow—often more than a foot deep; it was scary driving for miles through those dense, silent forest lined roads, where we at every moment expected to be stopped. Along those roads were wrecked vehicles, American and German, and occasionally we saw searching parties from the graves registration units looking for bodies to be buried. On the few days when it wasn't snowing and the sun shone I saw fighter planes chasing each other at great heights like dragon flies with their vapor trails painting elegant white lines against the blue sky. Often this distant playful duel terminated when one of the curves changed into a straight line, pointing directly to the ground—a beautiful, tragic casualty of the war.

Francochamps

After only a few days at Banneux-Notre-Dame we were delighted to leave Buzz Bomb Alley and move to our new station in Francochamps, about 20 miles southeast of Liege, where we saw lots of artillery damage and evidence of heavy fighting—burned out houses, dead tanks and wrecked motor vehicles pushed to the side of the road. One of my photos reminds me of a stop at a rail yard in Liege, where Col. Moss and I delighted a little kid when we let her wear a steel helmet and enjoy a chocolate bar.

When I refreshed my memory about the location of Francochamps—50 years after the events—by studying a 1993 road map of Belgium, the whole fascination of my arrival at our new headquarters site suddenly came back to me. I found myself in truly historical territory. About 3 miles north is the town of Spa, which in WW I had been the imperial headquarters of the German Army. Here the Kaiser abdicated and from here he drove to the Dutch border—a mere 15 miles—to seek asylum in Holland. In my mind's eye I could see the pompous field grey Mercedes touring car and the Kaiser's old chauffeur, whom I had met at the Berlin Royal Castle in 1938, when I showed Marion the sights of Berlin. He had told us about driving the Kaiser from Spa to the Dutch border, where he had surrendered himself to border guards. The last thing the Kaiser did was to instruct his chauffeur to take the car back to Berlin, because it was German government property.

Four events of our stay in Francochamps are indelibly impressed in my mind. First: When we arrived the weather was terrible with intermittent snow and sleet and thawing that made most roads very difficult to traverse. The highways were littered with wrecked trucks and tanks that had failed to stay on the narrow highways with one hairpin curve following the next. To get to the mess hall for chow we had to cross a highway on which trucks, tanks, tank destroyers, and heavy equipment were moving in an endless chain. To cross the highway was a desperate act. I remember standing there hungry and shivering, but lacking the courage to sprint across. On the other side of the road, at a distance of perhaps 200 feet, stood a hotel with an open terrace, which Ridgway had requisitioned for himself. I had to get past that building to reach the mess hall but I was still waiting for an opening to risk the dash across, when I noticed commotion on the terrace with army photographers setting up equipment. Suddenly the door opened and Ridgway held the door to let his guest step out and see the traffic rushing to the front. It was Field Marshal Bernard Montgomery, the hero from Al Alamein to whose army we had been attached during this campaign. Cocky and with the arrogance that had made him famous, he stepped briskly past Ridgway onto a patch of ice and fell flat on his face. He jumped up, helped by Ridgway and fortunately none of the army photographers used the opportunity to take a picture of "Monty," the British general most disliked by American soldiers. "Monty a Temporary Victim of the Ice" might have been a good caption for the picture that was never taken.

The second event involved my introduction to the B & F (Bath and Fumigation) Company. After about ten days of living without washing facilities other than those available from our helmets, we had acquired an intense aroma. To cope with this problem our headquarters provided a military solution that offered clean clothing and superior washing facilities. A B&F Company had been ordered to set up business nearby. They had found a reasonably clear river from which to draw water, and forcing it through some purification devices, they heated it in gigantic oil fired boilers for showers and laundering.

We were trucked to their establishment. Before we left we were told to remove all rank signs from our field jackets and shirts before lining up for the bath and to keep them to sew back later. Instructions were to turn in every stitch of clothing as we entered the unit and receive as we left reasonably similar clothing. The clothing we received—naturally all government issue—came from a group who had preceded us. An experienced F&B sergeant (probably drafted for that purpose from the fitting department of Brooks Brothers) approximated the fit and assisted us with the acquisition of clean clothes.

It was a glorious experience and I was awed by the ingenuity of the army's preparation for war. It was bitter cold outside and snowing as the first of about three groups of 80 enlisted men from our headquarters were herded into a large, pleasantly heated tent with duck boards on the floor. Men from the B&F unit divided us into groups of about twenty and directed us to big tables where we turned in every piece of clothing from field jackets to socks and handkerchiefs, keeping only our jump boots and dog tags. Naked, we walked on duck board passages into a nicely heated adjacent tent with about 25 shower heads. Along one of the walls were numbered boxes for our boots. The shower heads were fastened to wooden poles that supported the tent top. Attached to the poles were soap dishes with *Life Bouy* soap and a wash rag. A string with which we could activate a stream of pleasantly hot water started our cleansing action. In a matter of ten minutes we could scrub and shower ourselves to pristine cleanliness.

As we left the shower and stepped to the edge of the tent, clean, dry towels were waiting for us. Now, naked and with boots in hand we left the shower room to enter a room with large tables where mountains of freshly washed socks and handkerchiefs were waiting. On tables nearby, shirts, pants, and field jackets were arranged in heaps indicating three sizes: small, medium and large. It was up to us to pick something that might come close to what we had been issued originally and now had turned in. The clothes that we received smelled pleasantly clean but were not pressed, a matter that we soon remedied because several of our defense platoon heroes had electric irons which operated on the generator-produced electricity that followed us everywhere. In a couple of days most of us had replaced our rank indicia on our shirts and our clothes began to acquire in daily increments the perfume that would follow us for the next few months until we again met a B&F Company.

The third memorable event of my time in Francochamps came when I spied a notice on a bulletin board. It said that on Saturday we could, for a very reasonable fee, take a sulfur bath from the healing springs that had made the baths of nearby Spa famous for hundreds of years. I was one of the few to sign up. I knew from history books and occasional comments that the Spa in Belgium was the playground of royalty and millionaires. My imagination was running wild. I had seen splendor and luxury by paying fees for conducted tours of castles and palaces. But now for a puny entrance fee, I could be on the same level as a potentate—I would *use* not merely *view*.

The place was luxury incarnate. In a park-like environment were numerous buildings designed to accommodate people who were determined to buy back, at great cost, the health that they had wrecked, at great expense, by overeating. Some of the buildings had clearly been in use for many years, but the bath house, even though constructed during the last century, looked like a prominent Health Center. It had been updated and modernized with the most elegant bath equipment imaginable. I was escorted by an attendant in a white uniform to a large, tiled bath chamber with a gigantic bathtub—a full seven feet long and almost twice the width of American bathtubs, and very much deeper than any tub I had ever seen. From highly polished, gilded faucets, my attendant filled the tub with very hot water with a distinct sulfur odor. He let me feel the temperature and added cold water until I thought that I could manage. Then, as he let me lower myself into the tub, he warned me, our conversation was carried on in fractured French, of the powerful and exhausting action of the water. This, he advised, made it necessary for me to get out of the tub in half an hour at the most. He promised to be back after about 20 minutes, which was about what most people could stand taking their first bath. While he stood by I lowered myself into the tub wondering what famous men and women might have used this tub before.

After 20 minutes the attendant returned with an elegant, gigantic, white monogrammed bath towel, which had been pre-warmed. Now he led me to a recuperating room where I rested on a bed, covered with a clean sheet and a woolen blanket. As I departed from the building an hour later I felt a little disappointed—as if I had been in a never-never land where I did not really fit.

I had a little time left before the truck would take me back to our quarters and I used it to walk through the town to see if I could find something nice for Marion and the babe, who by this time had reached the age of one. I found a delightful dark cap, lined with white rabbit fur and a tiny baby cap. There has never been a cap in my family that was worn with greater pride and for a longer time. After about 25 years we reluctantly had to throw it out. The rabbit fur had lost most of its hair.

My fourth memorable recollection deals with the application for an officer's commission. Once my applications and the necessary paperwork for my promotion to officer status were completed, I had to appear before various field selection boards, whose officer members stamped me through with extraordinary speed in order to get back to their main job of fighting the Germans. The officers of the XVIII Airborne Corps certified:

> His quality of leadership, character, moral fitness and efficiency were found to be excellent. The applicant possesses the necessary military and professional training to qualify him for appointment as Second Lieutenant, AUS.

On January 15th, equipped with this endorsement, I went to a large field hospital of the First Army in St. Vith for my physical. St. Vith had just been cleared of the Germans after some brutal fighting, and the hospital had finished most of their urgent casualty work, so that they could check me from stem to stern. I still have the medical report, which shows me to have been in good physical condition. The medical officer who examined me was young, perhaps younger than I. We talked as he carried out this routine task. He told me that only two days ago this place was a madhouse with streams of casualties coming in, being attended to and then flown to major hospitals in England. A photo that was attached to my application has the inscription: Picture taken 8 January 1945 in the field in Belgium. It shows me standing bare headed, lined up against a brick wall—looking slightly uncomfortable, almost like a man expecting execution.

The Inspector General, knowing that I could manage French, asked me to accompany him to a small nearby town where he had to investigate a complaint against American airborne soldiers. For the whole period of the war the town had owned an air raid warning system that was activated by a fairly compact electrical unit not much bulkier than a big typewriter. It had always been in the mayor's office where he himself switched it on and off as needed, and it had enabled the inhabitants to reach the shelters. When the Germans fled after four and half years of occupation, the town was occupied by the pursuing Americans, and they installed themselves in the mayor's office. When the Americans moved on, the alarm-unit was missing. The next morning the mayor found a typed message on his office stairs:

> AVAILABLE: Air raid warning system.
> PRICE: 12 bottles of brandy.
> Deposit brandy at bridge at village entrance.
> No brandy—No system

There was no question that the men who had sent the message were some of those who had been assigned to our corps, but we could identify neither the unit nor any of the men. Inquiries led nowhere. The mayor had not considered raising the brandy, because he felt that the "Liberators" would not stoop so low and do such a mean thing. My French was good enough to get the story across to the Inspector General and both of us felt sorry for the local people. The villagers did not get the unit back. Jeeps frequently passed the bridge, but no brandy was ever deposited. After a few days the unit was found in the creek—no longer usable. War is hell.

I was able to resolve another case more equitably. One morning a friend of mine from the defense platoon came to consult me about an "act of liberation" (the common phrase for looting) that he had carried out. He wanted to get his loot back to his girlfriend in the States, but there was obviously something that bothered him. From a filthy bag he pulled a beautifully engraved antique silver plate about 15 inches in diameter. It did not take more than one glance to realize that he held in his hands a platter that had been used for centuries for dispensing the Holy Supper. Written around the edge in classic gothic letters was:

Unser taeglich Broth gieb uns heute.
(Give us our daily bread)

It was obvious that my friend had entered a German church in the area just occupied by American troops and pocketed this precious old plate from right off the altar. I suggested that he waste no time and get it back to where he had picked it up. If he were caught with it, I assured him that no one in the Judge Advocate's section could save him and that General Ridgway would not lift a finger for him. He took the plate back and to show his appreciation for my gratuitous legal advice, pressed one of my shirts.

Raeren

From Francochamps we moved north to Raeren, our last headquarters during the Battle of the Bulge just a few miles South of Aachen. As we proceeded to the new site we passed through destroyed areas around Eupen and Malmedy, which had been defended by fanatical German SS units. In December of 1944, seventy disarmed American prisoners-of-war were machine gunned and killed by German SS troops, which suddenly gave the city of Malmedy a grizzly fame.

As we moved north we passed some of the enormous fortifications that Germany had erected at its borders to keep the American tank armies from reaching the Rhine River. To make passage impossible thousands of slave laborers had constructed endless interlocking rows of steel-reinforced cement obstacles, dubbed dragons' teeth. This defensive wall, named with Wagnerian melodrama the *Siegfried Line*, was to guarantee that no enemy would ever set foot on German soil. The photos that I took at the time have the same qualities as those I had taken years ago of the Chinese Wall. Newer attack techniques had already made these monumental defense structures obsolete before the first cement form was cast.

By the time we reached Raeren, we were almost at the German border and the front had stabilized. The great last hurrah of the German Army had been spent at enormous cost in men and material, by both sides. Both sides needed time for regrouping. The crossing of the Rhine, which Hitler had promised would never happen, lay ahead. There were small skirmishes here and there, but the front was quiet.

Once settled into the routine of the new quarters, still in Belgium but within sight of Germany, we had time to think about improving our lives. We were tired of C-and occasional K-rations, which provided sustenance but not much variety. So, Col. Moss suggested that I test my German and see if I could not rustle up something like eggs, milk, perhaps a little fresh meat and potatoes in exchange for the greatest barter goods of all times: American cigarettes. Actually the assignment turned out to be much simpler than I had anticipated. A woman on a farm that seemed untouched by the war, looked thoroughly frightened when our jeep stopped in front of the house and I, armed to the teeth, approached her. When I greeted her in German and told her that she did not have to fear us, that we were with the American troops that had just occupied the area, she nodded understandingly. When I asked her if we could perhaps exchange some cigarettes for fresh milk, some eggs, a little butter, potatoes and even some meat, she looked greatly relieved, motioned me into the house and her spotless kitchen. She gave me two dozen fresh eggs, some fresh milk, which we poured into some empty wine bottles, a bag of potatoes, which had been stored in the basement of the house, a piece of fresh butter and a nice slab of bacon, which she had hidden in a metal container in the adjacent barn. The three packs of Lucky Strike cigarettes that I handed her— in terms of purchasing power of that time about $60 made her feel richly rewarded. She directed me to a butcher shop in the next village, where cigarettes would certainly persuade the butcher to find some fresh meat. Her advice proved correct. I returned to Raeren with my acquisitions that included seven large Schnitzels, one for each of us including the faithful jeep driver. That evening our section had a banquet for which Colonel Moss and Maj. Moroney contributed the liquor and some wine.

When we got back to our quarters after that glorious meal we heard that orders had been issued for our return the next day, February 14th, to Epernay our main French headquarters for rest and recuperation. The travel instructions directed us along a straight route leading us past Reims back to where we had come from six weeks ago. When I inspected the map I realized that by making a little extra loop in the opposite direction, we could sightsee Aachen only 10 miles away, and I would incidentally return to Germany for the first time since leaving in 1939. Actually it would extend our return trip by about 40 miles and perhaps three or four hours. I was convinced that in the general confusion of such a major move, the delay of a small section such as ours would never be noticed. Colonel Moss, to whom I presented the idea, listened to my suggestions and felt that it was a reasonable plan and a unique opportunity to see the place where Charlemagne, that great medieval ruler over France and Germany was buried. He was convinced that the people in Louisiana, where the Code Napoleon is still honored, would fully appreciate his decision to go.

The Return of the Native

As we approached Aachen we saw a scene of destruction the like of which I had never seen or imagined before. Pictures of Stalingrad had given me an idea that war can turn a city into shambles, but actually seeing, smelling, and experiencing it was something different. We drove through town, not very fast so that we could observe and take some snapshots. A church in the center of town appeared almost intact except for a burnt-out steeple, which probably had been used as an artillery observation post. On a place not far from the church was the statue of some king on horseback. His horse had a good many holes and his proud glance and gesture were in sad contrast to the picture that lay before him—a field of ruins as far as he could see.

Our jeep had no trouble negotiating the streets because we drove on sidewalks, and squeezed between craters and cracked walls. Upon inquiry we learned that the cathedral was at least in part standing, so we followed the directions and quickly found it. Of all the cathedrals it is probably one of the most famous in Germany, because it is the burial place of nobody less than Charlemagne and the site of the coronation of the first of the Hapsburg emperors.

We walked inside. The center part, almost intact, was used for religious services; a side chapel was roofless and had been boarded off. I entered through a small door. Debris covered the floor, portions of the lead-framed windows were missing, some were scattered all over the floor; the high carved wooden chairs were covered with pulverized mortar and half hidden under the roof that had fallen down. The high altar was empty and the crucifix gone; but even in this scene of utter destruction the walls with the gothic window holes, the ship-like quality of the whole section, still retained the feeling of a church, a mute witness that people had worshiped here, and would go on doing so. The statues of the saints up on the walls reminded me of Naumburg and Bamberg. They were hidden under protective covers of wood and may have survived, along with the famous diamond studded pulpit, hidden under a stone enclosure, which a provident bishop had erected in time. I walked toward the high altar. The sunlight barely penetrated through the remaining portions of the colored glass windows that were covered with a thick layer of dust.

I picked up a piece of red glass with its small frame of lead—truly a relic. The tomb of Charlemagne was untouched, as was the big chandelier that Charlemagne had given to the church. The tomb is under the pulpit and for my money pretty badly designed. I knew that Charlemagne was buried in Aachen, but hadn't realized that he was buried in the cathedral.

I was interested in seeing what the German people would seem like to me after my absence. The people seemed servile when you talked to them with firmness and an air of authority. I noticed it in men more than in women; men in Germany seemed to be more easily impressed than women. Once you have talked to the people for a short while, they assume the attitude of people who have been bitterly wronged and who are in a bad jam through no fault of their own. Since they are usually likable people, this technique of bartering for sympathy seemed to produce quick and satisfactory results with GIs who just cannot be hard boiled. People did not seem hostile but instead rather pathetic. A woman who explained the church to me later on prayed in front of a side altar. I would have been interested to know what she prayed for—did she ask for strength to carry on? Or for humility? Or for forgiveness? Or perhaps for a chance to get even with the Nazis? Or to get even with the Americans who had wrecked her hometown and made her a beggar? I will never know but what was apparent was that she acted like a person who was not aware of having done anything wrong and who had a *right* to be treated with consideration and sympathy.

And so I re-entered, after an absence of six years, the country in which I was born and had lived for the first 28 years of my life. I could not have known then that the sites and events that I would witness soon would make the day in Aachen look like a mere misfortune.

R&R—Rest & Recuperation

We found our quarters in Epernay as we had left them. But the next morning there was a surprise that demonstrated why General Ridgway was such a respected field commander. When we came to the mess hall there was a tube of brushless shaving cream and a pack of Gilette razor blades for each of us, a reminder that soldiers must look sharp at all times. And when we lined up for chow we could not believe our eyes: Fresh eggs—as many as we would ask for—any which way—scrambled, sunny side up, flipped, big slabs of bacon, sausages, pancakes, maple syrup, toast, butter, jam. And did we eat after having been on field rations for six weeks!

That morning after breakfast we all assembled for a short speech by General Ridgway. He reviewed what we had accomplished and told us that the real job was still ahead of us. He concluded with this remark: "Gentlemen, you have done very well. The next time I expect you to do better."

Aside from finding various ways of touring the champagne manufacturing facilities of our landlord, I remember mainly that the winter was bitter cold. For several weeks after we had returned, every night at about 10 a lone German plane arrived, setting off wide alarms. Wild antiaircraft fire followed to keep him from smashing the bridges over the Meuse with his bombs. We dubbed the guy "Bed check Benny." But now our airforce had a new night fighter known as "The Black Widow" stationed at a nearby airfield. Bed check Benny arrived with his methodical punctuality and the Black Widow took care of him. We could sleep peacefully now.

I enjoyed being in Epernay and used the opportunity to practice my very rusty French. One day when I sought directions from an elderly man, we got involved in a friendly ex change and upon inquiry he told me that he was a "greffier." My French was not up to that fancy word and after some palaver I realized that he was the clerk of the local court, in charge of maintaining the trademark registry for champagne. He told me that he had in his office labels dating back to the time when champagne was invented—around

1775. We made a date when I could come to see the labels. It sounded like a wonderful opportunity—and it produced an insight into French mentality that was quite startling.

Armed with a few packs of cigarettes, a few cans of pipe tobacco and some Hershey bars, I appeared at the courthouse at the agreed upon time and found his office. He was very pleased with the largesse that I had brought and he showed me the interesting labels going back almost 200 years. He spoke of the German occupation and how the Germans had bled the French by means of the black market. Nothing of value was available otherwise and the Germans were in reality controlling the black market. I expressed astonishment, but he maintained that the German practices of syphoning off all capable Frenchmen as slave labor and controlling the black market were the true causes for the total demoralization of France. I sympathized with him and said I hoped that the French would rise again under de Gaulle and restore the glory of the nation. He felt complimented and as I got up to leave, he asked me if I could help him buy some gasoline and that he would match any black market price because he knew that our gasoline was the very best. When I replied that I unfortunately could not help and thereby contribute to the further exploitation of the French nation, he looked depressed.

My next adventure almost landed me in jail. No sooner had we returned from the Battle of the Bulge where I had taken several rolls of film, when Col. Moss insisted that he wanted to see the pictures. I told him that we had to be careful and that I did not want to send them to the PX because the censor would most likely kill all of them. He merely said, "See what you can do." So, one afternoon I went to a photo store in Epernay and asked them if they would develop my films. They refused outright, saying they had orders from the American army that they were not permitted to develop any films brought to their store by American soldiers. When I asked them if they had a darkroom and developer and fixer they said yes, but that they believed that they could not let me use their shop, because they felt that it was against the law. I went back to the office and told Col. Moss that the matter was risky. He thought for a while and then said: "Go back and see if you can't weasel yourself in and develop those films."

I went back and said to the lady that I wanted to use their darkroom and that it would be all right. She shrugged her shoulders and showed me the place. They had a nice darkroom equipped with good modern equipment. Entering the room I turned on the red light. In about 45 minutes I should have the films developed and be out of the place. I could put the wet films in a glass jar that I had providently brought along. Back at the office I could rinse the films and dry them at leisure. I was pleased when I saw the images appear in the emulsion under the red light. The dragons teeth of the Siegfried Line looked terrific. I had just dumped them into the fixer when I heard some commotion in front of the darkroom door, which as a protection I had locked from the inside. There was the excited voice of the lady and I recognized the bark of the headquarters military police lieutenant who began to rattle the door of the darkroom and said: "Sergeant, I know you are in there and you better come out quick." I shook the films wildly in the fixer, dumped them into the water tank and then pushed them into the water filled glass jar, while proclaiming that I was hurrying as fast as I could, but that I could not find the light switch.

When I came out there was Lieutenant Smith of the headquarters military police platoon who said: "You are under arrest and you are in one hell of a lot of trouble." With me gingerly holding my glass jar with the films, we drove back to headquarters in his jeep. As we were driving, I said to him: "Lieutenant Smith, before you book me, maybe you would want to see Colonel Moss in the Judge Advocate's section." We stopped at the section; I was very scared. Lt. Smith walked into the office where Junior came to attention and bellowed: "ATTENTION." Junior, Ristow, and Harry Leykauf had jumped up and stood at attention while Lt. Smith said, " Lt. Smith, Headquarters Military Police to see Colonel Moss." With that the door opened and Col. Moss appeared, greeting Lt. Smith like an old friend and seeing at the same moment that I was discreetly holding the jar with the films—the corpus delicti right in the Judge Advocate's office! Without showing any concern he asked Lt. Smith to come into his office and he closed the door. Our hearing was then considerably better than what it is today, so we heard a conversation that went about like this.

Col. Moss offered Lt. Smith a chair, and asked casually what the problem was. The lieutenant, obviously uncomfortable, began haltingly to tell that he got a telephone call from a very excited woman at a photo shop in town that an American sergeant had been there and had pressured them into using their darkroom to develop some film and that they were afraid that this may be against regulations. He had immediately gone down there and found a sergeant from the Judge Advocate's section in the darkroom. He had put him under arrest and was about to book him, when the sergeant had suggested that before doing that he should perhaps come here. There was an inordinately long pause. Finally we heard Col. Moss's voice saying: "Lieutenant, I think that you acted properly when you arrested my sergeant; in your position I would have done the same thing." His friendly voice went on after another long pause, "How long have you been with this outfit, lieutenant?" The lieutenant answered: "I've been with them since they were organized at the Presidio in California in 1943." Col. Moss continued smoothly: "I guess you like the outfit even better now since General Ridgway took over last August?" The lieutenant answered: "Yes, sir, indeed." Col. Moss now speaking very slowly and almost humbly continued: "Lieutenant Smith, let me explain my dilemma to you. The sergeant was with me during the Battle of the Bulge and he took many pictures for me. The films that he was developing were these films. He had warned me that his doing the developing was risky but instead of saying, 'Don't do it,' I let him go ahead. Actually, Lieutenant, you ought to book both of us." There was a long pause. The lieutenant said, "I see, we better forget about it." They both got up and Col. Moss said, as he escorted him to the door, "Thank you lieutenant, I shall not forget you." Lt. Smith smiled at me as he left and later we often met—as friends. He now had two friends in the Judge Advocate's Department.

Forget about the Champs Elyssees, the Arc de Triomphe, the Louvre and Notre Dame, the one thing to see in Paris, according to staff sergeant Mitch, was the Follies Bergere, with whom he had danced before the war. For the next week or so after our return from the Bulge, getting a one day pass for Paris was a routine matter and almost all of us spent a day there. Everyone who got a pass got a briefing from Mitch with particular emphasis on what to look for at the Follies. Like everyone in headquarters, I had heard from Mitch the complete account of his reception at the Follies when he had shown up in his paratrooper uniform as one of the first to get to Paris. He had been mobbed—so he claimed—by the dancing girls who remembered him and loved him to death as the clearly remembered, wonderful young American dancer of the time before the war. Our truck driver who had also managed a pass in the first group—fully briefed by Mitch—came back having been to the ballet and raved about what he had seen. He was fascinated by the fact that the dancing was performed by many beautiful woman and all of them topless—a fashion not as yet commonplace in U. S. entertainment. This was something that he had always hoped to see at the Burlesque shows in Chicago, but they never had more than one topless dame on the stage. It obviously had made a deep impression on him, and it served as a cheerful topic on days when there was nothing cheerful to talk about—and there were many of those days ahead.

It was my first visit to Paris and I was overwhelmed by this glorious city with its wide streets and the friendly acceptance that an American uniform then generated—the liberation of Paris had taken place about six months before. Harry Leykauf had come too and we wandered along the boulevards, climbed the stairs to the top of the Arc de Triomphe and enjoyed the panorama of the city. We made our way to Notre Dame and in a side street found a restaurant that served horse meat—clearly identified by the figure of a horse next to the sign RESTAURANT. We had been told that we were not permitted to eat at any place other than the GI- mess hall and at restaurants that served horsemeat, because French food supplies were still severely rationed. For some strange reason horsemeat was in ample supply. The mere fact of sitting at a table with a tablecloth and napkins and eating with decent utensils from a plate instead of from our mess kit, with wine and glasses completing the setting was sheer luxury. The meat tasted just fine, the potatoes were every bit as good as the dehydrated ones that we had eaten, and the red wine from the carafe made us feel civilized.

I recall visiting several bookstores in the hope of finding a short volume by Vercors, entitled *The Silence of the Sea*. The book had been published by Les Editions de Minuit by a resistance printer during the occupation. It had been a best seller of sorts and a translation had been published in America by MacMillan. Finding it was a hopeless task, but I found at least one book published by Les Editions de Minuit which used up all my French money. Disgruntled I found on one of those book carts along the Seine a small law book and traded it for a pack of Camels. That I had acquired a first edition of the French Civil Code printed in 1804, when Napoleon was still consul of the Republic, was something that I discovered many years later.

Returning to Epernay from Paris we felt that we had seen one place that had managed to survive Hitler's madness almost intact. Within a few weeks we would join the final push to put an end to what he had attempted to do to our world.

Rumors of what we could expect upon entering Germany were flying high. *Stars & Stripes* reported that Hitler had created a "redoubt" around Berchtesgaden where he would offer a resistance such as the world had never seen before. Whole mountains filled with dynamite would be exploded to crush attacking forces like avalanches. Thousands of young dare- devil Nazis, who had sworn to die for the cause had been organized in groups called "Werewolves." They would create havoc with the invading forces. We heard that very thin steel cables were stretched across streets at night to decapitate the four men riding in jeeps. Our intelligence people had heard about this grizzly plot and while we were in Epernay all of our jeeps were modified by a wire cutting device that was mounted on the front bumpers. It gave them a ferocious look, but I never saw or heard of a case where this instrument of war was ever called upon to perform.

Shortly after we returned from the Bulge, Maj. Moronoy left and was replaced by Captain Ward. Col. Moss and Maj. Moroney had never hit it off very well. They were very different people. The colonel was a free-wheeling country lawyer who had learned much about life and the law from Huey P. Long and the politicians of Winfield, Louisiana. Major Moroney was a New Dealer who had found his way into a comfortable job with the Federal Deposit Insurance Company in Washington. He was a good lawyer when it came to banking problems, but the court martial work that was our daily diet did not match his training or liking. We dealt with the common problems of army life and discipline: Insubordination, AWOL, desertion, drunkenness, theft, assault, and all the gnats and warts that show up when men are cooped up for a long time- and sometimes rape and murder. Major Moroney lacked courtroom experience and was slow in raising objections or going for the jugular and Col. Moss needed an aggressive and feisty attorney who could shoot from the hip. And so Captain Ward took over from Major Moroney. I was sorry to see him go. He had been the officer who had censored my mail for a long time, and he was easy on my letters. With the mass of letters that I sent, I had the feeling that he was almost enjoying an ongoing soap opera. Later, after I was appointed a lieutenant and transferred to Wiesbaden, to the War Crimes branch, we would meet again.

CHAPTER 8

GERMANY

THOSE SIX WEEKS in Epernay after our return from the Bulge, were typical of army life. Sit and wait. Of course, there were a few general court-martial proceedings. It is unthinkable that among the thousands of men sitting around waiting and fretting, there would not be some crime or blow- up. An army of draftees almost invites situations where an enlisted man would call an officer a jerk or go AWOL because he met a lovely French woman, or break into a jewelry store because he had to own that necklace—all events that would lead to criminal prosecution in civilian life and now to court-martial. Major Moroney and Captain Ward, who replaced him a few weeks later , were the prosecuting attorneys and Harry sweated blood and water when he had to read and transcribe what he had jotted down. He depended on my recollections and my carefully kept notes.

We had the feeling that we had been forgotten. Every day we read about what was happening, but others did it. On March 7,

1945, *Stars and Stripes* reported the capture of the intact Ludendorff bridge over the Rhine at Remagen and the ever expanding American beachhead on the Eastern bank of the Rhine. Two weeks later our corps' airborne divisions had been attached to Montgomery's command and had crossed the lower Rhine at Wesel to bottle up the Ruhr in a gigantic pincer movement—the war was being won by others while we sat in Epernay.

Finally on April 1, came orders to march. After a ride of two days and some 200 miles, our convoy delivered us to Dillenburg, a small town at the southern side of an enormous net that the allies had put around the Ruhr Valley with all its industrial and war making potential. A vast German army commanded by General Model, one of Hitler's leaders in the Battle of the Bulge, had been ordered to fight to the last man. Model tried but when he saw that his armies had no chance to break out of the encirclement, he committed suicide. His armies surrendered, leaving the road to Berlin virtually undefended.

Coming from Epernay along almost the same route that we had followed from Aachen only three months before, we crossed Luxembourg and reached the German border at Echternach. The town was mauled by artillery fire, with gaping holes in the walls, caved in roofs, every window broken, and totally deserted. There was not a soul to be seen on the streets. A wooden plank bridge spanned a river and replaced a stone bridge that had been dynamited and had collapsed into the river. On the bridge was a sign:

ENTERING GERMANY
Be on your Guard

Crossing the Rhine at Bonn on the way to Dillenburg I had my first encounter with a **Treadway** bridge. The principle was simple. Army engineers placed numerous large boats—perhaps twenty feet long and six or eight feet wide—into the river next to each other until they spanned the river. They were fastened to each other by metal tracks, wide enough to allow passage of heavy trucks, and tanks and foot soldiers in each direction. If any of the components failed, replacement was quick. A bridge across the Rhine took less than 12 hours to build.

When the bridge at Remagen had been captured intact, our engineers had built a Treadway bridge right next to it, so that our forces could cross just in case the Remagen bridge might be destroyed by the German Air Force, as Hitler had promised. Josef Goebbels, the German propaganda mouthpiece, seeking to minimize this disastrous development for the Germans, calmed the German public by asserting that the bridgehead was about to be liquidated by heroic German troops (which was, of course, a lie). He said that the Fuehrer himself had ordered specially trained navy divers in black rubber suits to creep along the bottom of the Rhine, and dynamite these hastily constructed temporary bridges causing terrible losses to the enemy. It was typical Nazi propaganda and pure invention, but when our truck slowly moved onto the Treadway bridge at Bonn, I remember tensing up. It was night. Searchlights were moving back and forth across the water. Balloon barrages floated over the bridge to prevent low flying planes from dropping bombs. The water looked dirty and cold. Our truck made unfamiliar, wobbly motions as it slowly crept along, and all of us had our eyes riveted on the Rhine River, which flowed peacefully and provided no signs of daring underwater divers.

We did not reach Dillenburg that day and found quarters, which we shared with a tank outfit of the famous 1st Division that had been fighting nearby all day as part of the Ruhr encirclement. I was glad that I could creep into a corner of a room assigned to us and go to sleep. Junior, always eager to explore and see what was going on, had asked me to join him, but I had declined, feeling that it was curiosity that killed the cat. Junior returned quickly from his exploration quite scared and shocked. A nest of German snipers had suddenly opened fire on a passing American tank unit. Big commotion in front of our billet followed. Tanks rattled to and fro and there were calls of "medic, medic." One of the tanks came to halt a short distance from our billet. They lifted an officer out of the turret—it was General Rose the assistant commander of a tank division. A sniper had picked him off as he was directing a tank attack.

Next morning we moved on to reach Dillenburg and found that our advance detachment had again chosen well. We stayed in the buildings of the Prussian Stallion Service, which had been organized centuries ago to guarantee the availability of good cavalry horses for the army. With tanks available now, the stallion service was no longer the thriving enterprise it once had been. We occupied the rooms of the stable grooms and ate in the big arena where the horses had been exercised. With no tables we ate sitting on our helmets. It was pleasant with the smell of peat and horse manure adding memories of horse shows and farm stables. In the distance we heard artillery fire but nothing memorable happened. But the war was unpredictable as last night had taught us.

My letter to Marion from Dillenburg mentions that I observed for the first time the vast flood of emaciated, desperate people fleeing West. Speaking to some of them, who seemed to form an endless wave of humanity, I realized that many of them were foreign laborers who had been brought against their will to work in Germany's war industries. Now they were using the first chance to flee the terror of Nazis and communism and were braving sleet, mud and icy winds to return to France, Holland and Belgium. But I was astonished that many of those fleeing West were Slavic people who wanted to get away from Russia. Communism to those who knew it was no better than the Nazis.

On April 12, after about a week in Dillenburg, we moved some 20 miles North to Siegen, an old city protected on all sides by hills. It had served as a Regional Induction Center for the German Army. When we entered the town it was still burning. It looked like one big piece of pie splattered on the ground. SS troops had initially defended it and only a few hours before our arrival had fled as our advancing infantry brought up artillery. By this time a burning town and smashed houses did not impress us as much as the news that came from a loudspeaker as we arrived: **President Roosevelt Dead.** Most of us remembered the precise moment when we had heard the news of the attack on Pearl Harbor. And so it was with April 12, 1945. As we got off our truck we heard that Franklin D. Roosevelt had died that morning at Warm Springs, Georgia, three months to the day after he had returned from Yalta. The man who had first realized what a world dominated by Hitler would mean and had acted on this awareness—dead, when victory was almost at hand.

Walking to the center of the town which seemed totally deserted, I saw the modern building that had housed the German Army Induction Center for that area and went inside. It was empty. What I noticed instantly was evidence of panic and apparently loss of all sense of reality. In front of the two story main building, which had been cut into a hill was a half circle paved plaza, with a diameter of about 75 feet, enclosed by an elegant wrought iron fence. To defend this administrative army center, the Germans had stationed two heavy machine guns in the center of the plaza. To camouflage them, metal filing cabinets and large metal wardrobes had been placed around the machine guns. When I arrived they were loaded with cartridge belts properly inserted. Not certain that the metal cabinets would withstand American assault weapons, the defenders had resorted to packing the whole area with books that had been brought from the library and heaped pell mell about 3 feet high around the machine guns.

When the SS troops saw our armament approaching Siegen, houses being hit by artillery fire, and buildings starting to burn, they had fled. I was probably the first American soldier to arrive on the terrace of the abandoned Induction Center. For a moment I stood there and contemplated what must have gone on in the minds of these people to think that they could protect two machine guns from modern assault weapons by filing cabinets and books. These people were totally mad.

I bent down and the first book I picked up was volume one of a seven volume *History of Frederick the Great*, by J. D. E. Preuss, a well known German historian. It was the first massive study of Frederick, published in 1831, forty-five years after his death. I had read much about this great Prussian King whom I admired. The title leaf of the volume that I held in my hand disclosed that the book had once belonged to the library of a German regiment and had then become part of the historical collection of the Induction Center. I was about to drop it and pick up some other volume, when for some reason I turned the pages to the acknowledgments. And there was the statement that my great great grandfather, who had been the director of the Royal Berlin China factory had provided information on how Frederick had created the Royal Berlin China Factory to keep his subjects from buying the famous Dresden China. Buying goods abroad was not good for the Prussian trade balance and so Frederick was determined to stop it. As evidence that mistreatment of Jews is not really an invention of the 20th century, I saw Frederick's edict that required Jews who applied for a marriage license to provide a receipted bill to prove that they had purchased china from the royal china factory, Frederick's pet factory.

Suddenly this book was something worth having. The innate sense of acquisition—say larceny—overtook me and I began pawing through the mountains of books to retrieve all seven volumes of this monumental opus. I found them, dragged them to my quarters, found wrapping paper and string and sent them to Marion, but not before I browsed some more in the books. Four of them were documentary volumes, which gave many of Frederick's edicts, proclamations and file notes, most of them written in his peculiarly ungrammatical German spiced with perfect French, and all of them seasoned with an unusual wit and an ill concealed pessimism about the character of his subjects.

The books accompanied me for almost fifty years. Often I had occasion to check historical facts, particularly those relating to the first international treaty of friendship that in 1786 the United States of America was able to conclude with Frederick's Prussia. No treaty ever entered into by the United States had more famous signers on the American side: John Adams, Thomas Jefferson, and Benjamin Franklin. In 1993 I gave the books to the library of the University of

Cincinnati, where scholars can now enjoy them—a rare find in an American library.

The photos that I took and the maps that I kept show Gummersbach and Wipperfuerth as the end stations of the Ruhr campaign where our corps established temporary quarters. Writing the name Wipperfuerth reminds me of an event worth recalling. We were billeted in the county commissioner's plush home and office, and I remember sleeping in a bed with sheets, an unbelievable luxury. One of my buddies from the Defense Platoon woke me in the early morning. He had wasted no time doing what many of us did immediately upon hitting a new billet: casing the joint. Carrying a huge cardboard box he arrived at my bed with an expression on his face as if he had found the gold treasure of the Nibelungen, and said, "Look at this Von, I think I've got it made." The box had stood in front of one of the offices and it was filled with paper money—millions and millions of German marks. He saw himself already a wealthy man returning to America with riches beyond imagination. His return to earth came when I told him that the whole box contained worthless German inflation money, which in 1922/23 could not even have bought him one sweet roll. Looking at him at that moment was like seeing a tire lose air rapidly. Wistfully he said, "Gee, it would have been great," and then with a sad smile he added, "I'll let you have all of it," and left. Looking at that heap of inflation money reminded me of that time when as a boy of eleven I had worked for two back-breaking weeks on a farm picking potatoes and could just buy just one sweet roll with my earnings. It was a time when a wheelbarrow of money or more was needed to buy a loaf of bread. That catastrophic inflation had wiped out the German middle class and contributed much to the desperation that brought Hitler to the scene. I took the money and sent it home to Marion, who was bewildered when she saw it. Years later when she was a graduate student at the Annenberg School of Communications in Philadelphia, she examined the money and wrote a paper that she called: *The Money is the Message*. I later catalogued and sorted it to give it to the University of South Florida as instructional material for students who want to know more about inflation.

By the middle of April the Ruhr valley was safely under allied control and we were turning East. It almost seemed as if we were no longer concentrating on pursuing the German army but on occupying as much land as possible before the Russians got to it. We came to a stop in Uelzen, northeast from badly destroyed Hannover. The long awaited German collapse was at hand. No longer was there any noticeable resistance. We moved at a pace slower than walking because most roads were clogged with refugees and displaced persons. Most of the people fleeing West were Germans from East Prussia and Silesia who had been overrun by the Russians. Their families and pathetic possessions were loaded on hand wagons, baby carriages, horse drawn carriages and occasionally tractors pulling a farm wagons. In addition with concentration camps now liberated everywhere, their emaciated freed inmates, readily identified by their striped prison garb, were moving along the streets resting in fields and begging for food.

As our truck crept East I remember watching the faces of the people, wondering if I might suddenly recognize a familiar face—perhaps a brother or sister, a relative or friend—but even if I recognized someone, would I jump off my truck to say hello?

My hopes of being commissioned as an officer suffered a severe setback. With the end of the war in Europe in sight the army felt that they really did not need additional lieutenants. My buddies consoled me and said that I would probably get out sooner if I did not get a commission. In letter after letter I wrote about my despair at being so useless. I knew the army desperately needed interpreters but I was not even asked to help out, because I was interpreting for court-martial matters only.

Every move to a new station—and it seemed at times as if we were moving every week—was a tough and physically exhausting job that left me totally drained because everything had to be done on double time. The most important pieces of equipment were two small Franklin type stoves, four heavy manual typewriters, the boxes of books and preprinted forms, and the usual office supplies. In addition we had to move all the bedding and baggage for ourselves and the officers. For weeks we had toyed with the idea of constructing plywood boxes with handles to facilitate our lives. But the question was always how could we get anything like that built in a country that seemed stripped clean of everything.

When we settled at Uelzen, finding a carpenter to build boxes was high on my list of things to accomplish. The town had suffered little damage. We had just settled into our quarters and were enjoying city-supplied electric light, when suddenly the lights went off and we heard our generators being activated. Someone from the headquarters' engineering group suddenly showed up at our section and said "Von, we need you," and with that we were off. We drove to the local electric power station and demanded to see the manager. He was frightened when he saw all of us in steel helmets and with weapons. We asked him why he had interrupted electric service. He knew that the supply of electricity had suddenly stopped, but he merely said, "Kein Strohm, Draht kaputt" [no current—wire broken]. We asked him where the line was kaputt and who had done it. We suspected sabotage. He knew nothing and said that he could only tell us which line provided power. He could not deliver it until the line was repaired. An electrician on duty was produced and we said we would take him and a repair truck to find the break and repair it. The electrician refused to go. We realized that he was the man who would have to climb the pole and he was scared that someone would turn on the high voltage and leave him hanging on the wire—electrocuted. The manager had turned the current switch off until the line was repaired and said that he would sit by the switch and not permit anyone to touch it until the repairman was back. It was not enough; the guy refused to go. I realized that he was afraid that some wild American would walk in with a gun and tell the manager to turn the juice on or else. The man's fears were understandable. Finally I suggested that I would obtain from our headquarters six armed guards who would protect the manager and would shoot anyone who came to mess with the switches. That would assure that no one would touch the switch until I brought the electrician back alive. That, and my assurance that I clearly understood his problem and fears, did it. We set out and after about 5 miles we could see where the lines were down. The big glass and ceramic insulators securing the power lines had been busted and the wires had dropped to the ground and shorted out the line. It had not been sabotage, it was merely enthusiastic American troops flushed with victory engaging in target practice. The electrician climbed the big pole, a helper had the spare parts ready, and after a couple of hours he had the lines up and properly secured. We drove back and relieved our guard detachment at the power plant. The manager turned the switch, and as in the creation "there was light." The poor electrician felt that I had saved him from being fried alive.

Earlier to calm the repairman, I had spoken to him about other matters like carpentry, and in the course of our conversation he had given me the name of a good local carpenter, a piece of information that proved valuable very soon.

At this time, with the war not yet over, we were still very careful in all of our dealings with German civilians, because we had been given "Special Orders for German-American Relations". The key points of the instructions by General Bradley (sounding a little pompous 50 years later) were:

THE OCCUPATIONAL FORCES ARE NOT ON A GOOD WILL MISSION

*Never trust Germans, collectively or individually

*Defeat German efforts to poison your thoughts or influence your attitudes

*Avoid acts of violence, except when required by mili tary necessity

*Conduct yourself at all times so as to command the respect of the German people for yourself, for the United States and for the allied cause

*Never associate with Germans

*Be fair but firm with Germans

A letter I wrote on May 1, 1945 from Uelzen discloses that I, at least on that day, was still very much the obedient servant who read and obeyed orders to the last crossed "t" and dotted "i." But it also discloses that my adventure with the repair of the power line had resulted in an unexpected success.

"My attempt to get boxes built in town has finally been crowned with success," I reported. It is not nearly as simple as it sounds, and as I tell you about this job you will realize the complications. The electrician whom I had met had told me that a carpenter shop was open for business. I met the manager who was quite willing to have the work done provided we could obtain authority from the local military government. I needed an order signed from our headquarters; this order was passed on to the military government of the place, who in turn ordered the town mayor to see to it that the boxes were built. The mayor issued orders to the man who was to do the work and that poor guy immediately proceeded. Order in hand he obtained plywood, nails, screws, and all the other ingredients from suppliers who were permitted to deliver only against such orders. This procedure, cumbersome as it may seem, offered the advantage that military needs were taken care of first, and also that civilians could not deplete the meager stocks of available supplies. It took a lot of running around and often the temptation to say: "Get the thing done," while touching the rifle for confirmation was very great, but then I always remembered that that is exactly the way fascism works and that thought made me shy away from such action. Naturally I could get things done more easily than anyone else because I could tell the people specifically what I wanted and how I wanted it. The puzzled question of the natives "Are you an American?" I always ignored, and I carefully avoided talking with them except on authorized subjects.

When I showed up with the boxes, I found that the Corps was to have its first murder trial. At the end of the Ruhr campaign, an American infantry soldier had wantonly killed a German civilian. Col. Moss told me to pick up two eye witnesses near Wuppertal. He indicated that it would help if I asked them to explain what had happened at the site and keep careful notes to assist Captain Ward who would prosecute the case. It looked like a drive of close to 200 miles, so I would be back with the witnesses by six or seven in the evening. We would spend the next morning with the witnesses and Capt. Ward and could have the trial in the afternoon. Then I could take them back to Wuppertal the next morning.

It was cold when the driver and I took off in a light truck that had two facing benches with room for four passengers. We had an ample supply of five gallon jerry cans of gasoline to make us mobile and independent. We had with us a thermos with hot coffee, some GI blankets and K-rations for ourselves and our passengers. We made good time and found the small farm of perhaps thirty or forty acres near Wuppertal. There was a farmhouse with a little garden in front, and in back a small pond perhaps 50 feet in diameter on which a few ducks were feeding. The barn housed some cows, pigs, and two horses. There were some chickens; a dog was barking as we stopped in front of the house. As I got off the truck, a woman of about forty dressed in work clothes with a kerchief over her head opened the door.

I asked her for her name. It was the name of one of the two women for whom I had a subpoena to appear as witnesses. The man who had shot her father, I explained, was now a prisoner in Uelzen where the American army would try him for murder. I told her that I had come to take her and her mother to Uelzen as witnesses and that she would probably be away from the farm for 2 1/2 days. Meanwhile the mother, a grey, weary looking woman of about 65 had come out of the house. I requested them to ask their neighbors to take care of their animals while they were away. I then asked them to relate to me the events of the day on which the old man had been killed.

The daughter took off to arrange for neighbors to take care of the animals while they were away. The mother motioned me into the house. The house was immaculately clean. It had an entrance hall with a kitchen to the right and a probably rarely used living room to the left. There were two bedrooms. At the end of the hall was a small bathroom with a tub and coal fed water heater. The old woman was still in shock from the events now perhaps ten days in the past. Haltingly she talked to me. There had been fighting in the distance and they had heard artillery fire and also machine guns. On their farm and in the whole area there had been no German or American soldiers until this American soldier showed up. He came alone and had a machine pistol. He was unsteady on his feet and smelled of liquor. He spoke little German and asked her husband: "Du Soldat?" Her husband, 67 years old and dressed in his farm workers clothes said: "Nein, kein Soldat." The American soldier then demanded to go through the house. He walked into their bedroom. On the wall he saw a faded photo of her husband as a man of about 40 in the uniform of a German soldier of World War I. He became very agitated and said: "Du Soldat!" Her husband attempted to explain, but the soldier repeated, "Du Soldat" and ordered him out of the house. Then the old man was forced to walk into the cold pond with his arms raised. The soldier then raised his machine pistol and shot him in the pool. It was a shocking story told without emotion or tears. The old woman said that the daughter had run to get help. A jeep with military policemen had arrived very quickly and arrested the soldier and made a report. She asked me why she had to go—her husband was dead. When I said it was necessary so that the soldier be punished for what he had done, she shrugged her shoulders.

When the daughter returned from the neighbors she asked if they could have a little time to put on clean clothes and if there would be enough time for them to eat before leaving. I opened a K-ration for them and showed them how they could make some coffee from the coffee powder. Both were glad to see the 5 cigarettes in each of the K-rations—not to smoke but to have for barter.

I helped them onto the truck and covered them with GI blankets to protect them from the cold. It was a long and shocking ride. They had heard on the radio of the destruction that the war had brought to Germany, but now, for the first time they saw what had happened to their country. They saw destroyed towns, big camps of

German soldiers as prisoners-of-war, busted vehicles and tanks, the endless streams of refugees, despair everywhere—quite a contrast to their untouched corner, where, except for this terrible murder, the war had not disturbed the cozy communications over the fence and the daily exchange of gossip.

We arrived after supper and I reported to Col. Moss and asked if I could get supper for them served at a table in a corner of the officers mess, where they would have plates, knives and forks. He was not sure and said he'd better check with General Ridgway. He came back, embarrassed, "Let them eat from mess kits—but not in the officers' mess." So I asked the cooks to prepare supper for them, and brought it to them in two borrowed mess kits in a corner of the place where we ate. A room with two beds with sheets had been secured and I promised to be there for breakfast, when they would get bread and coffee. I was tired and depressed when I entered our office. However, there was good news for me. A telegram had been delivered:

SON JON PAUL BORN APRIL NINETEENTH 6:02 AM
SEVEN POUNDS THIRTEEN OUNCES ALL FINE
ELSA MUELLER

It was the only cheerful news I received that day. So suddenly I knew I had a son. I had no idea what he might look like and how long it would be before I would see him. But it was something great to wait for.

The preparation for trial was quick and simple. Of the trial itself I remember little except that the soldier, now sober, seemed sad about what he had done. I wondered if he had been influenced by the propaganda that had been passed out. There was nothing at the trial that indicated his defense counsel had even given that possibility any thought. It did not come up at the trial. He was found guilty of manslaughter and sentenced to a long prison term, which like most of these sentences was probably later shortened when he was invited to volunteer for assignment to a fighting unit.

The next morning found us again on our truck returning to the farm. The weather was milder. The old woman was silent and withdrawn. Her daughter told me that her husband, who intended to take over the farm after the war, had been killed in Russia. With her father, they had just managed to keep the place going. Now with him gone and without help they would have to sell it. When we arrived at the farm I helped them off the truck and escorted them to the door. As I said goodbye to them, the daughter motioned me to wait a moment. She went into the house and came out with a brown paper bag with six fresh eggs which she handed me saying: "You were very nice to us and my mother and I want to thank you. Take this." I was deeply touched, but I remembered the instructions about dealing with Germans and told her that I was not allowed to accept them, because it was forbidden by the army. But I told her "I will never forget your kindness." She smiled and I knew that she understood.

As I write this in 1994, thinking back to what I did next, I shudder at the risk that I undertook, having read and studied everything that concerned fraternization, and the punishments for practicing it. I directed the driver, a charming black, to return to Uelzen by way of Wernigerde in the Harz mountains, a matter of adding perhaps 100 miles to our trip, because I wanted to see my mother's sister Herma. I hoped that I might gain from her an idea of what had happened to my family—I feared the worst, that they had all been caught by the Russians.

Up to that moment I had thought that I had steeled my self sufficiently to accept anything that might happen to my family. But when I saw day after day the pitiful masses of German refugees who were escaping capture from regions over run by the victorious Russians, I was no longer certain that I would refuse all help to my kin if the situation came up.

I told the driver where we were going and why. If some military authority, most likely a roving Military Police patrol, should stop us, I would talk us out of the inquiry by saying that we were on our way back from Wuppertal to Uelzen and that we had heard that the roads a little farther West were better than those terrible roads over which we had come on court-martial work, for which I had the documents in my pocket.

I realized, of course, that if by chance, I discovered any close relatives—a possibility that clearly existed—I would not be able to do anything for them, unless I disclosed this to my superiors. But I had the distinct feeling that if such an event would happen, they would help me. The overriding fear was: God, do not let my relatives be caught by the Russians. If that had happened I knew I would never see them again.

We made good time on that ride to Wernigerode. In several areas the winter had given way to spring and hawthorne trees in bloom reminded me of Below. We drove into Wernigerode a small town where my mother's sister had lived since 1921. And now I stopped in front of the house that I remembered from a visit twenty years ago; the street was empty. Windows were closed; it was very still. With my steel helmet on and the carbine slung over my shoulder, I got out of the truck walked to the closed entrance door.

My heavily censored letter describes my state of mind and the details of my meeting of my relatives in Wernigerode. I put ***** whenever the censor removed passages because he felt that I was giving away classified information.

". . . . As I approached it, I felt a tightness around my neck the like of which I have not felt for a long time. When I drove up the last steep hill my heart was beating like a steam engine and I almost blacked out—then I stopped in front of her house, rang the door bell. Irmgard, her daughter looked out of the window and said 'It is Werner' and she almost fainted. They were down in a second and Aunt Herma embraced me in the middle of the street ***** I stood dumbfounded—should I have warded her off—mother's sister? I did not. ****** Irmgard had two little kids playing around her feet. I gave them practically all the pictures I had of you and of Helene—so please replace them, they were my birthday present to them and I felt so humble that I could not do more for them—just a few cigarettes I was able to scrape out of my pocket and 3 chocolate bars. Their questions came rapidly and I told them about you and Helene and JP, who was our just born son Paul. From Aunt Herma's comments I remember one specifically because it was the only straightforward admission of guilt that I have ever heard from a German. She said: "Knowing about the concentration camps, I am afraid to look a foreigner in the face; there is no honor in a German and the only thing we have left to be proud of are the people we knew to be honorable and who have died. They are better off than we are. What do we have to live for?" They looked like people who had suffered mentally. Irmgard had been a beautiful woman in her day, she was now smoking cigars left over from her dead husband and her boys were offering to beg American soldiers for cigarettes for "mama." The colored driver had intrigued the kids, who referred to him as the Moor. Tante Herma was surprised to see me treat him like an equal and tell her that he was a nice guy—which he truly was. And then they gave me news that came like **Gone with the Wind,** and I think I will be lucky if I can come out of this with my mind completely intact. "

"This is the news: Father and mother decided to stay ** **** regardless. Probably they felt that they were too old to undertake the Treck. Gerd and Alix with their children did not get away from Below, the permission to leave came too late, so they had to stay where they are with their children and since all large landowners have been executed so far, their fate is dark. Ruth's husband, who originally lived in Hannover and moved to Pommerania, did not get away so Ruth, he and their little child remained where they had lived—in Pommerania. Ilse, with her four children had no chance to get out so, she is there, with her fate probably the same as that of the others. Margarete had made arrangements—see enclosed letters—to trek West and perhaps is somewhere -but where?? ******* Claus has been seriously wounded in Russia, an abdominal wound that should have been fatal by all precedents. By sheer stamina and luck he pulled through although he will probably be an invalid for life. He had transfer orders to Karlsbad and it depends now upon the circumstances. If that town was taken by the U.S. then he may be our PW."

There followed the same news of uncertainty about my relatives in Breslau, Berlin, Marienwalde—no hope—all of them caught by the Russians.

After giving me this message of disaster, Tante Herma went into the house to bring me the letter from my mother, which had arrived ten days before, just before all postal services had collapsed. While Irmgard and I awaited Tante Herma's return, little Micha, the younger of Irmgard's boys, totally confused by the warm welcome I had received by his mother and grandmother and by my fluent German, concluded that I must somehow be a well armed German soldier. He asked me with bright eyes and charming eagerness: "Uncle Werner, did you kill one or two Americans?" When his mother put her hand over his mouth, I said "No Micha, I did not kill any but your mother will explain it to you later." Tante Herma handed me my mother's letter and said: "Keep it, it may well be the last writing that you will ever see of hers." She and Irmgard embraced me and I left after a visit that had taken less than an hour—during which I took five snapshots. When I read the letter from my mother upon my return to Uelzen, that evening, I wept. I placed the letter in my wallet where it accompanied me for many years as a token of good luck.

Our return trip to Uelzen went without incident. I reported that I had delivered the two witnesses to their farm, that the neighbors had taken care of the farm animals, and that I found everything in order when I left.

****

The May first *Stars and Stripes* had a headline three inches high that read:

HITLER DEAD

It was true that Hitler was dead, but the newspaper report that he had died in battle had been picked up from the German radio and was false. The Germans wanted to let Hitler enter into history as a man who had died fighting with his soldiers. In reality he could not face the music and had committed suicide. So, my letter, having been fed falsified, heroic fiction instead of the cowardly truth of suicide, envisions already the scenario for a "Hitler myth after death."

My letter in which I gave Marion as much news as the censor would let me say, reads: "Surely that was a good piece of news, but I was sorry that he got away having something like a Wagnerian death. Surrounded by his cohorts he was apparently killed in his place in Berlin. It will be interesting to learn the details. Having died the way he did, he will obviously become a martyr and hero; that is just the stuff on which German mysticism thrives. Remember Barbarossa, Roland, Siegfried, Alarich, Teja and all of them? That is what they blamed Willy II for and now that they had a chance they saw to it that history would not repeat itself. It would have been good if a bunch of liberated Germans from some nearby concentration camp had come up and strung him ignominiously on the nearest lamp post."

"That he was killed on May 1, is a significant fact. He was the man who used May 1 regularly to make his speeches against communism on that day. To be accurate, it was on May 1, 1933 that I saw Hitler for the first time in the flesh. Naturally it was unavoidable seeing him in the movies and in many other places but to see him in person, it was necessary to stand in line and wait. He held his first million person meeting on the Tempelhof field, the area that has served as an airport for the city. . . . It was an enormous affair and for hours and hours the surrounding streets poured humanity onto the field with banners and signs and bands and all the tam-tam of a big party affair. The front of the reviewing stand was reserved for massed groups of SA and SS and the stand itself was a mass of flags. I was on one of the side stands, maybe 100 or 150 yards away, together with Mrs. Treymann and we were watching things with binoculars and were surprised by the ecstasy into which so many of the people fell, once the magic voice came over the radio. Of the speech I do not recall much, but it seems that at that time he announced the plan for building the Autobahn and also outlined the compulsory Labor Service for boys and girls. Naturally his speech was spiced with remarks against the menace of Bolshevism, and today I am wondering if he thought perhaps of that day 12 years ago when he was fighting the Russians in Berlin."

Strange Encounter

There was never a day without surprise and adventure. When Bob Jordan, my favorite among the men of the defense platoon, was excited, he was often difficult to understand, because he stammered. So I could hardly make any sense out of his waking me and showing me an elegant silver engraved zippo type lighter and repeating over and over again: "A ggggift from that son-aaaof a bitch Gerrrrman genneral."

After I had examined the lighter and recognized it as a fine piece of German craftsmanship, engraved with initials and a family crest, I gradually heard what had happened. Very near to our command post in Uelzen was a large abandoned German air force field which our engineers had surrounded with enormous rolls of barbed wire to make it into a reception area for the thousands and thousands of surrendering German troops. Fighting on the Western front had essentially ceased and only on the Eastern front were desperate attempts made to stem the Russian advance to enable fleeing German troops to reach the allies and avoid capture by the Russians, which meant Siberia. For days a never ending stream had brought more and more of these desperate and totally demoralized troops to this camp. The majority of them had thrown away weapons and military equipment.

Bob had been given a jeep and a detachment of soldiers to keep order as the German soldiers were arriving around the clock. He was on the night shift sitting in his jeep when a large convoy of big field grey Mercedes cars with their headlights blazing approached. He got out of his jeep, machine pistol ready, raised his hand and made the convoy stop. From the first car a German general stepped forward and seeing Bob said in halting English: "This is the staff of Fieldmarshal von Mannstein and we want to surrender to a General of the American army." Bob, utterly surprised and not willing to show this, brusquely said: "Just a minute, stay right there," fiddling with his machine pistol and reaching for his pack of cigarettes. To calm himself he pulled out a cigarette. At that moment, the general reached into his pocket and offered Bob a light from the elegant silver lighter. Bob got his cigarette going and then put the lighter in his pocket. The general, too frightened to ask for his lighter back stated that there were 18 general officers who wanted to surrender. Bob blew a whistle and ordered a few of his men to take over his post. He told the general to get back in his car and to tell the other officers to turn off their lights and not to move until he was back, warning them that his men had orders to shoot.

He drove to Ridgway's quarters and reported. The officer at the duty desk told him that the general was asleep and had asked not to be disturbed. Bob was told to put the generals in the big enclosure along with the rest of the German prisoners. He had driven back to the camp, told the generals to get out of their cars and walk in single file into the enclosure to join their troops. Now he wanted to have me come with him and have a closer look at "his" captured generals inside the enclosure. He would take me there as soon as I could get permission for this mission. We were away in a few minutes.

It was probably an exaggeration to claim that the XVIII Airborne Corps had taken a half million prisoners, as *Stars & Stripes* reported in the issue of May 5. When Bob Jordan and another man from the defense platoon and I drove up to the airfield with all those German prisoners-of-war, it was a scene such as I had never witnessed. It was a sunny spring day. The gigantic airfield was covered with field grey German soldiers, among them a few women in uniform. Most of them were lying on the ground in various states of exhaustion. All over the field the familiar American Listerbags were hanging from the three poles that supported them, providing safe drinking water. A big army tank wagon made the rounds to refill them as the prisoners stood in line waiting with their canteens. The airstrips from which the German planes only recently had taken off were deserted. They were too hard for comfort and the only places not covered with humanity. One group of men had gotten a little fire going. They had taken off their uniform jackets and were using their knives to scrape the lice from the seams of their uniforms into the fire. The burning lice made a crackling sound. A woman soldier with a pair of German Army Zeiss binoculars hanging around her neck, handed them to me when I told her that she would not need them any longer. There was no visible hostility to us as we, heavily armed, walked around. What we saw were the pitiful, beaten remnants of the once arrogant Nazi armies that we had seen in the propaganda films as they marched at the height of their glory in the victory parade along the Champs Elysees.

There was no sign of the generals and so we walked to the administration building where we hoped to find them. At one of the low brick buildings leaning against a half open door and enjoying the warm spring sun, was a German first lieutenant in an immaculately tailored uniform, with riding breeches and long, black, highly polished riding boots. He wore no cap, was clean-shaven, his blond hair neatly combed, like a picture from a fashion plate. I recognized him; it was Harro Wuerz, a friend of mine from my law student days in Berlin 12 years before. We passed him and after we were about 50 yards away I said to my companions: "Did you see that German officer? I went to law school with him in Berlin in the early 30s." They were excited and insisted that we speak to him. We did. As we approached him, he looked at us with a sort of disdain on his face. When I said: "Lieutenant Wuerz?" recognition flashed over his face and in impeccable English he said: "Rather peculiar circumstances under which we meet again, Mr. von Rosenstiel." They were indeed peculiar circumstances. In 1932 he had told me that he had been an exchange student in the States and how easy it was to obtain a scholarship. It was he who had directed me toward America. Both of us had changed our careers since. I had managed to get away from Germany. He had abandoned the law and became interested in film production in Dr. Goebbel's Ministry of Propaganda. When he inquired where I would go now that the war was over, I mentioned that our unit would return to France. With an ugly smile he said, "I can give you the name of a girl friend of mine in Paris—I will have no longer any use for her." I nodded and replied "I won't need her either," and we walked away. After that encounter our desire to see the generals was gone.

VE-DAY

At the beginning of May we made our last move to Hagenow in Mecklenburg, a small town about 100 miles west of where I was born. To get there we crossed the Elbe River again on a Treadway bridge. The Eastern side of the Elbe was covered with a sea of refugees, who were hoping to manage a ride in the fleet of small rowboats that were moving back and forth across the 150 yard wide river, which people suspected of becoming the border of the Russian Zone. Allied troops were still pushing East and were occupying land for another 20 miles until they reached a line, which the Russians had established after meeting fierce German resistance. Rumors of the end of the war in Europe were flying around. It was only a question of days now, we were told; there was quibbling between the Allies over "when." On the 7th we had totally reliable information that the war would end the next day but we were not allowed to speak about it or get drunk. When the official news of VE-Day broke we were washing our laundry.

We had been billeted in the house of an educated lawyer whose library I enjoyed even though he had joined the SS. In his basement we had found a large cast iron kettle which could be heated with firewood so that we could boil our filthy clothes. I took photos. They look funny now. It would be some time before I would explain to my children that VE-Day for me and my buddies was LAUN-DRY DAY. On the whole the soberness and lack of enthusiasm was surprising. Apparently the uncertainty of who would stay, who would go to Japan, and who would go home was too much in all our minds to allow us to really relax and be happy. We had formed a friendship based on being involved in a grim business. As I went to bed that night, my mind walked back to the day when I was drafted more than two years before and when the war looked so endless and also so hopeless. Now with the end here, my main thoughts centered on the future with Marion and the kids and on the ways I could keep all of us happy and content. And mixed with it were thoughts of the sights of concentration camps, wrecked houses, endless roads filled with refugees, frightened women, disillusioned prisoners and cocky Nazis. Certain sights of the war were written on my mind with indelible ink and I was certain that they would always remain with me. And what my memory should lose, I was confident that my camera would retain and preserve.

Shortly after we moved to Hagenow, Col. Harry P. Cain, the civil affairs officer of the corps, became a very important man. In anticipation of occupying Germany, the army had attached to all major units civil affairs detachments, to organize the administration of enemy territory. Col. Cain, whom we secretly called "Light Horse Harry" because of his dashing appearance, was a man of action and purpose. He had taken a leave of absence from his job as mayor of Tacoma, Washington, and volunteered for military service. His ambition to become Senator for his state (which in fact he later achieved) gave him something rarely seen in the army, an attitude of "CAN DO." He now was responsible for administration of the Hagenow territory.

A few miles from Hagenow the Germans had operated the recently abandoned Woebbelin concentration camp that had housed several thousand inmates. Colonel Cain drove there immediately, having not had a chance to see a concentration camp before, and he found several hundred unburied bodies in various states of decay, many stacked like cord wood. For him and all of us this was a sight that would stay with us as long as we would live. Col. Cain was a man of action *and* vision. He meant to impress allied soldiers as

well as German people with the terror of Nazism and its consequences. Like all of us he wanted to combat the strange fact that no
German civilian that we met would ever admit that he knew anything about concentration camps and the horrors that took place in
them. He was determined to make Germans see the horror of concentration camps whether they wanted to or not.

With Gen. Ridgway's approval he organized public burials of
the dead found in the Woebbelin concentration camp in the three
major towns over which the corps had jurisdiction: Schwerin,
Ludwigslust and Hagenow. The project was set into motion on May
7 and was concluded in Hagenow on May 8, VE-Day.

If Germans had not actually seen concentration camps, it would
be difficult to conceive of a more drastic instruction course than the
one that Col. Cain had designed. He wanted them to experience the
horrors of these camps. He made the men and women physically
handle the emaciated, tortured, disfigured and often half decom-
posed bodies of the victims, and bury them.

The main participants in this burial project were the inhabitants of these three towns, and the allied soldiers who were invited as
witnesses. The three mayors had been ordered to conscript all men
between 18 and 70 to report to city hall. The strongest of them were
ordered to dig 144 individual graves on a large lawn area in front of
the Town Hall that would from here on be preserved as the town's
memorial burial area. The men who were not needed as grave dig-
gers would be transported to load the bodies of the concentration
camp victims on army trucks and accompany the bodies on the ride
from Woebbelin to Hagenow and unload them there, while the whole
town watched.

All women of the town had been ordered by the mayor to bring
a wash basin, clean linen and soap with which they would wash and
clean the concentration camp victims before they would be lowered
into their graves with the help of all participating Germans.

At a print shop Col. Cain had pamphlets printed in English and
German for distribution to all participants. I saved mine as a memento of a gruesome, tragic event. It reads:

STATEMENT

Delivered at Hagenow, Germany on 8 May 1945 at
Public Burial Service for 144 dead uncovered at
Woebbelin Concentration Camp

Public burial services were held in Ludwigslust, Hagenow and Schwerin on 8-9 May 1945 for victims of German persecution who died in a concentration camp situated at Woebbelin. The address represents the attitude of the Allies toward the conquered. Allied soldiers are determined to make impossible the recurrence of German practices which led to the development of concentration camps of which the one at Woebbelin was a fair example. Let each German understand that regardless of his station in life, he carries a responsibility for helping to create a self- respecting, law-abiding and decent Fatherland.

The Burial Sermon

"In these open graves lie the emaciated, brutalized bodies of 144 citizens of many lands. . . . They were driven, starved and beaten to slake that unholy thirst of the German war machine. When possessed no longer of the will or ability to work or fight back or live, they were either tortured to death or permitted to slowly die. What you witness in Hagenow today is but a small example of what can be seen throughout the length and depth of Germany.

"Untold numbers of allied soldiers and German citizens shudder before similar burial services as you shudder now. The Allies shudder because they never dreamed that human leadership supported by the masses could so debase itself as to be responsible for results like those who lie in these open graves. You Germans shudder for reasons of your own. Some of you having been a party to this degradation of man kind, shudder for fear that your guilt will be determined, as in fact it will. . . . That world isn't content to believe that what we are horrified about was the work of any small group of German gangsters, maniacs and fanatics. That world must, as it does, hold the German people responsible for what has taken place within the confines of this nation. . . . If there be a soul within the German nation, it will rise now to make impossible the doing of such future wrongs. If there be not a soul in the German nation, its future is forlorn and totally lacking in hope.

"The bodies in these graves came yesterday from Woebellin. . . . In death these bodies are receiving from Allied, Christian hands the decent, humanitarian and spiritual treatment they didn't receive in life from German hands. As we listen, Allies and Germans alike let us ask an understanding which Germany must find if there is to be a future life for her.

"In a service last Sunday, held in the German Cathedral in Wismar two thousand Allied soldiers . . . prayed 'for the German people, that they may be rid of the burden of false teaching and one day take their place again among honorable people.' "

While the preparations for the funerals were made I took pictures of what I saw. Nothing that I had experienced or seen before drove home to me more vividly what Hitler's Germany was all about and what it had done. From my short service in the German Army I had no illusions. Life in Germany was always cheap and men were expendable. But now I actually saw that Germans, re-made in the image of Hitler and his men—perhaps some with whom I had gone to school, had captured thousands and thousands of people from all over Europe like animals. They had then, without any hesitation deposited them in concentration camps like Woebbelin and then worked them to death throwing away their wasted bodies like broken furniture. And in their perverse sense of method and order they made those still alive stack the bodies of those who had perished, like cord wood. If I had not seen it with my own eyes, I would never have believed that Germans could force other men to live and work under conditions worse than those of animals selected for slaughter.

As I stood there watching the victims of this system being unloaded, I hoped that before the world would turn again to other things, someone would go after the people who had organized and carried out these horrors. Men who had engaged in such deliberate murder must account for what they had done and hang. But there was also a curious underlying fear. Was there a possibility that the Nazi system, the beginning of which I had seen and observed until 1939 in Germany, may have attracted some of my own friends and relatives to perform such grizzly deeds?

It also occurred to me then that later in my life I would undoubtedly meet people who would assert that the pictures and movies taken of concentration camps and the like were all forgeries and that in fact none of this had ever happened. They would state that it was just Jewish anti-German propaganda. I am glad I took these pictures on May 9, 1945 in Hagenow of the victims of the Woebbelin concentration camp to remind me that I must never forget. Once or twice when I have had an opportunity to talk about what I saw during the war, people have challenged me and I have been glad that on a hunch I brought my photos so that I could show them the pictures I took in Hagenow as evidence of how it really was.

After VE-Day

With the war in Europe won, the pursuit of victory and the need for discipline that had driven that gigantic American war machine instantly vanished. Censorship was the first restriction that disappeared. All letters written by enlisted men now passed the censor without comment. The strict rules of NO FRATERNIZATION were the next to go by the wayside. Cigarettes and chocolate became the friendship currency. The front page of *Stars & Stripes* still had an occasional reference to the war in the Pacific, but we all knew that Japan would not last forever either—even though not a person had knowledge of the atom bomb. The real news were the plans for demobilization and the point system that would determine who would go first and who had to stay. Length of service, time overseas, number of children, participation in battle engagements, those were the factors that were discussed—and of my friends there was no question that Junior was the one who had the most points.

But the army still had a few matters of high priority on their roster: How could we liberate the American soldiers who had become prisoners-of-war of the Germans and were now being held by our allies, the Russians? Less than 100 miles from where we had come to roost was the gigantic Barth Stalag (German abbreviation for prisoner-of-war camp), a gigantic German installation where over 10,000 American airmen, shot down over Europe, had been kept—some since early 1942. General Ridgway knew of the camp, and being accustomed to moving his airborne forces with the vast number of troop transport planes at his disposal, felt that it would be a simple matter to send someone to his Russian counterpart to tell him that we would like to pick up our men in Barth. He thought we would send the planes in and fly the men out and arrange for their immediate return to the United States. It looked so logical and simple and in Colonel Moss, trained by Huey P. Long, he had the precise man who would be able to persuade anybody.

Neither General Ridgway nor Col. Moss had ever met a Russian, and dealing with the Russians was a new game. We merely knew that the name of the Russian general who commanded the Russian troops opposite us was General Rokossovski, the victor of Stalingrad. We were also completely unaware that the Russians considered their own soldiers who had been captured by the Germans as cowards who were either to be shot or sent to Siberia.

A captain from our headquarters who was fluent in Russian, Col. Moss, and I climbed into a jeep to meet the Russian General. The colonel would tell him of our concerns and what we had in mind. We had not as yet any experience in dealing with them, and did not know that to the Russians all Allies looked the same. At the border, where our armies had met a few days before, we were surprised and pleased to see Russian escort vehicles waiting for us as we entered Russian territory. We were not aware that word had been sent that we were coming. We concluded that the Russians wanted to show us how welcome visitors from the allied armies were. At breakneck speed we and the Russians proceeded for about 10 miles over country roads. It was obvious that the Russians considered Germans who happened to be in the way expendable. We passed through village after village noticing a totally frightened and subdued population that hoped not to be hit by a Russian vehicle.

We halted at a large brick house with military vehicles including many motorcycles parked nearby. Upon our arrival about 20 officers, many showing rank insignia, appeared. The man in charge—obviously the general—wore no cap, but the high leather boots that identified all higher Russian officers. He leaned on a walking stick. Next to him stood a dour looking political commissar with the typical commissar cap and badge. Our interpreter introduced Col. Moss as Gen. Ridgway's representative. We were ushered into the farmhouse, where a table was set so accommodate about 30 people. The long table was loaded with perhaps thirty bottles of different types of hard liquor (no two bottles the same, much of it brands like Benedictine, Cherry brandy, Kirschwasser, Cognac, Kuemmel—clearly brought together from various houses and restaurants in the neighborhood). There were mountains of black bread, pickles, salt herring, sausages and ham. Before each place were glasses (again a large variety) and plates. Enlisted men stood by to replenish the table. We were surprised to see how well they were prepared for a visit from their American allies.

Col. Moss and the interpreter were seated next to the general, the driver and I were placed with some Russian enlisted men at the end of the table. Four or five seats were not occupied. The moment we were seated, the general got up and welcomed the American brothers-in-arms and toasted the great American President Roosevelt. Our glasses were filled, we got up, immediately downed the contents to the last drop and sat down. When the interpreter whispered to the general that the American President was Truman, the general, without showing the least embarrassment, had the glasses refilled. We all got up again, downed the second glass for President Truman and sat down. Now Colonel Moss rose and through his interpreter proposed a toast to that great Russian leader who had helped the

Allies to win the war, Marshal Joseph Stalin. Up we jumped and downed the third glass when suddenly in front of the building we heard an enormous commotion caused by arriving vehicles. The general excused himself, left the table and walked outside to see what was going on. It turned out that this great reception had not been arranged for us but for a British general. Our Russian escort at the checkpoint had mistaken us for the expected British general and had rushed us to the reception. Then, when the British general showed up about half an hour later the mistake was discovered, and a new escort was provided. Now the real party could start. It was only a minor problem—more liquor was produced, the British general took the place of honor, next to the Russian general, Col. Moss was moved to the other, less important side and now the Russian general honored Churchill, and the British general toasted Stalin and by the time we had that much honoring done, each of us had downed at least five glasses of assorted liquors and eaten some of the pickles and bread.

The driver and I had excused ourselves for a few moments during the interruption caused by the British general's arrival, and once behind the building we freed ourselves of the imbibed liquor. I thought it was particularly important that our driver remain operative in case we would have to go on to Barth. Meanwhile Col. Moss had approached the reason for his visit and learned that the general whom we had met was only a minor sort of general and that the man who had the authority to rule on such an important matter was Marshal Rokossowski, who had his headquarters some 25 miles further north. After a few more toasts to the victory and to affirm our profound admiration for our comrades-in-arms, we were escorted to the next place, to which advance information had been telephoned, so that ample liquor and food were ready for us upon arrival.

Our driver, who had gone for a second visit behind the barn, assured me that he was capable of getting us there safely and so we arrived at the "Great General's" headquarters. He had made his headquarters in an elegant castle near Parchim and had set a table very similar to the one that we had just left. Too busy with more important matters, he could not see Col. Moss, but a lesser general would be our host. There followed the same series of toasts, the drinks and delicatessen were the same. Our mission had accomplished nothing except that all of us could now claim that we had seen the Russian and had been drunk twice in one day. I remember our return to Hagenow and my utter despair about getting the runaround. I could not see how we could persuade the Russians to let our planes land at Barth and take our airmen back, and I could clearly see what was in store for Germans living under the Russian occupation.

From that brief interlude on the Russian side I brought back something that until that moment I had only read in books. A nation that has occupied the territories of its enemies and has abused and devastated them can only expect harsh retribution. That is what the Russians were doing now, we could clearly see that as we visited them. And worse was to come.

Col. Moss asked me the next morning to join him again on another try. I declined, and he understood and took Junior. They made it all the way to Barth—with a Russian escort. At the Stalag Col. Moss and Junior were received like liberators, even though they could achieve nothing, but the mere arrival of Americans was an enormous lift for those prisoners. Junior took the names of hundreds of our airmen and their home addresses and promised to mail the news to their families. He was busy for the next few days. The prisoners stayed until Eisenhower got together with General Zhukov, Stalin's commander for the Russian troops in Germany, to resolve the impasse several weeks later. It was clear that the alliance was coming unglued. Having had a peek behind the Russian curtain, and still under the impression that my whole family had failed to flee from the Russians in time, I was in deep despair.

Walking With a Lucky Foot

With our headquarters spread over a large area, I was often used as a courier. On Saturday, May 19, I was on a routine trip when I saw on the map the name, *Lauenburg*, which was a small town about 35 miles from Hamburg and Luebeck, near one of the large bridges over the Elbe River. The bridge at Lauenburg was one of the few that had not been dynamited. The name struck a memory cord. When I was still a child, my mother had told me the first tragic love story that I ever heard and in it the name, Lauenburg played a mysterious part. Annie von Maltzahn, my mother's cousin and contemporary whom I knew well as a young girl of about 18 (in 1895), had been involved in a passionate love affair with a very wealthy, dashing young man. The love affair ended tragically when he died and Tante Annie swore that she would never look at another man. She did not—as far as I know—but my mother also told me that when the will of her lover was opened he had willed her a valuable piece of land with beautiful buildings on it known as "Der Fuerstengarten in Lauenburg." I had never seen the place nor did I know whether my aunt had ever lived there—as far as I knew she divided her residence between Berlin and her farm in Pommerania.

Before returning to Hagenow I stopped at a country inn where I located a 1942 telephone directory of the neighbor hood, which included Lauenburg. Under "von Malzahn, Anna," I saw for the first time the printed name, "Fuerstengarten" as her address. Of course, that directory had been printed three years ago, and a lot had happened since, but I persuaded my driver to make a little detour so that I could stop in Lauenburg. We found the address and I arrived in front of a building complex with expensively constructed field stone buildings that could be closed off from the street by a large wrought iron gate. I was a bundle of nerves. Would she be there? Would she be still alive? She would be close to 70. The moment our car stopped we were surrounded by children who had jumped up from a long driveway that was covered with straw and served as a resting place for a large group of refugees. They assured us that Fraeulein von Maltzahn was in the garden and pointed in the direction where I would find her.

With my carbine slung over my shoulder and my steel helmet on my head I went first to the massive stone house and rang a bell next to the heavy oaken door with a tiny shutter that was covered by wrought iron bars. The shutter was opened from the inside. I could merely see two eyes peering intently at me. And then in the typical inflection of someone from the middle of Pommerania, I heard a voice saying "Oh, Herr von Rosenstiel, I would always recognize you!" It was Aunt Annie's old maid, who had known me from the time that I learned to walk. She sent me to the garden, where Aunt Annie was checking the plantings.

I saw her white hair in the distance and walked past people resting on straw that had been spread on the ground. All of these people looked totally dispirited and clearly frightened by the appearance of an armed American paratrooper who could only mean danger to the woman who had sheltered them. As I walked toward her, two younger women who had been with her saw me coming. They almost ran to intercept me. In stilted English they asked: "Sir, what do you want here?" When I replied in fluent German: "I want to see my Aunt Annie," they almost fainted. By that time Aunt Annie had recognized me—we were in each other's arms. Of course the news of the nephew from America spread like wildfire from group to group, but I was not concerned with answering questions, I needed answers and so my first question was "What do you know about my family?"

Aunt Annie had housed my sister Ilse with her four children for ten days very recently. Originally Ilse had reached safety in a little village, Bickhusen, just three miles East of the Elbe. There she had caught her breath after her perilous flight from Pommerania. Soon after their arrival the allied military government had emptied Bickhusen of all German refugees to accommodate Russian refugees. They had sent all of the German refugees—among them Ilse and her children—across the Elbe to Lauenburg. There Ilse had established contact with Aunt Annie and had found shelter until the military government relocated her back to Bickhusen four days ago.

That was good news, and Aunt Annie also knew that my sister Margarete with her two small children had come through Lauenburg some weeks before and was headed west to an address that she gave me. Of Gerd's wife she had heard that she had reached Luebeck, but there was no news about him. It was a great day and I returned to Hagenow hopeful and encouraged.

In Hagenow I told Col. Moss about my discovery. He was almost as astonished about this miraculous coming together of recollections and combinations as I. The next day was Pentecost Sunday, so in an outpouring of comradeship he immediately assigned our jeep and driver to me for the next day and wished me luck. That night I did not sleep much. At breakfast the next morning I had little appetite and I could not keep my hands from twitching. By 8 A.M. we were on our way and found the tiny village just east of the Elbe River, almost inaccessible because of terrible roads. Bickhusen was administered by a British military government unit to which I reported. I told the officer that I was looking for my sister and gave her name. With a courtesy and matter-of-fact understanding that made me feel that chivalry was not dead, the officer assigned a sergeant to take me to the local Buergermeister. On the way the sergeant told me that he knew exactly who my sister was and that she wore glasses. The Buergermeister was indeed the right man to see, because Ilse had been assigned to his farm for lodging and food.

The Buergermeister joined us on the way to a barn at the other end of the farm where he suspected that we would find Ilse and the four children. It was a large hay barn, still partly filled with hay and we noticed that the place had been used as living quarters. She was not there. So, we turned around and walked back and entered a typical North German farm court with farm buildings and stables enclosing a square area in the center of which stood a large tree. Ten or twelve women sat on potato baskets in a circle peeling potatoes. They were busy and paid little attention when they saw the Buergermeister and the sergeant approaching. When the women noticed that we were looking for someone they were apprehensive.

I still did not see Ilse, because she was sitting with her back toward me. She was just asking "What is the matter?" when I said, "Is Frau von Schwerin here?" She stood up, turned around toward me, recognized me and said "Werner!" almost fell down, grabbed hold of me, shook like a leaf and had trouble suppressing tears and a fainting spell. The sergeant beamed and said: "Good luck to you, fellow. I'm leaving you now." The two of us walked arm in arm—we both needed the support—to the barn where she was quartered with her children. She had not aged much in the six years since I had seen her last, a little heavier and some grey hair but she was much more in command of her children than I remembered. Now she ordered them to be quiet and not disturb us, and they obeyed. Her daughter and her youngest son were there. The older ones were in a meadow guarding horses.

The daughter, then fourteen years old, had recognized me at once—and then the news spurted forth from Ilse. She gave me addresses of people who could help me track down all brothers and sisters. When her husband Albert, the idol of my youth, had been killed in a November 1940 raid over London she had moved back to their farm in Pommerania. When the Russians approached she had loaded some possessions on two small wagons and had fled west. They had survived ice and snow, strafing attacks by low flying planes, and impassable roads and had just settled in this little village when they were temporarily evacuated to Lauenburg to make Bickhusen available as a transit camp for Russian displaced persons. To facilitate this transfer they had been told to leave their possessions in Bickhusen. So she had moved to Lauenburg and had stayed at Aunt Annie's before she was shipped back to Bickhusen, which had then been vacated by the Russians. Nothing was left of her possessions except five silver spoons, Albert's photo and Ritter Cross decoration, the old family Bible, and her address book. Those were her worldly possessions when I found her. Despite her misfortunes, she was something of an inspiration. She said: "Well, we are now harvesting what we have sowed—Albert always said it would end like this—but as long as I can live and keep going I shall manage somehow." The children, who by this time had assembled, looked thin but healthy and were terribly excited having an American in their midst. But I could not stay, no matter how much I wanted to, because I had to continue my search for the rest of the family. Before I left, I took a few pictures, one of them of my sister with her daughter Ehrengard, shows her with a pensive smile—perhaps she thought: "Miracles do still happen."

Zooming along the Autobahn to Hamburg we found the first address, heard from a housekeeper that Ilse's friend was attending Pentecost services in a nearby church, drove to the church and arrived at the very moment when the services were finished. Ilse's friend, whom I recognized immediately, was astonished when an armed American soldier honked the horn of his jeep and walked over to welcome her. The visit lasted not more than five minutes and brought me the assurance that Gerd and his family had managed to escape the Russians. She knew that Alix and the children had come through Hamburg and that Gerd might still be in Luebeck where he had fled with his friend Dr. Runkel.

In Luebeck I found Dr. Runkel, who had escaped with Gerd at the very last moment from Below. Hitler's orders had been to stay on the land and fight no matter how senseless the prognosis. When even the most devoted Nazis decided to flee, Gerd had given the top Nazi his car in exchange for permits that allowed him to leave his post. So, Gerd and Runkel and another friend had used Dr. Runkel's small car, for which he had saved emergency gasoline. They had reached Rostock, where they were halted by Gestapo agents who took them to their headquarters and told Gerd that he would be executed for having violated Hitler's orders and that his permit to leave was clearly a forgery. They had locked him in the basement telling him that he would be hanged in the morning. Dr. Runkel, saying that he happened to get a ride from Gerd, was not arrested and stayed to await the next morning. He came to the building and found it abandoned. The Gestapo men had fled taking Dr. Runkel's car. He unlocked the door to the basement, found Gerd and both made it to Luebeck, where Dr. Runkel's family took them in for a day. Then Gerd started out to reach the address in Holstein where he hoped to find his family. With this news I dashed back to relay the information to Ilse and immediately moved on to follow leads about Margarete.

I found a baronial estate a few miles west of the Elbe where I picked up the welcome news that Margarete with her children and several of my relatives from Marienwalde had briefly stopped there some weeks ago and continued on their flight West. When the lady of the house discovered in me an American soldier of fine German lineage, she brought her husband, who bitterly complained to me about the American occupants of his castle, who had used his place as a command post and had hung their filthy clothes on his valuable hunting trophies. He was sadly disappointed when I mentioned that this was war and I certainly could not help him. I headed back to Hagenow after having driven 340 miles that day. But now the future suddenly looked by no means so hopeless. However, when I returned to my post and reported back, I saw a map posted which showed for the first time the precise zonal borders that would establish which land would be occupied by the Russians and which by the Allies. **Bickhusen was to be Russian!**

Early the next morning I went to see Col. Cain, my unit's military affairs officer and told him that I had found my sister with her four children in Bickhusen, which within a day or two would become part of the Russian Occupied Zone. He already knew about this decision and mentioned that orders had been received to stop all westward traffic over the Elbe. American and British MPs were turning away all people trying to cross the Elbe and enter the Western Zone. When I explained my problem and told him that I could relocate my sister with my brother in Holstein he readily offered to sign whatever orders were needed to get her out of Bickhusen. He stated that we could justify the transfer as being in the interest of the United States. I never typed a faster set of orders. He signed them and I affixed seals and stamps all over the paper giving the documents a very important appearance. He also thought of issuing orders to the motor pool to give me a command car large enough to accommodate my charges. As I left he stopped me and suggested that I take enough K- rations to feed myself and my passengers and get an MP arm band that would give me more status when I would have to cross the Elbe bridge.

Getting transportation from my friends in the motor pool, a large supply of K-rations at the mess hall, and an MP armband took me no time at all and by 9 A.M. I was back in Bickhusen, where I found Ilse with her children at her hay loft. I told her to get in the car with everything that she still had, which was really nothing. She could not take the horse and the small wagon; that was something she had to sacrifice. The military government officer to whom I showed the orders, smiled and wished me luck and off we drove to the bridge. It was lucky that the MPs at the bridge recognized my shoulder patch and respected my carbine and stern face and, of course, the MP arm band and the orders enumerating the five Germans who had to be transferred "In the Interest of the United States." The driver was the one who had driven me on many missions during the Bulge and since we left Epernay. I knew I was in good hands.

Ilse wore a grey skirt that had been made from Albert's winter coat and a dark heavy jacket. The pictures that I took of her and the children are stark reminders of what traveling over terrible roads harassed by attacking planes, creeping under wagons for safety, and having no facilities for washing or mending torn clothes would do to one's appearance. Whenever we drove through towns I sat in the front of the car with the driver, the carbine between my legs, giving the impression of attending to serious government business. But the moment we were again in the open, Ilse filled in the events from the time since I had seen her in March of 1939 when she was living with her family in Berlin, where Albert was pilot for the Air Ministry. She had left Berlin after he was killed and relocated for more than three years in Iven, trekking West when the Russians approached. For a few days following the assassination attempt on Hitler's life in July of 1944, she had been arrested and kept for questioning. She knew nothing of all of these events and was allowed to return to Iven. When I suggested that she write her impressions of her days in Iven and the trek she promised that she would try to get it on paper. It was one of the last things she did before she died. I typed her manuscript and sent the original to Joachim, her oldest son, when he was old enough to treasure it.

Stars and Stripes had contained an article about a fire raid on Hamburg that had devastated the city and killed more than 10,000 civilians. Now, driving through, I saw a city where the devastation of a fire raid had left mile after mile of houses burned to the ground with nothing left standing except the chimneys. They had been constructed to resist heat and now provided the ghastly picture of endless fields resembling blackened asparagus stalks, mile after mile as far as the eye could see.

Ilse filled in the record of many of the relatives and friends who had been killed or ended up as prisoners. She related how on all the large estates that we had known the owners (she included) had buried their silver and valuables in the hope of getting back there some time to dig them up. Now fifty years later, when the return to those farms is possible, I am waiting for somebody to report success. One of her sons has been back several times to Iven, equipped with ever more expensive search equipment, but the results continue to evade him. How would someone identify a place where he hid the stuff fifty years ago, when all landmarks are gone and treasure hunters have had their day?

After a ride of about six hours we finally reached Wulfshagenerhuetten the place that had been given to me as Gerd's destination. It was a tense moment as we turned from the road onto the estate wondering if our information about his address had been correct. We halted in front of an enormous castle, where the arrival of an American vehicle created immediate excitement. I got out of the car, armed with my carbine and walked into a hall where four well dressed women were enjoying tea. There was an expression of fear and defiance on their faces as I entered. I noticed that upon my arrival one of them had hastily rushed to the next room to make a telephone call before she rejoined the other women. They were perplexed when I said "Is Mr. von Rosenstiel with you? I would like to see him." One of the women left to find Gerd. At the very moment when I had expressed the wish to see Gerd, the telephone in the other room rang and the lady who had previously made the call ran to answer it and called, "There is a call for Herrn von Rosenstiel." They all looked utterly dismayed when I said, "I'll take it," and proceeded to the phone. The lady who had said that Herr von Rosenstiel was wanted looked as if she must prevent me from answering the phone, but desisted when I walked to the phone, took the receiver and said in German, "This is Herr von Rosenstiel, but there is some confusion here." The voice at the other end said: "Do you have some problems with looters?" At the moment in which I said: "There is no problem here. We do not need your help," a second door to the room had opened and there stood Gerd. I will never forget the expression on his face—he looked as if he had been hit with a hammer. It is impossible to reconstruct what must have gone through his mind, when he heard me say, "We do not need your help." His eyes were glassy and he seemed not to recognize me when I walked up to him. When I shook his hand, he bowed slightly and in a voice almost without sound he said: "Werner—you here— what do you want?" Was it possible that he thought that I was a looter or had come to haunt him? When I told him that I had brought Ilse and her children, he seemed even more confused and said: "Do you know anything of our parents and of Ruth?" I could only nod. It was hard for me to think of the energetic, forceful man I had last seen in 1939. Here he was, white haired, nervous, in a state of total confusion and bewilderment, an almost unbelievable change from the man I remembered. Without another word he turned around and left.

I went back to the car and helped Ilse and the children into the house. We had brought K-rations for each of them and the driver and they enjoyed the excitement of opening those brick like cardboard boxes made waterproof by a thick layer of wax. Inside there was manna from heaven -luxuries unheard of in the Germany of 1945: a piece of chocolate, a raisin bar, a tin of beef, graham crackers, instant coffee powder and cigarettes, the new currency. Alix had come from her room in the attic to join us and mentioned that her children would not be coming down as they lay with high fever in an attic room suffering from scarlet fever. I explained to her that by sheer good luck I had found Ilse and I hoped that Gerd would not try to harass himself or me with the fact that I was an American soldier—we just did not have time to explain. I said I had joined the American army in its fight against Hitler because it had seemed to me the only right thing to do. She agreed instantly, promised to talk to him and apologized for his state, adding that he was so depressed and exhausted from what he had been through and by worries that most of the time he was close to tears.

What Gerd had been through was enough to break almost any man. But I did not have the time to listen to any explanation. I had to find the British military administrator, deliver the order from my headquarters to him and ask him to make food and lodging available to feed five more hungry mouths—all of them members of my family. After a quick bite, I was off to Gettorf. From there the British detachment sent me to their Command Post in Eckernfoerde where I would have to turn in my orders. It was not far and I reported to the commanding officer, Major Ormsby, who read the orders and asked me to identify myself. My dog tags and a written order that Col. Cain had given me so that I could draw gasoline, food, and quarters convinced him that I was genuine. When I appealed for his help, he made a statement that has remained with me. He simply said: "If you were good enough to fight in the American army we certainly can look after your family." When I mentioned that Gerd was an experienced farm manager who had administered large estates in Pommerania, he wrote on a little slip of paper:

Order

Gerd von Rosenstiel is directed to report at Headquarters
in Eckernfoerde at 8 A.M.,
May 21, 1945.
Major Ormsby, Commanding

He handed me the slip, and with a friendly smile said: "I'll speak with him tomorrow morning and look after your sister and her children." With the order in my hand I thanked him, saluted and left to deliver the order to Gerd.

How lucky I was in having found Major Ormsby I found out much later. The next morning after he would interview Gerd and have some quick checks run on him, he would appoint him to administer the large estate that Gauleiter Lohse, the Chief Nazi of Holstein had managed to acquire with Party funds. Gerd would stay in that job until his death in November of 1952.

By the time I returned to Wulfshagenerhuetten from Eckernfoerde, an incredible change had occurred. Ilse and Alix had convinced Gerd that I was a God-sent blessing and that he should put his mind to work to provide me with facts that could help them. I handed him the order and told him to leave the next morning early enough to be in Eckernfoerde by eight. He understood and showed me a sheet of paper on which he had outlined his education, employment and activities during Hitler's rule. Miraculously he had a letter from a French prisoner-of-war, who had worked in Below and for whom he had obtained a medical discharge that had enabled him to return to Paris. In that letter the man, Robert Legros, a jeweler, had thanked Gerd for his kindness and the understanding with which he had treated him and other prisoners. I quickly made a translation of the letter from French into English and laboriously printed a curriculum vitae that would help Gerd make a case for himself. The address of Legros I copied into my little notebook and I visited him later when I was in Paris.

In the course of writing this document I learned that Gerd had not joined the party and had been denounced, but the local chief party official had always supported him because finding a replacement for him would have been impossible and would result in reducing the food production by at least 40 percent. Despite the risk, Gerd had helped numerous people and given them shelter and food, the most famous one of them was Werner Fink, a famous cabaret manager whose license had been revoked when he did not meet the Party line.

I am proud of my brother, who withstood the blandishments of the Hitler system and who pursued the honorable course with which he had been brought up, knowing full well the risks that came with it. Clearly there were during Hitler's times men who were not Hitler's willing executioners as would be postulated in 1996 by people who had not lived through those times.

There was nothing more that I could do and I had to get back to my unit, so I said goodbye to them, promised that I would be back as soon as I could make it, and promised Ilse that I would take a picture of Albert's grave near London, if I could get back to England; she had slipped me a little note with the address and his grave's registration to be sure that I had the right information. Before I got back in the car, I took a few pictures—Gerd was smiling and Alix was with him. Suddenly the future began to look more manageable. I waved at them as we turned to reach the highway and saw Ilse with her four children waving at me as she had done so often when I had left Iven. I did not know then that it would be my last look at her.

It was about 10:30 at night when we made it back to Hagenow. I was tired and beat. Junior was still awake when I walked into our billet. The unit had been transported back to Epernay already and except for him they were all gone. We were scheduled to follow three days later. In my absence word had been received that my commission as a lieutenant had come through and Col. Moss wanted me as his assistant. Even my four battle stars would not get me home yet. The army would keep me until I had amassed the needed 85 points.

Dead tired as I was, it was some time before I fell asleep. Before I dropped off I thought of the incredible events I had lived through—the war was over now. I had come through it unscratched, certain that four of my brothers and sisters were safe. I had hope for Ruth, the one sister still in Russian territory. All of them were paupers who had salvaged nothing but their lives. Only the future would tell if they had enough energy left to start from scratch. Whether and how I might be able to help them I could then not even contemplate as I returned that evening. I had a wife, two children, and a small job. Two days later a letter to Marion showed a remarkable revival of my optimism when I wrote: "..with you behind me and St. Jude [the Saint of the lost causes] looking over my shoulder, we will and must succeed" in doing something for them. My faith in making it in America was then as unshakable as it is today. Maybe my note to Marion sounded like whistling in the dark, but I was convinced that somehow I would prevail.

On May 24, 1945 Junior and I boarded a C-47 and we were back in Epernay two hours later.

CHAPTER 9

A SECOND LIEUTENANT IN SEARCH OF A MISSION

OUR COZY QUARTERS in the *Moet et Chandon* champagne factory in Epernay felt great when Junior and I returned there on May 26th. It would be a few days before the paperwork with my lieutenant's commission was completed, but we knew it would come, so no one cared. Spring was in the air and sooner or later we would all get back home.

The most important task for me was to develop several rolls of film that I had taken and to make a photographic record of our war experiences for the six members of our section. Everybody wanted to see what my camera had immortalized. Junior became my dark room assistant. The album was a photographic narrative covering our time in Europe from August 1944 to May 23, 1945. I look at it fifty years later surprised at what I see and what I then had thought essential.

When I returned to our office from being sworn in as a second lieutenant on June 9th, my enlisted friends had prepared a special reception. They jumped to attention when I entered the office and saluted me with brooms, which they had secured for the occasion, held at "Present Arms" and we celebrated the event with champagne. I was told that I would soon be transferred, but nobody knew where and for what.

On to Paris

On June 19 my orders to go to Paris came. I said good-bye to my many friends—they were returning to the States to head the invasion of Japan later that year, and I would be left to do work in Germany until I had enough points to get home. Junior and Harry Leykauf remained my life-long friends. I met Major Moroney again when both of us worked in an office of the War Crimes branch in Wiesbaden, but of all the many other people whose names still appear in my diary I saw none—acquaintances made during war are that way.

In Paris I reported to Brigadier General T. J. Betts, the Judge Advocate General for the European Theater of Operations in Europe (ETOUSA). He had an elegant office that had served a German general before. A West Pointer, small in stature he was an ambitious martinet. With Germany defeated he was angling for a plush job in the U.S. Army of Occupation and had his heart set on the most coveted plum of them all: Director of the Legal Division of the American Forces in Germany and legal counsel to General Clay. The prestige and perks for a general in the Army of Occupation were something that appealed to officers who had been in the army for a long time and had never enjoyed a life of luxury. General Betts saw the possibilities, even if he did not correctly evaluate his own talents. In anticipation of the hoped for assignment, he had assembled a staff of capable civilian lawyers and career army officers who would go to Berlin as soon as the details of the occupation and administration of that city by the Allies were completed. He would then pull the necessary strings and get to Berlin and assume his dream job.

In the meantime he was in Paris waiting for the opportune moment. He knew that I was a lawyer trained in Germany and the United States, and he reasoned that it would be an ideal solution to have a man with such qualifications available just in case anyone asked a question about German law. And so I found myself as his aide sitting in Paris in the ante room to his office waiting for an opportunity to answer questions about Germany. They never came. I was billeted in the elegant Scandinavian building of the University of Paris (Cite Universitaire), which had been requisitioned by the US Army. I had wonderful quarters and lived in an essentially un-damaged city but I was unhappy without work and action. I was restless sitting in Paris. Patience was not one of my major virtues.

A local movie house presented a crop of American, French, and Russian movies from 11 A.M. to 9 P.M. daily, and soon I was able to calm my impatience by seeing many of the movies I had missed—among them Casablanca, Mrs. Miniver, Battleship Potemkin, and the Grand Illusion.

Back to Germany
Surveying the Records of the German Ministry of Justice at Fuerstenhagen near Kassel

Finally, on July 3rd as Colonel Pitzer, one of the officers on General Bett's staff stopped at my desk. He told me that the next morning we would fly to Frankfurt and go on to Fuerstenhagen near Kassel for a special assignment. A car would pick me up early next morning at my quarters.

On the plane to Frankfurt, Col. Pitzer started my briefing. Fuerstenhagen, he told me, was a village about 10 miles East of Kassel, next to which had been an enormous Nazi manufacturing complex with factory buildings and housing facilities for thousands of slave laborers. This plant, of which the allies had known, but had never been able to pinpoint for a bombing raid, was now abandoned. The machinery had been dismantled and shipped to Russia as part of their reparation claims. The empty buildings—in perfect condition—were now used as the Allied **Ministerial Collection Center.**

In an effort to learn as much as possible about the operation of the Nazi Government, the Allies, including the Russians, had agreed to bring all the files of German ministries found in their respective zones to Fuerstenhagen, and to transfer there as many of the ministerial top officials as were still available. All of these men were now living in the barracks that previously had housed slave laborers. But unlike the slave laborers they received three decent meals a day and were not abused, although they could not leave. They were considered privileged prisoners and were held for people like me who were charged with evaluating their files and finding, if possible, the skeletons in the closets.

Beginning in 1943, bombing of Berlin had laid waste to much of the city and made an orderly central German government administration from Berlin impossible. Whole ministries or sections of ministries had been transferred with their staffs to various smaller towns in Germany, which were less likely to be bombed. From that diaspora the German government had administered the Reich for the last two years of the war. At the end of the war these administrative units were discovered, packed up, and together with their personnel were shipped to Fuerstenhagen. Each of the ministries had been assigned a whole empty building where the files were now awaiting evaluation. One of the main purposes of surveying these files—now under exclusive Allied control—was to obtain from German sources evidence against German defendants for a war crimes trial, planned for later. My assignment, Col. Pitzer informed me, was to survey the files of the German Ministry of Justice. I was the first American officer to see those files. If in the course of my investigation I would find specific material useful in the prosecution of any of the major leaders of the Nazi government now in captivity, I was instructed to report it. Otherwise, I should prepare a survey of the existing files so that American personnel could use the files without the need of German officials. Finally he suggested that I report any material for which I could see some use in the now ongoing reorganization of Germany. He cautioned me not to let any German touch any of the records, because they might very well have a personal interest in removing incriminating material against themselves. I now had some idea what was expected of me, but I could not possibly have anticipated the immensity of what I would find.

A staff car was waiting for us at the Frankfurt Rhein/ Main airport. As we landed I saw on the airfield a plane of such gigantic dimensions that I believed it to be something like a specially designed flying moving van. It was my first view of a B-29, the largest plane then in existence—one of them would soon deliver the atomic bomb and end the war with Japan. Parked under each wing was a B-17, which until then had looked to me like a big plane compared with the C-47, which had been my mode of army transportation.

Our baggage was stowed away in the sedan and we were on our way to Kassel. My ride through smashed Hamburg at the end of May had already hardened me for the sight of Frankfurt. I had last seen that city in 1938, when I had admired the Paul's Cathedral in which almost 100 years ago the first futile efforts toward a democratic Germany had been made. Our car took us through endless streets of ruined houses and past the blackened ruins of that tragic monument of promise. Men and women were employed clearing rubble and neatly stacking bricks that might be used in reconstruction.

The Autobahn was in fair condition, except that almost every bridge had been dynamited, which forced us to make slow detours. The 120 miles took us four hours. Kassel looked worse than any city I had seen. The city had been the locomotive industry center of Germany and had been singled out for numerous raids, which had blanketed the city—now a heap of collapsed structures. We left the Autobahn at Kassel to reach Fuerstenhagen. The highway entered a pine forest and I noticed that we were riding on a highway protected from aerial sight by an endless canopy on top of which grew large pine trees. After riding for about two miles under this canopy we saw a large factory building completely painted with camouflage paint and on top of which was a dense forest of pine trees. This, then was the explanation of why the plant had never been found and bombed and had survived the war untouched. Our sedan left the road to stop at a building with a large sign **REICHS-JUSTIZMINISTERIUM**. We were at our destination.

An armed soldier at the entrance stopped us and requested identification and orders permitting us to enter. We came to a bare room without windows, about 40 x 80 feet, with a 15-foot ceiling. Large electric lights suspended from the ceiling provided illumination. Along the walls were stacked several hundred wooden boxes, all of them stenciled **RJM**, some of them already opened, others still nailed shut. In the middle of the room were three long tables with metal legs on which files had been heaped. Many of these files had bright red covers, which the soldiers later told me were for SECRET materials.

We were welcomed by four American soldiers who came to attention when Col. Pitzer entered. All were fluent in German and had been instructed to begin with the unpacking of the wooden crates. Everything that they thought could be of interest they were told to place on the three tables. Col. Pitzer introduced me and told the soldiers that I would be billeted in the inn at the village of Fuerstenhagen and was now in charge of all operations. He ordered them to assist me and see to it that I and my baggage, which our driver had deposited at the entrance to the building, be taken to the inn. He then turned to me and said: "Lieutenant, you are in charge now. Good luck!" and returned to his staff car. I was on my own.

The American soldiers waiting for me were young Jewish refugees from Germany, who had been drafted and because of their language skills, assigned to intelligence units. During the war they served as interpreters and had interrogated German prisoners. Now their knowledge of German provided me with invaluable help. I told them what my orders were and asked them to help me find all the important materials. We would meet every morning and I would tell them what I had planned, what I had found and what I was looking for, and where they could help me best. Being bright they were delighted to assist and instantly realized the important contributions that they could make and the excitement that was ahead.

They were itching to see my reaction to the red folders which they had already stacked on the three tables in anticipation of my arrival. They also mentioned that among the men held in something like protective custody in the barracks were 13 members of the ministry. All of them had been there for over a month and were anxious to explain and perhaps assist in an effort to facilitate their return to a normal life in the reconstituted Germany.

The *Red Files* proved to be of immense value. All of them contained material that the German judicial administration had wanted to keep secret. It was surprising how naive these German bureaucrats actually were. Obviously they had not, until the very last moment, anticipated the possibility of defeat and had made no preparations for the shredding of all incriminating material to prevent it from falling into our, i.e. enemy hands. It is incredible how effectively they had assisted us in our task of finding their government's skeletons.

All the hundreds of unopened boxes had stencil markings, which initially meant nothing to us. But when we opened one of the perhaps 50 boxes with the Code **RJM PERS A** and examined its content we realized that the code **PERS A** designated the personnel files of the judicial administration of Germany. What a find! If only all the files had come in, we thought, we would have had a complete dossier for every judge, prosecuting attorney, licensed attorney and notary in Germany. Actually these files were a wasted treasure trove. Having them would have facilitated finding the Nazi crooks as well as the responsible, untainted men needed for the reorganization of a democratic German judiciary. For reasons that I have never been able to understand very little use of this personnel material was ever made. It is well known that the judiciary in both the Bundes Republik and East Germany employed numerous badly tainted Nazi judges and prosecutors.

My collaborators had a jeep available and after I had glanced at a few of the *Red Files* I asked them to take me to the inn, where I would live for the next few weeks. The inn had always been operated as a guesthouse for this complex and now had been converted into an officer's mess with a mess sergeant in charge. Most of the rooms had been set aside for men with similar assignments for evaluating the bureaucracy of Nazi Germany.

As I sat at a little table in my room waiting for dinner to be served, the immensity of the job ahead of me began to dawn upon me. Less then six years ago, as a law clerk, I had been an employee of the Reichsjustizministerium. My years of training as a law clerk in the Nazi German Judicial Administration from 1934 until February 29, 1939 had been planned in this ministry, perhaps even by some of the men now held at Fuerstenhagen. It seemed possible that I might find my own personnel file. I might also discover the files of the judges who had trained me and find out where they stood and how they had weathered these six years. The *Red Files* would offer valuable leads, but above all I had hoped to find material on the events of 20 July 1944, when German Army officers had attempted to assassinate Hitler. Since I had known several of those involved in the plot, learning of the details and their fate was a matter of very personal interest.

In those three weeks I learned more about the German judicial system and German bureaucracy than I had in the years when I was involved in it.

The next morning, I met with my crew and one of them drove me to the barracks where I would find the staff of the ministry. A guard at the entrance to the barbed wire secured area checked my papers and directed me to the administration building. The area was filled with civilian prisoners who were milling around and enjoying the pleasant summer weather. The officer in charge of the camp already knew of my arrival and had assigned a small room with about 15 chairs for my meeting. Over a PA system he ordered all officials of the Reichsjustizministerium to report there at once.

And now I would meet my opposition. It was an eerie feeling to stand there, almost sensing the pulls and tucks of unquestioned obedience to higher authority that my long German training had imparted to me. All of these men had high rank in the judicial administration where I had served at the very bottom. And now wearing the army uniform of the victor I stood before them—I was by the mere coat that I wore the new unchallengeable authority. To eliminate possible complications, I had decided not to disclose my name. I knew that among the hundreds of inmates there could easily be one or the other who would recognize my name and perhaps approach me for some favor. By directing them to communicate with me through the camp commander I could also avoid complications.

The men whom I saw before me were a dispirited lot—most of them in the age range from 45 to 60. They had come from Greiz, a small town in Thuringia near the Czech border where they had been transferred during the last months of the war. Before that they had been evacuated to Prenzlau some 75 miles north of Berlin when in 1943 the bombing of Berlin had made operation there impossible. In early May an American unit had discovered and arrested them in Greiz. The army had shipped them and all their files to Fuerstenhagen just before the Russians took over, making them civilian prisoners. Disillusioned and frightened though they were by uncertainty about their future and lack of contact with their families, they were glad to be prisoners of the Americans and not of the Russians.

Standing now before them I said:

"Gentlemen: All of you have been employees of the German Ministry of Justice. I have been ordered to provide a report on the workings of the Ministry of Justice. Although I have a general idea of its organization, I feel that it is not sufficiently detailed. I expect you to provide the details that I must have. I am providing each of you with a writing pad and a pencil so that you can make notes. I want each of you to write for me three reports. This is what I need and want:

> 1. A brief carefully written **curriculum vitae** outlining accurately you're education and professional training. I want you to be specific about membership in the party and any asso-

ciated organizations—SA, SS- with dates of joining. Accuracy is essential and *will be checked*. Let me remind you that we have captured the complete records of the party and all its affiliate organizations and that I have access to those files. Falsification will be detected and will adversely affect your treatment here and the duration of your confinement and your future employment.

2. A carefully written **job description** showing all positions you held in the Ministry (with dates), and descriptions of duties performed in each job. I want to know the names of the persons to whom you reported and the names of those who reported to you. The report must also provide reasons for job changes, and give the file numbers and identifying designations for the files which you have handled.

3. A carefully written statement of **how you understand the Ministry of Justice to have been organized and operated.**

I shall pick up your essays one week from today, read your papers carefully, and then discuss them with each of you. If you have any questions now, please ask them."

There was complete silence. I continued: "If you want to ask me any questions about the three reports, please address them to: **SURVEY OF RJM** and have the administrative officer in the camp forward them to me." They nodded understanding, and I dismissed them.

Returning to our building I found my crew opening crates and adding *Red Files* to the heaps that I had seen the day before and which I had not yet read. They were eager to hear my reaction to the prisoners, but above all they were itching to show me a real hot file that they had discovered that morning. It was the smoking gun. They had found the notorious **COMMANDO ORDER,** and its discovery sealed the fate of two of the high German Army officers: Keitel and Jodl—then not as yet identified as defendants in the Nuremberg Trial. In 1941 when the Allies made frequent small intelligence raids into Nazi occupied Europe, Hitler directed his staff to issue an order, which in substance read:

> From now on all elements on so-called commando missions in Europe or Africa . . . even if they are to all appearances soldiers in uniform or demolition troops, whether armed or unarmed, in battle or in flight, are to be slaughtered to the last man. . . . Even if these individuals, when found, should apparently be prepared to give themselves up, no pardon is to be granted them.
>
> I will hold responsible under military law, for failing to carry out this order, all commanders and officers who either have neglected their duty of instructing the troops about this order, or acted against the order where it was to be executed.

What I saw was a clear violation of the provisions of the 1899 Hague Convention, which Germany along with most nations had accepted and never abrogated. The Convention was specific: "To kill or wound an enemy who, having laid down his arms, or no longer having means of defense, has surrendered . . . **is particularly forbidden.**"

The distribution of the **COMMANDO ORDER** had been made through routine army channels and since all matters relating to the defense of the Reich, were also checked for their legality in a department of the Ministry of Justice, the ministry had received a copy of the order signed by Jodl. By signing it he had written his own Hanging Warrant. Nobody in the Ministry of Justice had added a word of warning or reference to the Hague Convention, which they unquestionably knew. The only acknowledgment that it was a "smoking gun" was that it was made a secret matter and given a *Red File* folder.

I remember the shock at seeing this file. How could a professional German officer, who had been trained in the Kaiser's army and served in both World Wars, lend his hand to such a deed? From my pay book as a German soldier, which I had turned over to the FBI when they had investigated my loyalty in 1942, I remembered that it had contained a warning that it was a crime to carry out knowingly an illegal order. At that time it had meant nothing important to me. Many of my relatives had served in the German Army, among them my younger brother who was an officer in WWII. Would they, or perhaps more challenging *had they* actually carried out such an order? I knew of at least one historical incidence of a refusal to obey an immoral or improper order of the Prussian commander-in-chief. Frederick the Great had dismissed one of his generals who had served him for more than 20 years, for disobedience. During the Seven Years War (1756-63) Russian and Saxon troops had occupied Berlin, Prussia's capital, and done severe damage to the precious art collections and furnishings in the Charlottenburg Castle. When Frederick saw the damage his fury knew no end. Shortly thereafter the fortunes of war having changed, he occupied Dresden, the capital of the Saxon Grand Elector, who was allied with his Austrian enemy. Frederick now ordered General von Marwitz to empty a Palais in Dresden, one of the showpieces of Saxon baroque, of its art treasures and ship them to Berlin. Von Marwitz refused to obey, stating that he was a soldier not a looter. Stung by this remark, Frederick instantly cashiered him and sent him back to Prussia—never to regain his king's nod. He accepted the humiliation rather than do something that he knew was clearly shameful. His tombstone provides the classic answer: **Chose disgrace where obedience brought no honor** (Waehlte Ungnade, wo Gehorsam keine Ehre brachte).

Another *Red File* bore the signature of Keitel, who had also signed the **Nacht Und Nebel** (night and fog) **Order,** a similar violation of the Rules of Land Warfare, but even more perverse. As might be expected, Germany had experienced sabotage throughout Europe. To combat this, at Hitler's direction, plans were made for the purpose of reprisal, to pick up random people and have them disappear without trace. By accident much later, Allied search teams found liquidation records at the Mauthausen Concentration Camp.

These people had been brought there and killed. The records showed only their names, date of death and cause of death, like "heart-failure" or "embolism," not "bullet." Just by accident someone looking at the names recognized the name of one of the people who had been spirited away under the **Nacht und Nebel order,** and suddenly had the answer to what this was all about.

How could men coming from such backgrounds as Jodl's and Keitel's sign such documents? Both of these men were caught blatantly sanctioning the commission of war crimes, and I was certain that they would have to pay the price. I forwarded both files to the War Crimes Branch in Wiesbaden, from where they ultimately found their way to Nuremberg, where they were incorporated into the case against these two officers and the German General Staff.

My attention was soon engaged by other matters but I could not free myself from the question: How was it possible that a whole nation was ready to accept a moral code that simply abrogated the basic moral teachings that had been pounded into every German child for centuries? Was there not one decent honorable man left in Germany? It was on the last day of my assignment to Fuerstenhagen, when I came upon another *Red File* which demonstrated that even in Hitler's time there was at least **one** honorable man who lived by a code other than blind obedience rendered by a mindless vassal.

Around 1936 or 1937 Hitler began his campaign against the Catholic and Protestant churches which were offering resistance to the new Nazi code of morality. Reverend Niemoeller, a highly decorated WWI submarine commander who had become a Protestant minister in Berlin, refused to comply and was punished by incarceration at the Buchenwald Concentration Camp, where he was found by allied troops in 1945. The Catholic church was harassed by a vicious campaign that selected priests as targets for prosecution, alleging misdeeds such as homosexuality and currency violations. The newspapers were full of shrieking accusations against Catholic priests. Hitler's chosen cabinet was a selection of party faithful, who would perform whatever they were told to do without reflection on basic morality. There were two members in every Reich cabinet, however, who were not chosen for their devotion to the chancellor but for their professional competence: the ministers for the railway system and the postal service. It was common knowledge that the administration of those two portfolios required more than an enthusiastic salute to the Fuehrer. Both ministers in Hitler's cabinet had served Germany before Hitler came to power in 1933, and they were retained for their professional skills and experience. In 1937 Dorpmueller, the minister of Traffic (Railways), a devout Catholic, received an unexpected letter from the Party Headquarters in Munich awarding him party membership in the most exclusive party cell, the **Ortsgruppe Braunes Haus** in Munich, where Hitler's oldest and closest friends were recorded, and the **Golden Party Badge** which would place him on the same level as men who had joined the party when joining it involved a real risk. The letter, which we found in a *Red File*, was brief and courteous and read substantially as follow:

> Mein Fuehrer:
>
> I acknowledge my initiation into the ranks of the Party and the award of the high honor of the Golden Party Badge. Being a devout and practicing member of the Catholic church, I regret that I cannot identify myself with the Party and membership in the Ortsgruppe Braunes Haus, at a time when members of my faith are persecuted by the government authorities. I must, therefore, return the badge and decline the membership.
>
> Heil Hitler !
>
> Julius Dorpmueller

The man was not removed from his position and he saw to it that the trains continued to operate on time. It took guts to adhere to a code of morality, but apparently it was possible. What was it then that made so many abandon a moral code that we all considered part of our heritage? Was it greed, ambition, lack of pride, lack of civil courage? Perhaps it was the development of an irresistible terror mechanism that was so overwhelming that resistance was thought impossible?

The Noetling Black Marketing Affair

My team was itching to have me examine another *Red File* they had dug up. It was the 1943 black market scandal of August Noetling. The Noetling Company of Berlin-Steglitz was an old family enterprise predating the First World War. August Noetling was the proud owner of this prosperous delicatessen and wine business, where many Nazi cabinet members were his regular customers. Routine police checks in 1942 to monitor compliance with rationing regulations had disclosed that he also ran a lucrative black market operation of two million Marks annually, supplying VIP Nazis without bothering them about ration cards, etc. The police had been tipped off by local residents, furious at seeing top Nazis living high on the hog, while they had to get by with little. On top of that they were told of the need for sacrifice now that the war in Russia was not going so well.

The police commissioner of Berlin hearing about this, leaned on Noetling and his manager. The two admitted to their misdeeds and many irregularities in their bookkeeping. Initially the police commissioner chose not to pursue hints of improprieties by high government officials, fined Noetling 5,000 Marks for violating rationing regulations, and hoped that the matter would be forgotten. Noetling considered the fine of RM 5,000 a mere slap on the wrist, but feared that if it were publicized how well he had made out with this fine, he would have adverse reactions from the inhabitants of Steglitz who despised him for illegally supplying the government. Instead of letting the matter go, he filed a masterful appeal seeking a full judicial determination of his case in the local court, where he knew that he would be well served. When the matter reached the formal hearing stage, the police commissioner's operatives testified that they had the names of some 20 members of the top Nazi administration including Frick, Ribbentrop, Raeder and Keitel. Sud-

denly there was more to the case than the commissioner had suspected, or had cared to know. Noetling and his helper found themselves in jail. Noetling's two suicide attempts did not impress the
police commissioner who came down hard on him. Surprisingly a
flood of detailed disclosures now came to light. His very clever
appeal had been drafted by the presiding judge of the local court,
Dr. Gardiewski. Noetling, seeing that his game was up, offered to
provide itemized lists of what he had delivered and to whom—
including pertinent correspondence with high officials and their wives,
praising his devotion to his customers. Now the fat was in the fire.

The police commissioner realized that this was a hot potato,
and sent copies of the complete file to Dr. Goebbels, the Minister
of Propaganda, and to Dr. Thierack the Minister of Justice, neither
of them being reported as a beneficiary of this matter. In his letter
to Dr. Thierack the commissioner pointed out that it was, of course,
a violation of laws. But he also knew that it was not a simple matter
and getting rid of it discreetly was essential. He mentioned as an
embarrassing side issue that he would run into problems with his
own men if he had to order them to enforce the rationing laws
against residents of Steglitz, but not against the privileged members
of the cabinet.

Thierack had a very nasty job on his hands and acted coura-
geously. He wrote a full report to Hitler, mailing it to Martin
Bormann, Hitler's secretary and offered to talk to all of the people
involved to resolve the matter. By suggesting that no criminal action
be undertaken irrespective of what he would learn, he showed that
he had a clear comprehension of what was expected from him as the
Minister of Justice—solutions NOT justice. His letter concludes
that at most a monetary "**Busse** (atonement)" not a "fine" might be
considered. Bormann replied: Go ahead and tell them not to do it
again.

Thierack's file covering more than 100 pages contained his correspondence with these Nazi functionaries and their responses. The
letters from all these men, who should have been models for the
German people and particularly for the German youth, showed them

for what they really were—common, unprincipled people who did not even have the decency to say: I did it, I knew it was wrong, and I am ashamed.

Bormann finishes off the whole matter by the following letter of April 12, 1943

> Dear Dr. Thierack:
>
> You recently advised me that you had come upon two additional cases resembling the Noetling matter. Please keep me posted. Enclosed a photostat of a Directive of the Fuehrer dated July 14, 1942; it is essential that I as the Secretary of the Fuehrer be informed about all matters relating to prominent party members.
>
> Heil Hitler !
>
> /s/ Martin Bormann
>
> Enclosure:

> Adolf Hitler   Berlin
> ORDER
> All matters that implicate Reichsleiters, Gauleiters, Leaders of organizations, their collaborators or close relatives are to be reported to the head of the Party's Central Office (Parteikanzlei).
>
> s/s Adolf Hitler
> Headquarters of the Fuehrer July 4, 1942

I took the file and mailed it to the U.S. administration for Germany and suggested in a note that a series of articles could be written and fed into German newspapers. The file did not describe war crimes but it would show the German people who suffered, how they were deceived and abused by the very people who governed them.

Nothing of this case was ever utilized to show the Nazi Government for what they really were. Years later when I wanted to refresh my memory I wrote to the Bundesarchiv in Koblenz, where the file had come to rest. They sent me a microfilm. A comment in the file that Noetling had finally taken his own life was new to me. I must have overlooked or forgotten it. It made me wonder if that was really the way his life had ended. Could the Nazis have afforded to have that man stay alive?

For the next week I studied *Red Files*. None yielded material of value for the prosecution of war criminals, but they painted a grim picture of what life was like under the Nazis. For some administrative reason, all clemency matters were entitled to a *Red File*. There seemed to be mountains of them. I glanced at several hundred. All of the appeals were from persons who had been found guilty by the notorious People's Court and the sentence was death in every instance. The majority of these convictions were for acts that endangered the nation's power to resist her enemies, a crime that was often defined as "Defaitism." The answer to all appeals for clemency was simple: DENIED. There was no probing review of the evidence, of the procedure or of the conduct of the trial. The mere fact that anyone was charged with the crime and tried by the People's Court was justification to have him done away with.

I remember reading the first few files with a mixture of disbelief and fury. How could such judgments be passed and later be affirmed by trained, highly qualified judges, when the charges were so clearly trumped up and the defendants routinely denied competent defense counsel and prevented from saying anything? As I read on, I noticed that gradually my capacity for indignation diminished and was leaving me. My associates had experienced the same thing. After all every one of these cases had the same tragic ending **DEATH in EVERY CASE.** So in order to help me they told me that all these cases were the same—there were NO exceptions.

When I told them that I had, in February of 1939 seen Roland Freisler the notorious President of the People's Court conduct the final bar examination of five Referendare (law clerks) in Berlin, their interest in these cases was revived.

The Case of Erich Knauf before the Peoples Court

One of the soldiers brought me the case of Erich Knauf, which he thought was typical but also unusually informative. It illustrated perhaps better than any other file that I saw how the Nazi system had "open season" on all who might have retained any thought of their own. They were the real enemies of the Reich! How were these people recognized? Anybody who had ever shown devotion to democracy, been a member of the social democratic party, or expressed openly or by implication a criticism of Hitler or any of his henchmen was a menace to the nation and must be killed like a dog with rabies. From Hitler to the Minister of Justice, to the chief prosecutor and the Judge of the People's Court, the bribed witness, the jailer and finally the executioner there was a straight line of mania: Kill to save the Reich!! The case of Erich Knauf showed the trend but also the unbelievable turf fighting among Hitler's paladins to support this insanity.

By 1944 what little sense of justice may have been left in the Ministry of Justice, could and would be bent to the desires of anyone who had clout. Here Dr. Goebbels asserted himself. Hitler had made the Minister of Justice, Dr. Thierack personally responsible for the administration of the right kind of justice (i.e. death sentence) in every case that threatened the core of the Reich. Dr. Goebbels had been made Plenipotentiary for Total War in 1944 and was the one who reminded the Minister of Justice of his special duty for a death sentence in this case. He was a man who could not be ignored.

In 1920 Knauf, a veteran of WW I, had joined the social democratic party and actively supported the democratic forces of the Weimar Republic in Saxony when they crushed an attempt to restore the monarchy. Before 1933 he had written several books, one about artists with the title *From Daumier to Kollwitz*. In Hitler's time mentioning Kaethe Kollwitz in any favorable manner was in itself almost a crime, because she was a known pacifist and active opponent of militarism, having lost a son in WWI. In 1933 when Hitler came to power Knauf gave up his directorship of the German Book Club. Shortly thereafter he was arrested and sent for ten weeks to concentration camps in Oranienburg and Lichtenburg, because he had written a review of an opera performance which violated Nazi views of art. After his release from the concentration camp, he worked as manager of an industrial advertising company until the beginning of 1944.

A February 1944 air raid had destroyed the home of Captain Schultz of the Gestapo in Berlin-Kaulsdorf. Schultz, suddenly homeless, was assigned living space for himself and his wife in the house owned and occupied by Knauf, his wife and his friend, the cartoonist Erich Ohser. On February 22, 1944, soon after Schultz and his wife arrived, they reported to the authorities that both Knauf and Ohser were enemies of the state. Perhaps it had occurred to Schultz that death sentences against Knauf and Ohser would improve his living space.

On March 28, 1944 both men were arrested by the Gestapo and charged with the following crimes which Schultz had alleged:

(1) having suggested that Dr. Goebbels, the Minister of Propaganda, might have enriched himself by collecting a fee of RM 1,500 (mentioned in the newspapers) for writing an article for the *Reich*, which his office published, and for which Goebbels should have written without compensation,

(2) having declared that the SS was composed of a bunch of tramps, and

(3) having stated that: "A German victory would be our greatest disaster because according to Hitler's own words he would only then become a real National Socialist."

These accusations were cleverly phrased to bring prompt action. Questioning of the accused by the Gestapo followed. A file note of the next day to the Minister of Justice contains the disappointing news that both defendants denied having made these statements—but the reporter is optimistic that the Gestapo may well achieve a confession—and cheerfully adds: "There is always the testimony of Schultz."

On the next day, in the absence of **any** supportable evidence for a conviction Thierack is nervous. A summary of a meeting with him, made by one of his assistants states that the minister wants an early trial to show his control—but he also wants to review the matter with Dr. Freisler, the president of the People's Court, who will try the case. Thierack is anxious to have a meeting with Freisler before judgment is announced, so that he may have the possibility of recommending a modification of the sentence. Once a death sentence is announced by the court, appeals, because of Hitler's specific orders, are not permissible. Death sentences are always final and cannot be appealed.

The same day soothing news arrived from Dr. Thierack's chief of staff: "We always have Schultz and his wife available. They will testify under oath and make a good impression."

Enter Dr. Goebbels' associate—running roughshod over the Minister of Justice by going directly to the Minister's own man Roland Freisler. He blithely states that he has bypassed the minister and has contacted Freisler directly. There he received the disappointing news that Ohser has revoked an earlier partial confession and there is now no evidence sufficient to start the trial. Dr. Goebbel's associate is not discouraged. He informs the minister that in a day they will have matters under control. His conversation with Dr. Freisler concerning a preview of his judgment produced the following statement of principles: "President Freisler declared as a matter of principle that he would never make a prognosis for a judgment. However, he intimated that here two death sentences at least appear likely (taking into account, as I do [this is the writer's comment] the seriousness of the case, one could not reach a different decision)."

The next day—April 3, 1944—Goebbels' office writes to Freisler that except for a few sketches from Ohser they have no incriminating material and have not been able to dredge up anything derogatory—but they are working at it.

Goebbels' chief of staff reports on the same day to Goebbels:

"Thierack is dragging his feet and has asked for a conference for tomorrow morning. So, trial must be postponed. Thierack has been advised of your interest in the matter and your wish to speed it along. It does not look as if we can keep Thierack from having advance notice of the trial."

April 5, 1944: Goebbels' chief of staff reports to Goebbels: "Freisler has advised me that trial will take place on April 6 at 9 A.M. and that he hopes to have the judgment including supporting opinion in your hands early in the afternoon."

The prosecuting attorney, Dr. Metten, writes to Goebbels the next day: "There was some delay in the trial of April 6. The suicide of Ohser delayed the beginning of the Knauf trial by one hour. The trial itself was quick and simple. The Prosecuting attorney presented the government's case. The interrogation of the defendant by the presiding Judge brought to light that he had been a member of the Social Democratic Party. Knauf denied all accusations. The witness Schultz and his wife repeated their allegations. The imposition of the death sentence, which the defendant accepted without sign of emotion, is final since appeals against judgments of the People's Court are not provided."

"As soon as the judgment is written and signed, the file will be turned over to the Minister of Justice, who is charged with the execution of the death sentence—unless he should be inclined to pursue a petition of clemency with the Fuehrer."

The Reasons Supporting the Judgment

"It is easy to see how the accused arrived at his demoralizing and destructive comments when you hear that he said: Our victory would be our greatest misfortune, because only then would the Fuehrer become a real National Socialist. It is clearly the hatred against National Socialism and against our way of life that tolerates no compromise that drove him in that direction. His life turned back into itself. The circle of his political development has been completed.

And that man once held an important position in our cultural life. Such a man must deem it his honorable duty to discharge this higher responsibility.

We would not act as proper National Socialists if we would respond to this act of an infamous man by anything else but: This man must be put to death.

Since Knauf has been convicted he must also pay the cost of the procedure.

Dr. Freisler, President of the Peoples Court"

On the afternoon of April 6, 1944, Dr. Freisler wrote to Dr. Goebbels and sent him a copy of the decision.

The file ended with a bill for the costs of Knauf's prosecution. They were to be paid by his widow. The bill is revealing. There was a fee for the defense counsel of DM 81.60, even though his work is never mentioned and we do not even know his name. His stay in jail from April 6 to May 2, after his conviction to the day of his execution, cost Knauf's widow RM 44 for lodging and food. Payment for beheading was RM 158.18 in those days, and the charge was RM 0.12 for a stamp for sending the bill.

There was not a trace of justice to be found in the performance of the Ministry of Justice. They had achieved a substitute work ethic and found gratification in documenting their own crimes like docile, certified public accountants.

Annelore Leber, the widow of Julius Leber, immortalized 68 of those who resisted and paid with their lives in her book, *Das Gewissen Steht auf* (An Appeal to Our Conscience) published in 1956. Julius Leber was a prominent German labor leader and one of the many men like Erich Knauf whom Roland Freisler sentenced to die as an enemy of the state.

In Leber's book I rediscovered the case of Erich Knauf that I had read with horror for the first time in Fuerstenhagen in July of 1945. The photo of Knauf that accompanies Annelore Leber's account shows a man who appears relaxed. The picture was not taken during the trials as were many of those who were honored in that book. It reflects the dignity of a proud man, confident in the righteousness of his beliefs, whom even the vituperation of a man like Freisler could not subdue.

The last *Red File* dealing with these macabre matters was an application by the executioners for an increase of their cigarette rations to calm their nerves. To support this demand they asserted that the daily beheading or hanging of people was grizzly and unnerving work. Their petition was denied.

During the next two weeks I interviewed the thirteen employees of the ministry and prepared an outline that described the organization of the Ministry. Later that outline assisted in the prosecution of some of the employees of the Ministry of Justice before military tribunals. Thierack, the minister, like so many Nazis who had become shameful prostitutes in their profession, had committed suicide.

The majority of these former employees of the Ministry who now filed reports for me were dull professionals who had mastered tiny sections of the law and knew and cared for nothing else. Their records of promotion and membership in the party made it clear that by 1945 the Party had achieved its goal of total domination. As I talked to one after the other I was reminded of percussionists in an opera orchestra. Do the drummers in the pit beating their drums, realize the drama and excitement of what happens on the stage while they hit their instrument with measured precision—bum, bum, bum?

My hope of finding material on the trials following the assassination attempt on Hitler's life was not realized. Most of those files had been kept in Berlin and destroyed. But much later films of the events specially prepared for Hitler's amusement were found and preserved.

We found the complete code for the filing system, so that we could actually plan to set up a gigantic master file so that Americans could locate records that were needed. The most valuable discoveries were the personnel files of judges and lawyers. They would ultimately serve as the files of the newly created states and facilitate the discovery of the bad apples. Unfortunately little effort was made by the newly created states to remove those among the judges who had served the party instead of the law. Until 1980 the courts of the states continued to employ judges whose approach to justice had been formed during Hitler's times.

To put all of this material into acceptable shape was difficult, because we did not have the kind of facilities that are available today. There were no electric typewriters, word-processors, or copy machines. The only way to produce a report of 50 copies was to cut stencils and have those placed on duplicating machines that would run off the required number of pages. Fortunately the army had found me a German typist eager to do a good job, because if she failed she would be sent back to Kassel, where life was misery.

I still have a copy of that report, dated July 21, 1945. Its pages are yellow and brittle. When the cases against employees of the Ministry of Justice were tried years later, I occasionally had an inquiry about that report.

As I was waiting for my final report to be delivered I joined my soldiers in going through files. They were all preprinted greenish file folders with names and codes entered by hand. There was an almost medieval quality to these folders. To make tampering with them difficult, a special filing clerk had stitched additional material with needle and thread to the hard outer cover. If any of these threads was broken or cut, it immediately alerted one to the possibility that it had been tampered with. Loose-leaf binders, although known, were frowned upon, because they permitted manipulation of the file—and since the time of Frederick the Great no one in the judicial administration had ever stooped to manipulating a file.

Suddenly my eye caught the caption: *STRAFSACHE von ROHR*. The name rang a bell—he was a cousin of my mother and she had seen much of him in her youth. I grabbed the file and read a story filled with heroes, knaves, crooks, courageous women, tragic prisoners, bribed judges—enough material to gain a chilling feeling of what life really was under Hitler.

Joachim von Rohr, born in 1888, a prominent Pommeranian landowner, was a trained agronomist who had been a member of the Deutsche Nationale Volks Partei, a reactionary party that hoped for a restitution of the monarchy. He had represented his party in the Reichstag when Hitler came to power in 1933 and became an undersecretary of Agriculture in Hitler's first Cabinet. It took him less than six months to realize that he had joined a den of thieves and he resigned to dissociate himself from Hitler's crowd and devote his time to the administration of his farm. His act of disapproval did not pass unnoticed and landed von Rohr's name on Hitler's first famous list of "Enemies of the Fuehrer."

If in 1930, at the age of 42, he had not married a beautiful and charming woman of 20, the story would end here. Siegrid von Rohr, an impressionable teenager in 1926. had joined the Nazi Party when the Party was not yet respected and popular. She had a very low number on the party's roster, a fact that was significant and had made her a rarity. At the time she had also befriended an awkward chicken farmer by the name of Heinrich Himmler. In June of 1934 Hitler's chance to wipe out the approximately 1,200 people on his "black list" came when he had Roehm and his other alleged enemies shot. Joachim von Rohr's name was on that list. The police had orders to arrest him, but somehow von Rohr had been tipped off and had disappeared. So the police arrested his wife, very pregnant at the time, and hoped to coerce her into telling where her husband was. Himmler heard of this and immediately had her released from prison, asserting that the Nazi Party would never stoop so low as to force a pregnant woman to give up her husband. But it was a strong warning to the von Rohrs.

Aware that he was an endangered species, von Rohr stayed on his farm and limited his activities to growing farm products. Being over age at the outbreak of WWII, he merely reported to the army that he still held a captain's reserve commission from the last war. In early 1942 awareness that the Russian campaign was not a pushover began to dawn on many in Germany. Farming had become much more difficult because the war in Russia had siphoned off most German men who could bear arms. At that time the German Army held millions of captured Russian soldiers in prisoner-of-war camps without food, shelter or care of any kind for the simple purpose of extermination. Then someone pointed out to Hitler that letting these men die did not really benefit Germany—it would be much more sensible to use them as slave labor and work them to death. Hitler did not like to save Russians but saw the logic. Instructions were issued to the army to develop the necessary plans.

The army set up a program of offering large German farms contingents of 30 to 50 of these half dead Russians for farm work if the farmers could restore sufficient strength to these walking skeletons. The army would provide an armed guard. If the Russians lived, they could be worked as much as the farm owner desired. These men would not be counted against the quota of workers allotted to each farm. The army contacted von Rohr and he was delighted to get the manpower promised.

The Party, aware of the scheme, saw the opportunity for causing trouble for von Rohr, a man already once found to be unreliable. A Party member in army uniform determined to deliver von Rohr's scalp, brought the thirty Russians to the farm. They were housed and instructions were issued to feed them so that they would soon be able to start work.

The morning after they arrived, when von Rohr entered the barracks two of the Russians had already died. Their comrades had placed the bodies in large paper bags that had held synthetic fertilizer. Von Rohr called the army to report the deaths and asked for instructions. The army told him not to make a fuss, and to arrange for a basic burial in the corner of the local cemetery shortly after noon, when the village would not notice the activity. The Russians must dig the graves and handle the burials. He was to stay at a distance but would be responsible for not letting the matter be noticed.

When he returned to the barracks to issue instructions to the supervisor, he noticed that his wife, six months pregnant at the time, had seen the dead Russians, and had placed field flowers on the two dead bodies. Von Rohr instructed his secretary, who spoke Russian, to accompany the Russians to the cemetery and to read the rites of the Russian Orthodox Church, at the gravesite.

At the prescribed time the Russians carried the two bodies to the cemetery. Von Rohr followed at a safe distance of about 75 yards. He did not enter the cemetery, but could observe from a distance his secretary reading the rites for the deceased men. When he saw the Russians lower the bodies into the two graves he removed his hat. At this very moment, the military supervisor rose with a camera from behind the stone wall at the cemetery and took a snapshot of von Rohr holding his hat against his chest with his head bowed.

Later, the supervisor sent the picture to the local Party headquarters as proof of von Rohr's anti-government attitude. Removing his hat, he stated, clearly demonstrated von Rohr's sympathy for the Russian enemy. The Party, delighted to finally have a case, sent the photo to the district attorney in Greifswald, the nearest court, and demanded that criminal proceedings against von Rohr be initiated. The efforts of the Party to have him brought before the People's Court where convictions were assured, failed. But the Party used every device to smear von Rohr and to intimidate the judges handling the case.

The indictment charged von Rohr with *defaitism*, the newly invented crime of weakening the will of the German nation to resist the enemy. The word does not mean precisely "defeatism," but something more like losing faith in the mission of the Fuehrer. Von Rohr's wife and secretary were charged with having assisted him in this terrible deed.

When von Rohr read the indictment he realized the seriousness of his problem and concluded that he'd better remove himself from the scene. He rejoined the army on the strength of his WWI reserve captain's commission in the hope that after a few months matters would settle down and be for- gotten. While he served in the army nothing happened. He was safe. But on the day after he returned to the farm the Party was waiting for him and the trial in Greifswald got underway.

He hired an extremely well connected Nazi attorney from Berlin to defend him. But the Party, feeling challenged, exerted pressure on the court. The proceedings were, in effect, a show trial. The case was tried in December 1943 and von Rohr was found guilty of *defaitism* and sentenced to a prison term of eight months. Considering the climate of the time, he was lucky not to have been sentenced to be hanged. His wife and secretary were found not guilty.

Both the prosecution and von Rohr appealed the case to the Reichsgericht, the German Supreme Court. The prosecution sought a heavier sentence and a conviction of Mrs. von Rohr and the secretary. By this time the climate in Germany had become extremely unhealthy for people like von Rohr. He had learned that the case had been reported to Hitler and to the Minister of Justice, Dr. Thierack. The latter had informed the Supreme Court that the Fuehrer desired that the conviction of von Rohr not only be confirmed but the sentence be increased and that the acquittal of the two additional defendants be reversed. The case was assigned to Senate President Dr. Vogt, a highly regarded jurist. He was a Party member and had been the Reich prosecutor in the case against the Communists who had set fire to the Reichstag in Berlin in February of 1933. He had obtained the conviction of one of the defendants, a Dutch Communist by the name of Van der Luebbe. Vogt had been rewarded for his performance with an appointment to the Supreme Court.

Von Rohr retained one of the most prestigious attorneys at the Supreme Court, and on his advice had gone underground until a date for his trial in Leipzig was set. With the war going badly and conditions becoming more and more uncertain, ruthless Party organizations were resorting to administration of justice of their own— by gun. Both the Reich prosecuting attorney and von Rohr's attorney separately visited Senate President Vogt and reviewed the case in general terms. The Reich prosecutor stressed the importance of the case and mentioned the interest of the Fuehrer and of the Minister of Justice in seeing the conviction confirmed and the sentence increased. Von Rohr's attorney pointed to the inadequacy of the proceedings of the lower court and the failure of the judgment to meet even minimum standards of legal reasoning.

The case was heard with von Rohr present. The decision came as a great surprise. The Supreme Court had reversed the decision of the court in Greifswald as being legally defective, and sent the case to the court in Neu Strelitz for retrial because it was obvious that von Rohr could not receive a proper trial before the court in Greifswald. Von Rohr was held at a concentration camp until the court in Neu Strelitz could retry the case. The decision was a sensation.

Although it is doubtful that Hitler would have concerned himself with trivia like this while the Russians were advancing on Berlin and the Allies had landed in Normandy, his Minister of Justice immediately started an investigation of the five sitting justices. The judgment had been signed by all five and none of them was willing to talk. The file contained reports on the political and professional backgrounds of each of the five. They were not helpful. So, the Minister of Justice, to protect himself against a recurrence in other cases where the regular courts (different from the Peoples Court where conviction was always assured and not appealable), ordered that all five justices be relieved from hearing criminal cases and transferred to less important civil cases. That is where the case ended.

It was a tantalizing conclusion. What happened to von Rohr; what happened to Justice Vogt? For many years I had forgotten about the case until in 1958 a history teacher revived my interest by telling me that the German archives were very cooperative about making material of the Nazi times available. Although I was then involved in building an existence for myself and my family, the mere thinking of that case made me write to the Bundesarchiv in Koblenz, Germany inquiring about the file. They had it and offered to send me a photostat. There it was, but the decision of the Supreme Court and the investigation of the judges were missing.

During a visit to Germany later in 1958 I learned that von Rohr was still alive. He had been arrested after the reversal of his conviction. The new trial never took place. I established contact with him, told him about my reading of his case and sent him a stat of my file. A correspondence ensued, but he died before we could meet. Be-

fore he died he sent me the copy of the argument before the Supreme Court and the text of the decision of the Supreme Court. My
interest was rekindled. From his attorney, who had became a prominent judge in Germany, I learned that Dr. Thierack, Hitler's Minister of Justice, ordered Vogt, the presiding judge of the senate, to
come to Berlin for a reprimand for this obvious miscarriage of
justice. The Minister, furious, berated Vogt for having defied the
Fuehrer's wishes. He demanded that Vogt immediately file an application for early retirement so that having disgraced the Supreme
Court, he would no longer be a blemish on that institution. To his
surprise Vogt stuck to his guns. He refused to apply for early retirement and pointed out to the Minister that as a justice he was bound
by his oath of office to apply the law and correct errors of lower
courts. This was precisely what he had done in the von Rohr case,
because the lower court had neither understood nor correctly applied the law. Therefore, the case had to be retried. Whether Thierack
understood what Vogt had told him is not known, but shortly after
the end of the war Thierack committed suicide. Did it dawn upon
him that he was an accomplice to more crimes, including murder,
than any Minister of Justice in the history of Germany?

Vogt returned to Leipzig. He was left in his office. He was
given no work and when the Russians came a few months later, they
arrested him for having been the chief prosecutor of Dimitroff, one
of the Russians accused in the Reichtags fire. Dimitroff had been
acquitted. Vogt was sentenced to seven years in a penitentiary and
released in 1952. He went to West Germany to be with his son, a
physician. His son, whom I contacted, declined to answer any questions, saying it was too painful for him to even think about his
father's sufferings.

Reading that file in July of 1945 and pursuing the issues further,
made me see and understand how fragile is the fabric of the law and
of justice. Von Rohr was an opportunist, who managed to get through
Hitler's rule alive and to even wring some help from Hitler's law, but
Senate President Vogt was a real hero, a courageous man who clearly
understood what justice is all about.

CHAPTER 10

LOOKING FOR THE RIGHT PLACE TO DO SOME GOOD

WITH SO MUCH exciting work ahead of me when I left Paris at the beginning of July of 1945, I had not even looked at the orders that had sent me to surveying the records of the German Ministry of Justice in Fuerstenhagen. Now with that job behind me, I discovered that I was temporarily assigned to the headquarters of the U.S. Group Control Council, located in Hoechst near Frankfurt. What this Group Control Council was, I had not the vaguest notion. And so, on the first of August 1945, I found myself in Hoechst at their headquarters where the driver dropped me with my two bags that held all my possessions.

The army had requisitioned as our headquarters the main office of the Farbwerke Hoechst, an important part of the gigantic German IG Farben Industrial Complex, which stretched over several square miles. Housing for employees was located conveniently near the production facilities for dyestuffs and pharmaceuticals. All of this had survived the war without noticeable damage and the workers housing had now been taken over to serve as our quarters. The administration building, probably constructed before World War I, was an ornate structure displaying the pride and the money that had made many German inventors of medicine rich. Having worked in a pharmaceutical company in the States, I could hardly wait to see what they had been up to.

At the orderly room, where I checked in, I learned that the U.S. Group Control Council was the elite unit headed for Berlin to participate in the administration of Germany with our wartime allies. Naively I thought that General Betts had recognized my potential and had assigned me where I could do the most good, helping to reorganize Germany. It looked to me as if I had fallen into a dream job.

I could not have known that Gen. Betts's dream, that he would be named legal counsel for Gen. Clay in Berlin, was only a few days away. So I used my time to meet the key people in the group that he had selected for the dream job, and learned from them what would be our work in Berlin.

The leader was Col. March, in private life the head of a major Wall Street law firm, and now charged by the War Department to organize and staff the army's new Berlin legal office. He was a perfect choice because he knew how to find men with that curious combination of legal training, and an understanding of army and business psychology. He had a touch for politics, the rare quality of common sense, and above all what may be termed "street smarts." Col. March also had the ability to make people feel comfortable. He inquired about my training and background and assured me that there would be lots of work for me, once we were settled in Berlin. I saw myself already there. He introduced me to several of his associates, among them I remember a civilian employee of the army, wearing an officer's uniform without the army indicia, William J. Dickman.

Bill had been a successful lawyer in Berlin until 1938 when even his service in the German Army during the First World War could not protect him from Hitler's vicious persecutions. He managed to escape to Denmark just ahead of the Gestapo, and go to America. Through the Philadelphia Friends Service he was given an opportunity to study law at the University of Pennsylvania. Upon graduation in 1944 he had joined the Office of Strategic Services (OSS) and had returned to Europe. Now he was back in the legal field and applying his intimate knowledge of Germany, her people and institutions for the benefit of his adopted country.

His knowledge of German history and administration was profound. As a German lawyer he had established contacts all over Germany and the range of his acquaintances and his charm opened doors for him everywhere. When his friend Robert Kempner, once general counsel for the Prussian Police prior to Hitler, became Justice Jackson's advisor on German matters, he enlisted Bill's help to find defense counsels for all of the defendants of the Nuremberg War Crimes Trials. But the most unusual legal task of his career, which he later was too modest to mention to me, would happen in June of 1947. It was a rush job. With less than three hours available he drafted for General Clay the famous Control Council Law #46, which dissolved the State of Prussia. In Article I he wrote:

> The Prussian State together with its central government
> and all its agencies is abolished.

My friendship with Bill Dickman would last until he died in 1988.

My curiosity about what went on in this gigantic pharmaceutical plant in Hoechst needled me. I was aware that an American officer's uniform was an assured "open sesame" that would take me anyplace in this vast enterprise. So, instead of deterring me the signs "No Admittance" or "Do Not Enter—Work in Progress" invited investigation. I entered the first room marked "EINTRITT VERBOTEN," having heard a familiar hissing sound when I listened at the door before entering. I found myself in the presence of some 30 women, who were filling glass ampules with liquid and then sealing the ampules by activating Bunsen burners—which I had heard hissing—with a foot pedal. I inspected the labeling and found that they were filling a Bulgarian order for Neo-Salvarsan, the famous Ehrlich treatment for syphilis. My attempt to talk with the women failed. None of them spoke German. They were Russian slave laborers who had chosen not to go back to their homeland but hoped to do better for themselves in Germany, as I learned from their German speaking supervisor who seeing the American uniform was docile and explained to me what was going on. When I asked him if he hoped to be able to ship the finished job to Bulgaria, he smiled and said: "I'm not sure, but we have plenty of use for the stuff right here."

On August 9 the bubble burst. My newly made friends and associates received orders to go to Berlin, but I was transferred to the War Crimes Branch in Wiesbaden. President Truman had appointed Mr. Fahy, a civilian lawyer, to go to Berlin to assist General Clay as Legal Counsel. Gen. Betts was left with the uninspiring task of assembling material for the war crimes trials that were scheduled to be held in the fall in Nuremberg. Since I had been assigned for only temporary duty to the Berlin contingent, he could keep me.

For the next four weeks I fretted about ways and means of getting to Berlin. I wrote to Col. March, who attempted to get me transferred, but General Betts was not willing to lose me in what was clearly a turf fight. On one of his visits to Wiesbaden he sat me down and told me that he was getting tired of my communications with Col. March. It was entirely improper for me to correspond privately with Colonel March and he wanted me to withdraw my request for transfer to the Legal Division in Berlin. If I did not do so at once, he would have my loyalty as an American citizen investigated. If I would withdraw my application all would be forgotten and I would be sent to Nuremberg to work with Colonel Fairman, who was assigned to the staff of Justice Jackson. That threat did it. I had endured plenty of opportunity to be investigated before— enough to last me a lifetime, and so I caved in.

Simple calculation also told me that within five months there was nothing, not even the worst that General Betts could dream up, that could keep me from going back to the States. I just would have to wait.

Wiesbaden, where I would now be stationed, was the capital of the former state of Hesse and had always been a very nice place. It had been a town where people went to "take the baths" and relax from the stresses of business life. The outstanding hotels, medical facilities, a gambling casino and even a charming little opera house, where a minor Duke had maintained an opera company had attracted people. Except for one V-bomb with a faulty mechanism which had been launched nearby, and turned around to attack Wiesbaden instead of London, the town had not suffered any damage. The army with a keen eye for the comforts of life in a badly mauled Germany, had made it the center for the newly created War Crimes Branch and for the U.S. Air Force.

Since I was assigned for permanent duty, I was given a room in a private house overlooking a park near the office that had been requisitioned for me. I ate at an officer's mess at the nearby Rose Hotel

It was a lucky break that I had not been billeted in the officers quarters for transients, a former German Army barracks at the outskirts of town. The announcement of the Japanese surrender (VJ-Day) on August 15 hit the papers and created a wild orgy of shooting and drunkenness. One transient officer scheduled for return to the United States had been assigned a bunk for one night on the second floor of the transient officers quarters. The drunken officers on the first floor, in their joy over the end of the war and not aware that the second floor was also in use, emptied their 45 pistols shooting at the ceiling. The next morning brought the sad news that the officer on the second floor had been killed in his bunk.

My first assignment at the War Crimes Branch was to translate into German the English text of a trial manual to be used by German attorneys who would be licensed to defend German defendants (war criminals) before American Military Courts. The Manual made

American law and court procedures applicable to such trials. It was a fascinating translating job because much of what the German attorneys had to do was totally unknown to them. For example, the manual had to explain to them that the defense counsel under American law had the same rights for information as his opponent, the prosecutor. Also completely unknown to the German judicial system was the right of the defense attorney to cross-examine the witnesses for the prosecution.

Once I had completed my translation, I was plagued by doubts that I had actually produced a workable tool for a German attorney who suddenly had to apply American criminal procedure. Although I had a basic knowledge of German and American criminal procedures, I was certainly not an experienced defense attorney. To resolve my uncertainties, I visited the president of the local German court in Wiesbaden and told him that I needed his help and experience with my project. The man, whose name I have forgotten, was delighted to lend a hand. Establishing friendly contact with an American was not only a guarantee of access to cigarettes, it added prestige. For the next week or so we met daily for work sessions, during which we made countless changes and improvements and in the end crafted a manual, which was published and served as the model guide for German attorneys defending German War Criminals before American Military Courts.

The War Crimes Branch in Wiesbaden had become the depository of anything that American military personnel considered helpful for the prosecution of war criminals. Since no one knew what the prosecution wanted, everybody sent what came to mind. We were inundated with files and records from countless concentration camps, among them Buchenwald. I remember the day we received those grizzly lampshades that Ilse Koch, the wife of the Buchenwald commandant, had made from the tatooed skins of inmates whom she had ordered killed by injections to enlarge her collection.

It was not often that Germans showed up to assist us—to most of them we were still the enemy. But there were still other important reasons why Germans were reluctant to help. It was not just the dislike of snitching, it was fear of becoming ostracized by their fellow Germans if they disclosed some of the terrible things that they had witnessed. Among the older people there was also still the memory of the FEME organization, Klan type avengers who had carried out killings of those who had assisted the Allies after the First World War. With talk about FEME and Werewolves still fresh on their minds, Germans who would dare to come forth to speak were rare.

While at the office I met Hermann Friedrich Graebe, a German who felt compelled to testify despite his awareness of the risks. He now lived in Wiesbaden and had come because he felt it his duty to clear his conscience and tell us what he had seen. As manager of a German construction company in the Ukraine he had witnessed on several occasions mass murders of local Jews. He was shy and nervous when he came to tell us about these events. We suggested he write his recollections down, providing dates, names, locations and as much concrete, specific detail as he could recall. We would then evaluate his statement to see if it might be useful at a trial that would be held later. We also asked him whether he would be willing to swear to the truth of what he had written and even be willing to testify in court. After some hesitation he said that he would do it. He handed us his handwritten notes and we had his German text transcribed and typed. I now set out to translate it into English. It was undoubtedly the most horrid tale of cruelty that I had ever read. The terseness and simplicity of his narrative had created a chilling recreation of the event. I labored with the translation. It was the first detailed account of mass liquidation of Jews that I had read and I needed to retain the sharp image of the man at the scene. At the time I did not realize that later on my translation would be used as one of the most incriminating documentations at the Nuremberg War Crimes Trial. It shocked the defendants and became the document most often cited to characterize the true nature of Nazism.

Graebe's account of the events of October 5, 1943 in Dubno, Ukraine reads:

"Thereupon in the company of MOENNIKES I drove to the construction area and saw in its vicinity a heap of earth, about 30 meters long and 2 meters high. Several trucks stood in front of the heap. Armed Ukrainian militia chased the people off the trucks under the supervision of an SS-man. The militiamen were guards on the trucks and drove them to and from the excavation. All these people had the prescribed yellow badges on the front and back of their clothes, and thus were recognized as Jews.

"MOENNIKES and I went directly to the excavation. Nobody bothered us. Now we heard shots in quick succession from behind one of the earth mounds. The people who had gotten off the trucks—men, women and children of all ages—had to undress upon the orders of an SS-man who carried a riding or a dog whip. They had to put down their clothes in fixed places, sorted according to shoes, over and underclothing. I saw a pile of shoes of about 800 to 1000 pairs, great piles of laundry and clothing. Without screaming or crying these people undressed, stood around by families, kissed each other, said farewells, and waited for the nod of another SS-man, who stood near the excavation, also with a whip in his hand. During the 15 minutes that I stood near the excavation I heard no complaint and no request for mercy. I watched a family of about 8 persons, a man and woman, both about 50 with their children of about 1, 8 and 10, and two grown-up daughters of about 20 to 24. An old woman with snow- white hair held the one-year-old child in her arms and sang for it and tickled it. The child was squeaking from joy. The couple looked on with tears in their eyes. The father held the hand of a boy of about 10 years old and spoke to him softly; the boy was fighting his tears. The father pointed toward the sky, fondled his hand, and seemed to explain something to him. At that moment the SS-man at the excavation called something to his comrade. The latter counted off about 20 persons and instructed them to walk behind the earth mound. Among them was the family which I had mentioned. I remember very well a girl, black-haired and slender, passing near me; she pointed at herself and said: "23 years." I walked around the mound, and stood in front of a tremendous grave. Closely pressed together the people were lying on top of each other so that only their heads were visible. Several of the people shot still moved. Some lifted their arms and turned their heads to show that they were still alive. The excavation was already 2/3 full. I estimated that it contained about 1000 people. I looked for the man who did the shooting. I saw an SS-man who sat at the rim of the narrow end of the excavation. On his knees he had a machine pistol and he was smoking a cigarette. The completely naked people descended a stairway, which was dug into the clay of the excavation and slipped over the heads of the people lying there already to the place to which the SS-man directed them. They laid themselves in front of the dead or injured people, some touched tenderly those who were still alive and spoke to them in a low voice. Then I heard a number of shots. I looked into the excavation and saw how the bodies jerked or the heads rested already motionless on top of the bodies that lay before them. Blood was running from their necks. I was surprised that I was not chased away, but I saw that there were two or three postal officers nearby. Now already the next group approached, descending into the excavation, lined themselves up against the previous victims and were shot. When I walked back, around the mound, I noticed again a transport which had just arrived. This time it included sick and frail persons. An old, very thin woman with terribly thin legs was undressed by others who were already naked, while two persons held her up. Apparently the woman was paralyzed. The naked people carried the woman around the mound. I left with MOENNIKES and drove with my car back to Dubno."

I still have a carbon copy of my translation of that affidavit and another that Graebe gave us. A few days after he had completed his account he came to see me. It was obvious that he was worried about the reaction of people once his statement would become known. He was scared. He wanted to know if I thought it possible to get out of Germany and to America. I told him that his chances of getting a visa to America were slim, but that I was not an expert on the matter. I promised to make inquiries. Except for the lawyer who had handled my immigration matter, I knew nobody who might be able to help. But I remembered my favorite law professor, John F. X. Finn in New York and wrote him. He sent me the address of a woman associated with a prominent law firm in Washington. I wrote her about Graebe, sending her his affidavits and gave her what additional background information I could gather. I contacted Graebe and gave him the address of the woman. Shortly after that I was transferred to Nuremberg and I heard nothing further.

Forty-seven years later, in December of 1992 Telford Taylor's *The Anatomy of the Nuremberg Trials* was published. A footnote on page 245 provided an unexpected happy ending to the Graebe story:

> Defense counsel did not object to acceptance of Graebe's two affidavits. The portions read by Colonel Storey, though sufficiently shocking, do not comprise the most vivid passages, which were later read by Sir Hartley Shawcross in his closing statement, included in the Tribunal's judgement, and set forth here. Graebe, for his part, found life in Germany unpleasant and emigrated to the United States. He settled in San Francisco, where he died at the age of eighty-five in 1986.

And so, after 47 years I learned that my efforts on his behalf may have helped this brave man.

The heavy daily dose of horrible events of the Nazi era was utterly depressing. That I was able to put these events aside for even a brief period of time I owed to a curious coincidence. I had met

Eleonore Halbscheffel the owner of Der Kupferstich, a small art store in a shopping center in the center of Wiesbaden not far from my quarters. She ran an elegant and sophisticated store that sold flower and city prints, maps, rare books, and pages that had obviously been cannibalized from medieval church prayer books and hymnals. The displays in the window often changed; they were skillfully chosen to invite inquiry. Everything in that store spelled class and exquisite taste. All pictures had been carefully selected for their intrinsic beauty or interest. Mats and frames had been chosen to emphasize the pictures not to overwhelm them. While admiring the window displays I never saw any customers in the store, only some old people who seemed to offer pictures that the woman inside inspected with care.

One day, curiosity got the better of me and I entered the deserted store. The dark-haired, slender woman of perhaps fifty, whom I knew by sight, rose from a period desk where she had been reading. She greeted me in halting but educated English and inquired if I was interested in anything specific that I had seen or that she might show me. My reply in German broke the ice. I told her that I was stationed in Wiesbaden and had passed her store many times and enjoyed the elegance of her display and the manner in which every picture was framed. She acknowledged the compliment and was obviously relieved that we could converse in German. I was the first American who had entered her store, she told me, and mentioned that most Americans passed her place because they were more interested in war trophies, which she did not care to add to her line. Before the war English and French customers had often visited Wiesbaden. She was lucky to have survived the war and she was hanging on to her business in the hope that she could get it going again. Right now she, like everybody else, depended upon black market dealings because German currency had lost its value. Curiously the supply of excellent values was much greater than in normal times, because so many people sold heirlooms and valuable art in order to eat.

Among the pictures she displayed was one that I found particularly interesting. It was a hand colored print of Noerdlingen, one of the charming medieval towns that had long fascinated travelers who going south on the "City Road" from Bamberg and Nuremberg toward Rothenburg and Dinkelsbuehl to reach Augsburg and Munich. I bought it at that first visit, but not until Mrs. Halbscheffel had educated me as to why this picture was worth having. It dates back to 1574 when Braun & Hogenberg, two talented woodcutters had created a market for a series of views of privileged German cities (freie Reichsstaedte) that became popular. Later, after the art of copper engraving had been perfected, the classical city prints of Merriam took over the market and Braun & Hogenberg became collector's items. I still like to look at it with a magnifying glass. Like most towns of that time, Mrs. Halbscheffel had pointed out to me, Noerdlingen had an enormous church and outside of town as a reminder of law and order, the gallows. The picture hangs in our library.

Mrs. Halbscheffel was studious, had many reference books and many contacts. But she also had that rare gift of letting her clients self-infect themselves with curiosity that invariably led to a never ending search for more information—and purchases. A map that also hangs in our library is a good illustration of how it worked. Walking into her store one day I remember being arrested by a curious, early Italian map of Europe printed from a wood block. I had not seen it before. The terrain looked strangely familiar but it was clearly upside down. She knew that I was hooked. What was the explanation? The map was made before cartographers understood that cartography was not an art but a science. As such it needed a uniform reference method. That method was supplied by the German cartographer Mercator, who proposed that all maps, unless specifically indicating a different reference method, would show North at the top of the map. It was that map that triggered my interest in maps and led to my becoming a collector.

In 1958 I returned to Wiesbaden for the first time after the war. I was there on business and could not find the time to go back to the Kupferstich. But I reminded my wife, Marion that much of our collection of maps had started there. So, she ventured there to see what was still available. Mrs. Halbscheffel, was still at the Kupferstich and was doing well. When she heard my name, she rose to the occasion and sold Marion the Coronation print by Merriam of the Coronation Procession that brought Joseph I as German emperor to Frankfurt in 1658. The picture now hangs in our living room.

Just before I left Wiesbaden, *Stars & Stripes* ran a big advertisement for the first circus that would perform in Wiesbaden after the war, and American soldiers would be permitted, as an authorized and encouraged form of fraternization, to bring small German children to the show. As it now had become almost a habit for me I was again browsing in the Kupferstich. A young woman with two small children of about five or six entered. Mrs. Halbscheffel introduced her and told me that this young woman had been trained by the largest German antique bookstore, the Edelmannsche Buchhandlung in Nuremberg, which was owned by the Kistner family. If she could not find the answer to a question she would always turn to this young woman, her best source of information. When I saw the two small children, I remembered the ad from *Stars & Stripes* and asked if I might borrow the children for the circus. I explained that I could not invite the mother, because only children were allowed. After some initial hesitation, which was calmed by Mrs. Halbscheffel, who vouched for me, we reached an agreement. The next day I picked up the children and took them to the circus where they saw their first elephants and monkeys and were enchanted. I had the first chance to act like a father and found the initiation a charming eye opener to the pleasures that lay in the future.

Through Mrs. Halbscheffel I established contact with the Edelmannsche Buchhandlung in Nuremberg and with the Kistner family. Every time I visit Nuremberg, and that has been quite often, I always find myself in those great bookstores, and I never leave without acquiring something worthwhile.

On September 20, 1945 I received the mysterious order that I was assigned to War Crimes Investigating Team #6835 and directed to report to the Office of U. S. Chief of Counsel in Nuremberg.

CHAPTER 11

THE WAR CRIMES TRIALS IN NUREMBERG

ON SEPTEMBER 20, after several delays another lieutenant from the War Crimes Branch and I were ordered to drive to our new jobs in Nuremberg (as the U.S. Army had renamed Nuernberg for reasons that I have never been able to fathom). On the way from Wiesbaden we had to deliver Colonel Fairman to the Rhine/Main Military Airport so that he could accompany General Betts on his flight to Nuremberg. Col. Fairman, in civilian life a Professor of Law at Stanford University, had done much to calm the choleric general's antagonism against me and to make some intelligent use of my obvious willingness to work. At the airport, on the spur of the moment, he put me into one of the empty seats on the general's converted C-47. On arrival in Nuremberg, a waiting limousine whisked them to see Justice Jackson, but since I did not qualify for a limousine, I had to find my own way to town.

Actually I was not very enthusiastic about my new assignment, because criminal law had never been a field that had interested me. Somehow, although I knew that criminal lawyers were needed, I had always thought of them as people who had dirt on their hands. Since about 1942 there had been much in the papers about the need for War Crimes Trials and I completely agreed that the crimes of the Nazi leaders had to be punished. Hanging the principals seemed a most appropriate punishment after what I had seen during the war. Loose recommendations like shooting all German officers as the Russians were reported to favor, did not appeal to me as a good solution. What to do with Germany and how to prevent it from starting WWIII was a job where I had hoped I could make some contribution.

When President Truman announced the appointment of Supreme Court Justice Robert H. Jackson as Chief American Prosecutor, I was elated because I had the instinctive feeling that he would seek a fair trial. He had served as Attorney General, and just before Pearl Harbor had been appointed to the Supreme Court. I had heard him and Eleanor Roosevelt speak at a rally of the American Civil Liberties Union in New York, where he had counseled for calm and warned against seeing a spy in every foreign born person or any person with a German or Japanese name.

By August of 1945 I had read much about the various plans for a prosecution of the Axis war criminals. After protracted negotiations in London, the Allies had published the London Charter that announced the law and procedure under which the defendants would be tried for their crimes. The basic principles of the Anglo-American criminal law had been adopted because it was considered a fairer system than procedures available under German, Russian, or French law. In a way it was a clear rejection of Stalin's drum beat convictions of the Russian show trials and the models of injustice that the German Peoples Courts had dispensed. We knew from the very beginning that the London Charter had glossed over many basic disagreements that had appeared almost insurmountable. For example, the Charter, at the insistence of Jackson and over French and Russian objections, had made aggressive war and conspiracy a crime. That being the case how could Russia be a judge in this trial, as she had been herself involved in aggressive war against Poland and Finland? The Charter had solved it by expressly prohibiting German defense counsel to raise the defense of "*tu quoque* (you too)," which normally leads to disqualification of the judge who had engaged in such conduct. Thus Russia was assured of an undisturbed seat on the bench, but Jackson, having been overruled on this point bitterly resented the Russian presence and never missed a chance to show his disdain.

As I stood at the airfield in Nuremberg waiting for some transportation, I was slightly disgruntled with my fate but I was confident that my point score was growing every day and that by the end of the year I should be on the way home. As it turned out by the end of the year I was indeed on my way home, but in my wildest dreams I could not have anticipated the events that I would witness and experience before leaving.

The ride from the airfield to the city took about half an hour. By this time, after having seen Hamburg and Kassel I thought I had been hardened about bomb damage. The suburbs that we passed had been badly mauled. The damage increased as we approached the center of the old city. This was the first time I had entered a city that I knew well. My apprehension grew.

The bus delivered me to the Palace of Justice about two miles from the center of Nuremberg on the road to Fuerth, where I met my new boss, Lt. Col. Calvin A. Behle, commanding officer of War Crimes Investigating Team #6835. He was a lawyer from Salt Lake City, about 40 years old, of medium height with greying hair and a friendly smile. Married to Brigham Young's youngest granddaughter, he had two daughters and was anxious to get out of the army and back to his family and practice in Salt Lake City. But that was difficult because he had joined late, had served some time in Washington, had not seen combat and therefore did not have many points. It was a wonderful discovery that he too had had a wild run in with General Betts and that in our dislike of him, we were soul mates.

Almost immediately we developed a relationship that transcended the formality of army organization. Although I never would have dared to address him as anything other than "Colonel," we became friends. He was like an older brother. That friendship has lasted—there is no year in which we have not exchanged greetings or sent clippings that reminded us of each other, and occasionally we have visited.

He explained the job that was hidden under the name War Crimes Investigating Team #6835. From the beginning when the Allies had agreed on an international trial for the initial group of the Nazi War Criminals, it had been clear that this trial, conducted by all four war-time allies, would be a one shot affair. Despite its frightful destruction, Nuremberg had been selected as the place for the trial because it had been the spiritual center of Hitler's Reich where many of the most repulsive laws and actions of the Nazis had been proclaimed. It was already clear that future trials would be carried out by military courts of the Allies in their respective zones. But the task ahead, running a trial of this nature with documents in several languages and witnesses speaking many languages, presented problems that the U.S. Army had never faced before. General Betts was scared that he might be saddled with running such trials, and being ignorant of law outside the narrow limits of court martial activities he wanted to know how to do this. To find out how to do it was to be our job.

Col. Behle, a member of a large law firm and an experienced trial lawyer, was an ideal choice to investigate the organizational problems, and I could ferret out the bilingual matters. In a sense Behle would be the hunter and I his bird dog. General Betts, himself a regular army officer had only limited legal experience and had been advanced by war promotions to his exalted position. He had assigned a Col. Fairman who was familiar with international law, to Nuremberg to aid the tribunal and to coordinate our activities with Jackson's staff. He depended so much on Fairman's skills and finesse that the poor man spent most of his time traveling between Nuremberg, Wiesbaden and Paris to hold General Betts's hand. As it turned out, I was lucky again, because Col. Fairman treated me like one of his law students. Peggy Marchand Brown, a bright and efficient secretary of about 55, who had joined the WACs when her husband had died early during the war, managed his Nuremberg office.

The Palace of Justice

Our office was in the enormous judicial complex, now renamed The Palace of Justice. The star shaped jail, right next door, was filled with 1,200 Nazi prisoners who were guarded by a detachment of soldiers from the First Infantry Division and commanded by Colonel Burton Andrus. Since 1918 the complex had served as the convenient prison annex to the Judicial Center for the courts of Nuremberg and Fuerth. Before 1933, Julius Streicher, the notorious local Jew-baiter had been a frequent defendant in libel cases committed through his paper *The Stuermer* and had done time in the very jail where he was now again confined for the coming trial. During the war, the courtroom had served for the show trials of the feared Peoples Court, where the verdict was always predictable: Death by hanging.

Now, damaged by bombs and artillery shells and in need of major changes, it had been taken over by the U.S. Army and renamed "The Palace of Justice." Masses of German prisoners-of-war, guarded by armed GIs, labored over the reconstruction and assisted local masons in the repair work. Most important, however, was the conversion of the main courtroom into the most advanced communication center in the world. German defendants would be tried by a court that spoke three other languages but did not understand a word of German and had to rely on simultaneous translation services into English, French and Russian. And, since the defendants spoke German this added the fourth language. Aside from the technical needs, the room needed space for vast press coverage, visitor accommodations, German and Allied spectators and large staffs for prosecution and defense personnel. And telephone communications to all corners of the world were a must.

Our small office housed five people, Col. Behle as commanding officer, me as his assistant, a warrant officer who had to administer us, which was not really necessary, a typist, and a driver. We had two jeeps. Normally officers are not allowed to drive. But Behle and I, because our unit was small and our assignments were important, had special permits that allowed us to drive. This deviation from standard army practice led to numerous halts by Military Police whose hope to arrest us we routinely thwarted.

After a few courtesy calls in our building we went to the Grand Hotel, Nuremberg's biggest and most famous hotel, where reservations had been made. It was strange that we were quartered in the very hotel where Hitler had held forth during the gigantic party rallies—the Partei Tag conventions. The hotel had suffered one direct bomb hit and several minor nicks from artillery fire. The stairway that led to our wing was impassable but rickety scaffolding enabled us to reach our rooms. Mine was so small that I could barely enter the bathroom, but I did not complain, because I always had hot water. Hammering and construction noise began at 6 A.M. and ended at 7:30 at night. After I had stowed my stuff, we had lunch at the officers' mess and listened to two German piano players practicing Gershwin's *Rhapsody in Blue* for the night's performance at the Night Club—dubbed "The Snake Pit." It was not exactly Oscar Levant but it sounded like Gershwin. Then we walked back to the Palace of Justice—a 25 minute walk—and saw Justice Jackson accompanied by some civilians enter the Palace. He wore a dark blue suit, needed a haircut, and walked with the deliberate dignity of a senator at the time of Henry Clay, who wanted to be noted for re-election.

Unfortunately there was rarely any work. We sat down at our two large desks, both empty. On a small table in the corner was a typewriter. The enlisted men came in the morning and mid-afternoon to report, but there was rarely any work. Col. Behle was a superb typist who had absorbed the jargon of army orders. I soon found out that he was a master of composing (and typing) orders that enabled us to go any place in Europe. Those orders looked so authentic that they could pass the most critical army examiners. Actually the two of us were the main beneficiaries of the typewriter. We converted our typist into a competent factotum. Our movements in Nuremberg and all over Europe were facilitated by impressive, special passes with photographs that had been issued by Justice Jackson's office.

Out our window we could see the jail with its many cells. Beyond it lay the totally devastated inner city. Behind the barred jail windows I often discerned faces, male and female, but even with a pair of binoculars I could not identify any. Passing through a corridor I looked into the courtyard where two prisoners were taking their daily constitutional. A loud voice, reinforced by a bullhorn from across the courtyard, admonished me not to stop and look. I moved on without being able to tell whom I had seen.

General Betts and Colonel Fairman came to call on us in our office. We jumped up and came to attention, listened to what the general had to say and were astonished when he concluded his remarks by saying: "General Eisenhower will appreciate what you are doing." That was the last time I saw General Betts.

Revisiting Albrecht Duerer's Nuernberg

That afternoon I walked past the famous cemetery outside the city walls where Duerer and many other famous men of his time are buried. The place looked untouched as I remembered it from 1938. Passages between the graves had been raked and there were fresh flowers on graves. Even the famous decoration on one the graves, a skull with a movable lower jaw, was still operative.

I entered the old, historic city through one of the gates near the Burg with its fortifications and watchtowers that had dominated the city silhouette for centuries. People had warned me that historic Nuremberg was about 95% destroyed. But what I now saw paled anything that I had seen before.

Before the war I had admired Nuremberg as a place that had retained the appearance of the Middle Ages. Churches decorated with precious carved altars, massive fortifications and city gates and walls, torture chambers, elegant homes of wealthy merchants, and museums all added to the illusion that I suddenly had been transported back to 1500. Even the historic restaurants had contributed to this charming illusion. The waiters, dressed as if they had served Duerer, brought dishes that had been traditions in the city from time immemorial.

Now before me lay a field of ruins that looked as if an earthquake followed by a fire storm had flattened the whole city. I was amazed. I had heard that much of it had withstood the bombing attacks. Apparently when toward the very end of the war the mayor had surrendered the city, some crazy SS troops had attacked American troops that had been invited to accept the surrender. The U.S. Army had been withdrawn and ordered to deliver a devastating bombing attack and artillery bombardment, and so the city was reduced to charred ruins.

The Burg and the adjacent sections, ivy covered fortifications in 1938, now were in ruins, as was most of the inner city. The Duerer house just below the Burg, famous for its rakish gables and the bulls-eye glass windows, was so badly maimed that I expected to see it collapse at any moment. A piece of corrugated roofing had been used to board up the front door. The statue of Duerer, a short distance down the hill, stood defiantly among the ruins. Shrapnel had pierced his face and the ragged edge of his left cheek pointed toward the sky. Only the famous *Schoene Brunnen*, a fountain at the edge of the market place—for centuries one of the showpieces of the city—had survived untouched. The reinforced concrete structure built for its protection had withstood bombardment and fire. The city administration had the concrete shelter removed to give the inhabitants hope by showing them what Nuernberg once had been. The church at the other side of the market place with its famous organ and art treasures had collapsed with only a part of one of the steeples still standing.

The inhabitants went on with their daily tasks. On a pile of rubble I saw an English sign, so familiar in America: "JESUS SAVES." Right next to it I spied a sign in German: Marriage Brokerage Office. It seemed rather incongruous to start a marriage bureau in that environment. Most of the life in the inner city had gone underground—the basements that had not collapsed provided the only shelter. Everywhere I saw little temporary roofs that kept cellar dwellings from being flooded in the occasional rains. Wisps of smoke coming from stove-pipes that had broken through the rubble indicated that the people were cooking down there. I saw an old woman with small children who had collected bricks and pieces of metal and constructed a fireplace on which she heated some food. Here and there I saw wash lines with clothing drying in the air. A gnome-like man of perhaps 50 passed me, stopped for a moment, looked at me and said, "Wir bauen's alles wieder auf" (we are going to rebuild all of it), and disappeared into his basement abode.

Along a street of collapsed houses, I saw an elegant door entrance that had survived. It must have been the house of someone important in Nuernberg. I carefully climbed over the rubble to read a plaque that was still fastened to the small piece of wall next to the door. I could decipher: "14..-1519 Here lived Ludwig Krug, Albrecht Duerer's Teacher." The town even in its agony was still breathing the spirit of its greatest citizen.

First Meeting with Jackson's Crew and the Floor Show at the Grand Hotel

When I arrived at the Grand Hotel, Col. Behle asked some of the younger men to join us for a bull session. A mixture of gin and grape juice helped us get off to a good start. The first man I met was a navy lieutenant, Whitney Harris. He told me that he was working on the brief against the Gestapo. It was a difficult assignment because he had so much material—all of it in German, which he could not read. And there were so many people who had worked in Gestapo jobs, many of them right here in the jail, that he should interview. He really needed someone with a command of German who could lend a hand. I offered to collaborate at the very first moment. It was a challenging opportunity and I was determined to follow it up.

That first evening at the Officers' Club at the Grand Hotel was an eye-opener. I saw my first floor show as an American officer. Most of the German war criminals were in jail at the Palace of Justice, and now legalized Fraternization with Germans was in full bloom. The U.S. Army Officer's Club had taken over the dance hall of the hotel. It was arranged like a giant bar, with a small dance floor that also served as the stage for the nightly floor show. German Fraeuleins, selected for pleasing appearance, worked as waitresses and brought us drinks from the bar for which we paid with German occupation money. Tipping was done with cigarettes. Since a package of cigarettes had the purchasing power of about $20 on the black market, a single cigarette was considered a very generous tip. The Fraeuleins were continuously emptying the ashtrays on the tables to collect the cigarette butts. The tobacco left in the butts had high commercial value on the black market and was resold to people who rolled their own cigarettes.

Every evening, promptly at 9 P.M., livening up a rather depressing hotel, a forty-five minute floor show would be announced by the German MC, who was crude and obsequious. The show always started with a piano rendition of George Gershwin's *Rhapsody in Blue.* At the stroke of nine two superb piano players in white tie and tails sat down at two requisitioned grand pianos and began to hammer out the music that I had heard them rehearse when Col. Behle and I had our first lunch there. Then followed what became known at the Club as "The Meat Show," a lady dancer with scanty dress and considerable exposure. The next act was invariably a vocalist, accompanied by accordion or guitar. It was a rare evening where they did not drag up *Lilli Marlene* either in English or in German. The last act was always a group of acrobats that never failed to impress, because they had kept in shape and used their bodies with such precision and grace.

After one week at the Grand Hotel we were glad to leave that depressing and slightly nauseating atmosphere. We were assigned a billet at 31 Schlegel Strasse in one of the suburbs. The army had taken over undamaged private houses and made them into officers' billets, usually housing six officers to the house. Life in that billet provided us with a surprising number of unexpected experiences.

Two of our new housemates were technicians who designed and installed the complex translation equipment in the Palace of Justice. They had access to sensitive recording devices and they installed some in our living room. We now could record the conversations of the frequent visitors from a nearby holding pen, where Germans willing to testify to horrors that they had seen were kept. These German people loved to come to our house because it gave them the opportunity to talk to people other than their German colleagues, whom they did not trust and in many cases loathed. Since I was the only one who was fluent in German, I often interpreted. Some of the stories that they related were surprising.

One of the men invited to our house was a young German air force general who had been selected to go to Japan as the German air attache. In early April 1945 everything was set for his departure by submarine equipped with snorkel equipment which enabled the boat to remain submerged until it reached the South Atlantic. The general was not going with empty hands; he brought with him a disassembled Heinkel Duesenjaeger, the dreaded German jet fighter plane that at the very end of the war had created serious problems for the Allied bomber fleets. Hitler felt that his allies should have the best! The young general had been underway and under water for some time when on May 8, he surfaced for the first time. The antenna provided him with the welcome news that the war was over and the submarine must show a black flag in order to be escorted to an Allied base. The submarine was quickly escorted to a harbor, and the general was arrested and sent to Nuremberg. After we had elicited this story with the help of some whiskey, I asked him about some of his friends in the German air force and it turned out that we had several common contacts. At the end of the evening he mentioned that he had lived in Neubrandenburg. When I asked him how he liked the Reuter Stube, one of the town's most famous restaurants, he was surprised.

Interpreting for Goering—Observing Famous Nazis—Learning What Goes On

Being attached to Justice Jackson's staff gave us a certain glamour status. We were treated well wherever we showed up. On one of my first days in Nuremberg I made a courtesy call on Colonel Amen. The name was familiar from my time as a law student in New York. Amen was then Governor Dewey's popular racket-buster, who had obtained convictions of many Mafia members and a gang nicknamed "Murder Incorporated." He had now been recruited to head the U.S. interrogation and cross-examination team at the tribunal.

Col. Amen was flattered when I told him I remembered him well from his spectacular work in New York. He seemed delighted when I explained my assignment and told him that I was trying to learn how to organize such a trial and how to deal with the myriad of procedural and linguistic problems it entails. Certainly in his section I thought, there might be a way to find some help. And if he could use me, I would be glad to do what I could. He explained that most of the proof of the crimes committed by the defendant Nazis would come from incriminating documents that they themselves had signed and that had been found. That material was now being readied by Colonel Storey, whom I would undoubtedly meet soon. But, he pointed out, the prosecution also must be prepared for the cross examination of the defendants if in the course of the trial the occasion arose. He and his assistants, all highly skilled trial lawyers, had laid the groundwork for careful professional evaluation of each defendant. That was important because a trial attorney must know the strengths and weaknesses of his adversary before he starts his case in court, especially before he attempts cross-examination.

Not all of the attorneys who presented their case in court availed themselves of this valuable assistance, as I found out later. Unfortunately Justice Jackson was a prime example of those who did not feel that they needed this help. When during the trial Jackson cross-examined Goering, he was ill prepared for his task, botched most of the cross examination, and had to be rescued by Sir Maxwell Fyfe, an experienced British courtroom trial lawyer. Goering was a formidable opponent of superior cunning and intelligence, which Jackson had not anticipated. He, like so many people in Nuremberg, had viewed Goering as a jolly, fat drug addict interested only in good food and spectacular uniforms. But he had failed to realize the advantage that Goering, and for that matter, several of the defendants enjoyed. Understanding English but never admitting it, Goering could use the time that it took to translate the question into German to prepare for his answer. Jackson, to his dismay, found out that with Goering he did not possess the normal cross examiner's advantage of catching an unaware witness in a rapid fire interrogation.

Col. Amen asked me if I would be willing to interpret for him the next day when he would question Hermann Goering about some of his activities as one of the greatest art looters the world has ever seen. Goering, he told me, was a very sharp and difficult witness, who was hard to handle. He understood English perfectly well but he would never admit this. Recently Goering had come upon a clever, new way of throwing a monkey wrench into the interrogation procedure by making his usual interpreter, Richard Sonnenfeldt, a young Jewish refugee with excellent language abilities, gun shy. To rattle the interpreter and cause a real problem, Goering would use the following trick: He would say to the interpreter, "Please tell Colonel Amen that you have not translated to me what Colonel Amen has asked me." With this tactic Goering created distrust and achieved what he wanted: the end of the interrogation at least for that day. Col. Amen mentioned that they had obtained the complete record of Goering's art acquisitions and that it would be an interesting morning.

As a student at the University of Berlin I had seen Goering many times in his glory in Hitler's entourage, as head of the German Air Force, or as the Reich's Master of the Hunt. Early in Hitler's reign, no foreign dignitary could avoid the theater of being seen with Hitler's cabinet at the Tomb of the Unknown Soldier at Unter den Linden. For students at the Humboldt University next door, it was a free grandstand seat to a great spectacle.

Instead of a fancy uniform, bedecked with orders and decorations, a shrunken Goering now wore a simple Loden jacket that he had perhaps ordered years ago, when he weighed about 60 pounds more. The jacket, now several sizes too big, made him look smaller than he really was. He had the usual prison color, was clean shaven, had alert, fast moving eyes, and interesting, strong hands with well cared for fingernails, but his skin, especially at the neck, showed that he had lost much weight.

Now he sat on a wooden chair at a simple 4 x 10' table and waited for us as we entered. He got up. Behind him, also on a wooden chair, sat an armed guard who had brought him from the prison. Through a window across the table he had a good view of the ruins of Nuremberg. To his right, about 6 feet distant, was Col. Amen. I sat facing Col. Amen with Goering to my right. Next to Amen a stenographer took down the English questions and Goering's answers as I translated them. A tape recorder stood in the middle of the table to take down the complete interview. At the other end of the table facing Goering, sat James Plaut, the curator of one of the large New York Museums and now a lieutenant in the U.S. Navy. He had obtained all the records of Goering's art collections with complete information of the origin of each picture, the prices paid, etc. Lt. Plaut and Col. Amen had carefully prepared every detail of the questions that they would ask Goering and they knew in advance the answer to each of them.

The interrogation proceeded slowly and with the utmost precision, never giving Goering any opportunity to debate anything. In effect, leaving no question unanswered, Amen pieced together admission after admission concerning the gigantic art collection composed of extorted pictures. With devastating accuracy we could see how a man of moderate income who had joined the Hitler cabinet on January 30, 1933, had used his power as a government official to make himself overnight one of the greatest art collectors of all time.

In February of 1933 Hitler had appointed Goering Minister President of Prussia to take control of the Prussian police and the concentration camps. In the beginning these camps were holding pens for enemies of the people as defined by the regime. It was not necessarily Jews who were confined there, but people who had expressed or were rumored to have expressed reservations about the new government.

In 1934 Goering married the opera singer, Emmy Sonnenberg. It was an important social event. Goering passed word that the usual wedding presents like silver and porcelain were not desired. Instead, he was interested in enlarging the Hermann Goering Foundation to bring together art objects that ultimately would benefit the German nation—after he had enjoyed their possession during his lifetime. To accomplish this goal money contributions would be welcome. German industry and many people who wanted to bring themselves to the attention of this key man in the new government understood the message and sent cash. Goering now sat on a large fortune. He hired an art expert and a financial adviser, who visited Berlin's major art dealers to select pictures that would fit Hitler's art criteria. Emphasis was on German artists of the early 19th century. His team usually selected 10 pictures and then brought Goering to the art dealer. Properly primed, he inspected the pictures, expressed satisfaction and agreed to buy the whole lot. However, in view of the magnitude of such a purchase, he demanded a quantity discount of 10 to 20 percent, which the art dealer instantly granted. The pictures were immediately paid for by Goering's check drawn against the Hermann Goering Foundation. His team ordered the art dealer to keep the pictures at the gallery until they would receive word on how to ship them.

Many of the people who had been arrested and put into concentration camps were moving heaven and earth to get out. Usually through some connection they were directed to Goering and in many instances he found a way of releasing them. Now each of the grateful beneficiaries of Goering's kindness approached one of his associates and inquired how he could show his gratitude for the kind consideration that he had received from the Prime Minister. The associate would then inform the party that the Prime Minister was very interested in fine German art and that the gift of a picture might be a suitable way of expressing his sentiments. In fact, he happened to know that the Marshal had expressed particular interest in pictures that he had admired in a Berlin Gallery. He was now taken to the gallery and was shown one or two of the pictures, but was not told that these pictures were already Goering's property. The interested party now purchased the picture and paid the gallery the full price (not the discounted price that Goering had paid). The art Gallery cashed the check and sent the full proceeds of the transaction to the Hermann Goering Foundation. After all the pictures in the gallery were purchased for the second time, they were delivered to Karinhall, Goering's enormous Hunting Lodge in the Schorfheide near Berlin and at the end of this grandiose scheme Goering owned 10 pictures and the Hermann Goering Foundation got richer all the time. It was a carefully manipulated scheme that was repeated, time after time.

Goering knew of course, that such art acquisitions would not meet the standards of any ethics committee. But he was equally certain that manipulations of this type would not lead to the death sentence. He admitted all of it without any signs of interest, probably considering the matter a mere trifle in the context of all the crimes that he would be charged with.

Col. Amen thanked me for my assistance and suggested that in the afternoon I attend the interrogations of Dr. Karl Brandt, who had been the equivalent of Hitler's surgeon general, and that of Feldmarschal von Brauchitsch.

Brandt was an unusually good-looking physician, who as Hitler's medical director was responsible for an enormous euthanasia program. Soon after the outbreak of the war with Russia, the German army suffered heavy losses. When it dawned upon the military that they were critically short of hospital facilities for wounded soldiers, who had to be patched up to go back for more fighting, they turned to Brandt for help. Dr. Brandt suggested that vast hospital facilities were being tied up by incurable mental cases. He proposed that it was a simple matter to kill these incurable people by lethal injections and thus immediately provide 300,000 beds. Brandt admitted that he had hatched this plan and carried it out and he confirmed that if he were confronted with a similar problem again, he would act the same way, since it would help assure Germany's victory. By way of explanation, he added that the mental patients were incurable and merely a burden to the nation. That day I heard for the first time a mass murderer calmly admit his crime without the slightest remorse or embarrassment. He must have known that ultimately he would have to account for his deeds, and might be hanged, but he seemed unconcerned.

Later when the question of Hitler's sterilization program was raised, he readily admitted that he was in favor of it and was responsible for preparing the necessary directives. He had developed this program after studying precedents in other countries. With a sort of an amused smile, he added that he was especially guided in this approach by a decision of Oliver Wendell Holmes, a United States Supreme Court justice, who had endorsed this concept for sterilization of mentally defective persons. I related the substance of Brandt's interrogation at one of the many bull sessions we had at our billet. It was astonishing how often the issue was reduced to a remark like, "Well, if you are up against the wall and must save wounded soldiers to fight for a nation's life, putting insane people into pens may be a way of providing the needed beds. After seeing those poor, deranged people in the pens might there not come a time where killing them is more humane?"

Compared with the tension of the Brandt interrogation, the questioning of von Brauchitsch was pure theater. As the former chief of staff of the German Army he had to identify documents which he had signed. Before he accepted any document he pulled a monocle fastened to a black string from his vest pocket and placed the monocle in his eye, creating a distortion of his face. He then examined the paper, acknowledged or denied the authenticity, and returned the document as he released the monocle—again with a grimace—to his waiting right hand which he employed to catch the monocle and put it back into the vest pocket. No pressure, no admonition, no request to hurry could modify or speed up this monotonous, theatrical performance. As I watched him repeat this routine with the precision of a metronome this thought crossed my mind: How could a man like that ever have commanded the whole German Army?

The next day, as agreed, I helped Whitney Harris with the interrogation of Otto Ohlendorf, the high Gestapo official and commander of one of the infamous Special Detachments. This unit had followed the German army into Russia and had liquidated Jews and Communists using large trailer vehicles to gas them. Whitney was concerned that the numerous German documents that he had assembled studiously avoided the term, "killing" and instead continuously made reference to the "Resettlement of the Jews." He knew that behind the word "Resettlement" was hidden "Murder" but he needed confirmation of this for his brief on the Gestapo. A small room with a stenographer was ready for us. Otto Ohlendorf, guarded by a soldier, had been brought from prison and rose when we entered. In his ill-fitting prison garb he looked like the hundreds of prisoners whom I had been able to observe on their compulsory morning walks. Like most of the prisoners, he was glad to have a chance to communicate and seemed almost loquacious. Within minutes he told us that the word "umsiedeln (resettlement)" was, of course, the Nazi jargon for "resettlement in another world," which meant "killing." When Whitney, toward the end of the interrogation, asked him how many people he had "resettled" by gassing, he suddenly became uncertain and nervous and I noticed sweat drops on his forehead. Whitney and I thought for a moment that the enormity of his crimes had suddenly overwhelmed him. Then he got hold of himself and with sort of an apologetic smile he said: "You know, it is funny what happens to one's memory, I can't say with certainty whether it was 90,000 or 190,000 people whom we gassed at that time."

Every other evening there were compulsory lectures that provided insight into legal approaches, problems of proof, and historical background. Hearing and meeting new people almost every day, my letter of September 29 reflects our state of mind at the time.

> "It is an interesting fact that consciously or unconsciously the Jewish problem has become one of the main problems. I am entirely in agreement that it is perhaps the most terrible chapter, but I guess that what was done to the Russians, the Poles and the Czecks is probably on the same level or frequently even on a worse level. But none of them have as articulate a backing as the Jews and also, the number of Jews on the present prosecution staff is a certain explanation of the trend that seems to manifest itself everywhere."

Documents as Proof of Crimes

It had not taken me long to discover that the document center was the power source that provided the facts needed for this monster trial. In a large former courtroom with endless shelving, the army had made available a vast range of captured Nazi documents. A daily bulletin pinned to the door announced what new material had come in the day before. What was assembled here had been culled from nearly three thousand tons of captured German documents. More than a thousand documents were prepared by the American prosecution team and used at the trial. Here is what caught my eye at my first visit, as recorded in a letter:

> "Here we have innumerable documents of all the big, minor and midget guys. I spent the morning reading Rosenberg's private files on the church and on his special "Cultural Mission." He had been chosen to go with the

invading forces and immediately secure all evidence of Jewish activities—also masonic activities—in the countries overrun by the Nazis. The most valuable "evidence" of their [the Jews] dangerous activities were possession of old masters, valuable carpets, and other possessions that the Jews had the nerve to keep out of Goering's and Hitler's reach, thus willfully preventing them to "complete" their collections.

It is really a remarkable thing that these people [Rosenberg et al.] did their looting with a methodical and thoughtful approach that is otherwise found only in scientific research. Goering was most willing to offer his planes to transport the material back to Germany."

The next day I introduced myself to Colonel Storey's section, which was still searching for materials needed for the framing of the indictment. The work area was a large courtroom. On one side was a platform from which I could see the whole area. At 30 small tables I saw soldiers reading file after file from stacks on their desks. As soon as they had finished their piles they raised their hands and a new stack of files was delivered. All of them had complete command of German, some of them were Jewish refugees, as I later found out. Along the wall hundreds of boxes were stacked, all of them marked with code letters and numbers to indicate their origin. Careful records were kept to log the removal and return of every file. My first impression was that all of this work was performed according to a carefully thought out but essentially dull system that accounted for the origin and content of every piece of paper. But there was something else—there was a sense of urgency and of stalking important game.

Suddenly I heard a soldier say, "My God!" I got up from the table where I had studied some files that had been assigned to me and walked over. The soldier held the famous *Rascher File* in his hand. Dr. Sigmund Rascher, a member of the SS was a professor of medicine in Goering's Air Ministry, who had established a secret "laboratory" in Dachau. He was determined to find by scientific research methods how to revive pilots and sailors rescued from icy waters and, of course, half-frozen soldiers in Russia. With an unlimited supply of concentration camp inmates the design of a testing protocol was simple. Healthy inmates were placed into water tanks, the temperature of which was lowered with ice to resemble the target environment (sea—Russia). When the body temperature of the inmates, measured in the rectum, reached 86 degrees, most of them lost consciousness. The next step was the revival technique. They were placed into hot water tubs with temperatures varying from 105 to 120 degrees. A few of them made it, but most died. In another "scientific" series, they put victims of cold treatment between two lush gypsies—also readily available as test material in the concentration camp. Observation established that they occasionally came to, but did not regain body heat very quickly because as the report "scientifically" recorded, "They were apparently embarrassed to find themselves between two women." Later in a "control series," when victims were placed next to a single woman, the recovery was much quicker, although they never compared with the speed of recovery in hot water.

From among the many gruesome cases I recall another one. The file was marked: *Medical Experiments With Poisoned Ammunition.* There was an abundance of testing material available from the same source: The concentration camps. The question was: Would it be possible to transmit deadly poison by bullets, so that even superficial wounds would result in death? If that could be demonstrated, what a bonanza for the armed forces of the Third Reich! The stage was set for another significant medical advance. Inmates in large numbers were slightly wounded—just flesh wounds, nothing serious. The results were disappointing. The poison could not be transmitted in that way, not a single wound proved fatal. We thought the file could be used to prove crimes against humanity—until we turned to the last page. It showed photographs of the ammunition. It had been manufactured in Russia and had been captured by the German armed forces.

Finding Competent Translators

The greatest need at that time was to find competent translators who could quickly and accurately translate the hundreds of documents that were needed to support the indictment. Justice Jackson had cabled the Pentagon that he needed a large supply of them. The Pentagon placed ads for translators in many papers and had put applicants on planes without having made an effort to determine whether they were capable. So, one morning two plane loads of the people hired showed up for work in Nuremberg. There were two or three of us who had to determine whether these people were capable. Fortunately, I had concerned myself with problems of translation before. To earn extra money while attending law school, I had read numerous German manuscripts for a New York publisher to determine whether in translated form they could find a market in the U.S. Usually I made a sample translation of one or two pages to support my recommendations when I thought the book merited translation. Now I borrowed a stack of Nazi books from the library—like Rosenberg's *Mythos of the 20th Century,* a book of Goebbel's Speeches and Hitler's *Mein Kampf*—and handed each of the applicants a book, asking them to translate just two pages into English and bring their work to me the next day. The results were astonishing. Of the perhaps 75 people whom I tested, not more than 10 could do the job. Many of them were highly intelligent, educated people who spoke a fluent German and understood what the Nazi text said, but they were unable to recast it accurately into English. Those who could not qualify and for whom we could find no other use, had to fly back. I recall one man who had proudly applied for the job of an interpreter, probably the most difficult and taxing job of all the linguistic variations. When I asked him why he thought that we could use him as an interpreter, he replied with great pride: "I spick siven linguages, English die best." He had dreamt of great adventures, but I had to send him home.

Observing One Russian

The American presence in Nuremberg was overwhelming. The British had sent only a small and competent detachment. They were anxious to work, and since it was easy to communicate with them, I met several with whom I developed friendly contacts. Among them was Major Neave, a highly decorated officer who had succeeded in escaping from Colditz, one of the touted escape proof German prisons. Contact with the French and Russians, because of language difficulties, and general distrust did not exist. The only contact we had was seeing them in the new PX in the Palace of Justice. It was there that I had my only opportunity to observe a Russian during my time in Nuremberg.

Leaning against the PX counter was a young enlisted soldier from an Asiatic area of Russia. With his rakish cap, loosely fitting uniform blouse held together with a broad leather belt and his coarse boots, he looked like one of the horsemen from the tundra of Asia who had once terrified Europe. Like all Russians at that time, he carried a briefcase—it looked like a looted German model -and it was bulging with money. Russian soldiers had not been paid during the war, just fed and told once they won the war their pay would be delivered in German money in Germany. Now he was looking for something to buy in the American PX. Not knowing a word of English or German, he could not tell the women in the store what he wanted. He himself had no idea what he wanted because he had never been in a gigantic PX stocked with hundreds of items from cigarettes, candy, and nylon stockings to shaving cream, deodorants, peanuts, and gigantic light blue boxes of Kleenex. He stood there looking and calculating. Finally the size of the Kleenex box and perhaps the attractive shade of blue overcame his indecision and he pointed to the container holding boxes of Kleenex. The sales girl put it on the counter and he opened the briefcase so that she could select the correct number of Marks. Now he walked off carrying the big box probably wondering why it was so light. He left the PX and went along the hall where an alcove with windows invited him to stop. He did not know that I had followed him, hoping to see how he would react to what he had bought.

He opened the big box, which obviously was a shipping container for about a dozen boxes of Kleenex and removed the first individual package. Seeing the oval area with an arrow indicating how to open it, he punched it, reached in and pulled. The first Kleenex emerged, followed by a second, third and fourth as he pulled. The tempo of his pulling increased. Within a minute he had emptied the first box. I saw him hopefully opening the second and emptying it at greater speed; by this time he was surrounded by a growing mountain of Kleenex tissues. After attacking the third box with the same result, he kicked the rest of the box into a corner and left the littered alcove, shaking his head in furious disbelief. Did he think that the Americans had tricked him into spending a lot of hard earned money and buying something worthless which no heroic Communist veteran would ever care to own? Did he ever find out what it was that he had bought? My hunch was that he would never find out.

Making the Most of Weekends and Social Events

Every Friday saw an enormous weekend exodus as most of us looked for relief from the depressing atmosphere of Nuremberg. Franconia, with Nuremberg as its center, is loaded with medieval towns, history, art and culture, which I had seen and studied before I left for America. Now I could put this knowledge to good use. I became a popular tour guide for my boss and for many of the higher ranking officers. Col. Behle, Peggy Brown and Col. Fairman were always the first to ask for an excursion. Three events from those weekend tours have remained fresh in my mind.

A tour of Berchtesgaden to see Hitler's badly mauled Berghof and the Eagles Nest, which he had built with slave labor, was a must in those days. But the truly memorable event of our trip had to do with an attempt to purchase a pair of Bavarian leather pants. A fat major, who happened to be on this trip, had his mind set upon buying a pair of those pants. I thought it a strange desire that a man with that build wanted to be seen in leather pants, but he insisted. Very soon we found out that Berchtesgaden, which had been captured by the 101st Airborne Division had been picked clean. The stores were empty, there were no Bavarian hats, no fancy shoes or socks—absolutely nothing. I was ready to give up, but the major insisted and we entered a store that clearly had been a major supplier of leather pants. I asked the proprietor if he had a pair of Bavarian leather pants for the major. The owner looked at him and said: "NO." The major nudged me and said, "Give him the needle." So, to please the major, I said: "Look, if Hermann Goering came in here, I am sure that you would supply him with a pair of pants!" The man shrugged his shoulders and said "You know, from little scraps of leather in my basement I could probably put together a pair of pants for a little kid—but for the major no, and for Goering absolutely impossible." I replied "You must be kidding, you never made a pair of leather pants for Goering!" The man stung by my remark, reached under the counter and brought forth a stack of black order books with measurements. He looked at the dates, shuffled the books and sure enough there was the strong and familiar signature of Hermann Goering and above it the measurements—knee, thigh, waist and seat. When I read the enormous centimeter count for the seat and converted it to inches, my major said with an admiring sigh: "What a butt."

At another time I made a trip to Bayreuth, which was occupied by the 102nd Division. The gigantic Wagner Opera House with a stage that seemed large enough to allow dirt track races, was now disgraced by giant USO shows featuring hot mammas and crooners instead of Heldentenors. Wagner's house had been converted into an officers club, and instead of pictures of the Walkuere there were posters of Lana Turner.

In the *Trinkstube*, which had been renamed *BAR*, they served gin and coca cola. The "holy couch," on which Hitler often had been photographed with Winifred Wagner, was still in the living room. I could not resist sitting there for a moment. Years later on the 50th anniversary of Hitler's rise to power, I would be asked to give a lecture of my recollections of the Hitler times. In preparation I would set about looking up old *New York Times* reports for January 30 to about March of 1933, wondering if anyone had the slightest inkling of what was in store for the world. The staid *New York Times*, devoted to reporting ALL THE NEWS THAT'S FIT TO PRINT, would provide an amazing amount of coverage on the potential liaison between Hitler and Winifred Wagner, frequently seen in Bayreuth, usually pictured sitting on what we called the "holy couch." And I had graced that very same seat.

Among the American officers in Nuremberg were several who were determined to acquire porcelain to send to their families in Germany. The town of Selb about 80 miles from Nuremberg near the Czech border, was famous for its Rosenthal china and it was rumored they still had wonderful selections. Coming from a family that had been linked to porcelain through my great-great grandfather, who had directed the Royal Berlin china factory (KPM) in Berlin around 1800, I was always game for porcelain exploration. In Selb we met a local man who told us that there were several factories and that they even had a Royal Berlin China factory. The plant in Berlin had been totally destroyed so they had opened a factory right there in town.

Leaving the others to browse around, Colonel Behle and I went to the KPM factory, a modest plant with a few display cases. What was shown, however, was elegant. Obviously they had brought some of their designers and potters along when they came to Selb. What I saw was much more modern than the staid designs with which I had grown up. A young woman showed us what they had available. When I asked her if any of the people from Berlin were in Selb, she said she would ask Mr. Franke, the director, to come and talk to us.

A tall friendly man with horn-rimmed glasses came and inquired what he could do for us. I introduced myself and said that I was interested to learn what had happened to the Berlin factory and if there were any plans to go back to production in Berlin. Mr. Franke, listening attentively started by saying, "Did I hear the name of our

famous director who saved the Manufaktur during Napoleon's occupation of Berlin?" When I nodded, he continued: "Yes, we intend
to go back to Berlin. That is where we belong. Most of our forms
and patterns have survived; we'll start soon. Until we can get the
materials to rebuild Berlin, we must keep Selb, but all of us want to
get back." He looked at some of the display cases and said: "It's a
modest beginning. Please have the young lady show you what is not
yet displayed, while I attend to some business." He bowed with a
friendly smile and disappeared. A few minutes later he came back.
He had in his hand a nicely wrapped box which he handed to me
saying: "Let it not be said that the KPM is ever so poor that it
cannot salute one of the descendants of its great director." It was a
wonderful moment to see the spirit of that man. When I opened the
package upon our return I found a beautiful green vase with a light
relief of running deer. It still reminds me of that day and the man
who brought KPM back to Berlin, where I saw him several times
before he died.

After one of those excursions, Peggy Brown called me to come
to her office. Justice Jackson had invited members of his personal
staff, their secretaries and a few high officers to an informal cocktail
party at his house. She and Colonel Fairman had been asked, but
Col. Fairman was away and she did not feel that she could appear
without an escort. "Would you be willing to go, if I clear the matter
with Jackson's secretary?" she asked. There was not a second's hesitation. She picked up the phone, dialed the number, received permission and said: "We go!" That evening I drove her in one of our
jeeps to Jackson's very elegant quarters. Undoubtedly I was the officer with the lowest rank, but it did not matter after a while, because booze is a great equalizer.

Among the guests was Colonel Burton C. Andrus, the commanding officer of the Nuremberg jail and the master of its 1200
Nazi inmates. I had met Andrus during the war on the night after
our unit had crossed the Rhine on the way to Dillenburg. He, a full
combat colonel of the famous First Division (the **Big "1"**) ordered
people around, cursing and shouting. I had made myself as invisible

as possible. After I came to Nuremberg I learned that as a young infantry lieutenant after WWI, where he had earned his commission, he had for a short time commanded the army stockade at Fort Oglethorp, Georgia and established a fine record for tough and unyielding discipline. The army considered this brief exposure to prison management the perfect qualification to put him in charge of the captured Nazis. Before coming to Nuremberg the prisoners had been locked up in the Palace Hotel in Mondorf in Luxembourg, generally referred to as "Ashcan" where Andrus had been in charge. Having served under General Patton, he adopted his lacquered helmets for his own guards. Every picture of the trial shows Andrus' guards standing ramrod stiff behind the prisoners, displaying Andrus' beloved laquered white helmets.

All parties in Nuremberg followed basically the same pattern. A thank you to the host—then a move to the food table—far better than rations in the officers' mess.

During that time there would be polite conversation with the few ladies who were present and then the men would gravitate to the bar. Before long those men who had been actually involved in the war, of whom there were very few in Nuremberg, began to relate their most exciting war experiences. Since Col. Andrus had been a combat officer with Patton, he told how it really was and we all listened with rapt attention. Standing there I thought it would be nice if I said something complimentary to Col. Andrus. Flattery is always a safe way of gaining attention, and so I said: "Colonel Andrus, you are certainly a most remarkable man." He looked up at me wondering what I would say next—and I continued: "As the Commandant of the Nuremberg prison you have under your thumb undoubtedly the largest number of managerial talent the world has ever assembled in one place." He looked at me with slightly bloodshot eyes and barked: "They are a bunch of jerks, that's what they are." Colonel Andrus clearly knew how to deal with American soldiers by giving them laquered helmets and white gloves, but he vastly underestimated the German managers under his thumb.

Service of the Indictments & Unexpected Problems

The pressure to get the trial going was mounting daily.

I had spent most of my time with translations and with Whitney Harris, who was working to get the brief for the Gestapo case ready. Finally October 19, 1945 was the date set for the service of the indictments on the 20 defendants in Nuremberg. Gustav Krupp von Bohlen, senile and unable to stand trial, was served on the 23rd of October and Bormann, whose whereabouts were unknown, was served by publication.

Raeder and Fritsche were the only important Nazis who were not served with the indictments in Nuremberg. The Russians had caught them and had held them in Berlin. Peeved that the trials would not be held in Berlin, the city they had captured and where the war had ended, the Russians insisted that they would open the trial in Berlin by serving indictments on their two captives one day before the remaining 20 defendants would be served in Nuremberg. It was typical of the haggling between the Russians and the Western Allies and showed the problems with which Jackson had to contend. The Russians delivered the two men two days later.

I contacted Major Neave of the British delegation, who had been selected for the job of serving the indictments. We had agreed earlier that I could help him with interpreting. When I joined him, he had already served the first group of 10 defendants, among them Goering, Hess, Ribbentrop and all of the military men. We met in a small room in the prison. Major Neave had a stack of indictments before him. The English version had been typeset and printed on glossy offset paper. It looked very professional. The German translation, which was stapled to the English text, was typewritten and printed on duplicator paper. Each defendant entered the room, approached the table at which Major Neave sat, and was informed that he was being served with the indictment that contained a statement of the crimes with which he was charged. Neave informed each defendant that he had the right to his own defense counsel and that the trial would commence on November 20, 1945. After I had translated Major Neave's statement, the defendant was handed a copy of the indictment and then was escorted by his guard to his cell. When we were finished I picked up one extra indictment and took it with me as a memento.

Of the defendants for whom I interpreted, I remember three: Schacht, Speer and von Neurath. Schacht was outraged that he had been indicted and spouted forth that this was a great injustice and that his indictment was a sham for the sole purpose of acquitting him at the end of the trial, so that the Tribunal could assert that the trial had been fair. Major Neave, totally unimpressed by this tirade, merely said, "Here is your indictment. We do not need your comment. Please return to your cell." As it turned out, Schacht was indeed acquitted. Several years later I met him on a flight from Duesseldorf to Hamburg and reminded him of his 1945 remark. Unchanged—arrogant and self righteous—he said, "You see, of course, I was right!"

Speer accepted the indictment without any sign of surprise. He bowed politely as Major Neave handed him the indictment and turned around to be escorted to his cell. I visited Speer in 1976 in Heidelberg, ten years after he had been released from Spandau prison. The publication of his two books on the times of Adolf Hitler, which he had written during his confinement in Spandau, had made him famous and rich. During the years that I had regularly listened to Hitler's speeches, I was always irritated by his mistreatment of the German language. His Austrian/Bavarian inflection sounded like someone from the play "Das Weisse Roessl." When I mentioned this to Speer and expressed surprise that he, coming from a cultured family would not have been repelled by Hitler's language, he replied, "I could never be inspired by someone who talks like you."

Von Neurath entered, received the indictment, bowed politely and walked out. The reason I remember him was that he had a beard trimmed exactly like my father's.

On Monday October 22, 1945 at 9 A.M., and on every Monday morning, until the trial began, Jackson held a staff conference at which problems relating to the trial were discussed. I attended regularly because the conferences helped me understand the overall plan of the trial. Attendance was usually large; I recall perhaps 80 to 100 people present that day. Justice Jackson sat behind a table on a raised platform; next to him was his military executive officer, General Gill, and the chief of his legal staff Col. Storey, a tough man with a noticeable Texas twang. The staff conference opened with Colonel Storey reading a petition from Dr. Dix, the spokesman for all the defense counsels. He requested that each of the defendants should be provided with a set of the documents on which the indictment was based. At present, he complained, there was only one copy of the documents supporting the charges available for all of the defendants. Unless they were provided with this material, he felt that they could not prepare an adequate defense.

Justice Jackson, who had listened attentively turned to Col. Storey and said, "Colonel Storey, what do you think we should do?" Colonel Storey, after hesitating for but a few seconds replied, "Mr. Justice Jackson, we are going to hang most of the defendants anyway; therefore, I think there is not much to it. I would deny the petition."

I do not know what moved me to raise my hand and get up from my chair, but I said: "Mr. Justice Jackson, I agree with Colonel Story that he has evaluated the outcome of the trial accurately for most of the defendants, but I have no doubt that we are not going to hang any of the defense counsel, and they will be the people who will say whether we gave their clients a fair trial." Without saying a word, Justice Jackson turned to Storey and said: "Colonel Storey, please call General Clay and tell him to immediately send two companies with reproduction printing equipment to Nuremberg so that they can print the documents, which the defendants must have." Then he turned to me and said: "Lieutenant you made such a valiant plea, I would like you to take over the handling of the defense counsel for the next few days and keep them calm until the documents are available."

With that I had an interesting new assignment that led me to the defense counsels. One of them, von Papen's son and now his father's assistant defense counsel, I knew from a cram course for the first German bar examination that I had taken in Berlin in 1933. He recognized me and inquired how we might have met and was taken aback when I told him. The defense counsels were visibly relieved when they heard that each of them would receive a complete set of the documents, but shocked when I explained to them that for about one week they would have to manage with the one set. I told them that no one could use any document for longer than one hour. If any one of them would not comply with this rule, I would personally bar him from all documents until he received his own set. They saw that I meant business and complied.

Robert Ley's Suicide and The Magic Flute

The sensational news of October 25, 1945, was the announcement that Robert Ley, Hitler's labor management expert, and one of the indicted men had committed suicide by hanging himself in his cell. The blame was squarely put on Col. Andrus. Additional personnel were added to the guard roster. Every defendant was now observed 24 hours a day. Knowing how Ley had accomplished his hanging by fastening a piece of self-made rope to an exposed pipe in the toilet, precautions were undertaken to remove from all cells everything that could facilitate suicide. The prisoners had to sleep with hands visible at all times.

Life went on in Nuremberg; the absence of Ley was considered just one less problem to cope with. For the following Wednesday, October 31, the local opera company had announced the reopening of the Opera House for the U.S. Army with a performance of Mozart's *The Magic Flute*. Like so many German cities, Nuremberg had a state supported opera house, which in its glory—that is during the Nazi Party Rallies—had presented Wagner's operas to Hitler and his cohorts. Now the U.S. Army had decided to provide some entertainment for the large American occupation force and the foreign contingents. The badly hit building had been patched up and auxiliary heating equipment made the place tolerable.

I had a good seat not far from the imposing loge, which had been specially enlarged for Hitler and which had survived the bomb damage. In that loge all by himself sat Colonel Burton T. Andrus, the commandant of the prison, also in charge of the guard detachment. I was surprised that after the Ley debacle he had come to see *The Magic Flute*, a story in which an attempted suicide by hanging is presented in a love scene to Mozart's glorious music. Obviously he had never seen the opera and had no idea what it was all about. He sat there, pompous, erect and showing disciplined attention. Several soldiers serving on his prison guard detachment, whom I recognized, were in the audience.

The opera was well planned. They had a charming couple playing Papageno, the bird catcher, and his girlfriend Papagena. As part of the story Papageno appeared very depressed because he had failed to pass some tests that were essential for his advancement. Walking around the garden he was contemplating suicide by hanging himself with a piece of rope he had discovered. As he was just about to knot the rope around his neck, the audience—perhaps inspired by members of Col. Andrus's detachment—connected Papageno's actions with the hanging of Robert Ley and there was suddenly subdued laughter. Everybody turned to look at Colonel Andrus. He sat there like a stone, looking straight forward with his steel rimmed glasses, not acknowledging the reference to his recent failure. Papagena fortunately appeared in the nick of time and thus Papageno, different from Ley, survived.

Preparing for the Search for my Family

After the defense counsel had received their documents I was released from my job of keeping them from fighting. Everybody on Justice Jackson's staff was now concentrating on the opening of the trial on November 20, 1945. There was little work for us. Col. Behle had gone for a week to Prague, while I minded the shop and made plans for my visit to Gettorf, where I hoped to find out what had happened to my family. It was now five months after the end of the war, but I had not received a letter posted in Germany—there was no postal or telephone service. I had not heard a word from any of my relatives since I had seen them at the end of May.

An old fashioned method of communicating was in use everywhere: the Bulletin Board or anything that could be used for that purpose, like a large smooth wall, a leftover concrete bunker, anything that would accept a message. Occasionally I stood along with many desperate people reading the messages: names, locations, addresses, descriptions, all seeking somebody, hoping for words that in the past had been brought by the mailman. But there was no mailman—he was a casualty of the war.

In anticipation of my trip to Gettorf, I had begun to collect worn out clothes from all my friends, underwear, socks (with or without holes) and had purchased dyestuffs in little drugstores in neighboring towns. Black dye was in great demand, because with it Germans could change the olive drab color of the cast-off American uniforms given them, without later being questioned about the origin of the clothes. When Behle returned from Prague he cut my orders -showing his composing and typing skills:

Liaison Detachment, Theater Judge Advocate
Office of United States Chief of Counsel

U. S. Army
14 November 1945

Special Orders

NO 8

SUBJECT: Travel Orders

1. 2nd Lt. Werner H. Von Rosenstiel, 0-2026823, AUS, WP on or about 14 November 1945 from Nuremberg to Eckernfoerde, Germany, on War Crimes matters for a pe-

riod of approximately five (5) days, and upon completion of TD will return to his proper station. Authority is granted to vary itinerary and to proceed to such other places as may be necessary for the performance of his mission.

2. No enlisted man is available as a driver. Lt. Von Rosenstiel accordingly will travel by WCIT #6835 motor vehicle No. 2018811 (1/4 ton 4x4 Jeep) with trailer, which he is hereby authorized to drive. Rations will be drawn upon OCC Supply Officer.

Calvin A. Behle

Lt. Col., JAGD

Commanding.

Although I had gone to bed early the night before, I had not slept much. Uncertainty about what I would find of my family held me in a tense grip. I looked forward to seeing my sister Ilse. When I had found her in May, I had promised her that if I ever got back to London, I would find the Rippleside Cemetery in Barking, and bring her a photo of Albert's grave. I had written the grave's registration number in my notebook. In October I had used a short leave to go back to England, find the cemetery and take several photos that I wanted her to have.

As the crow flies, it is only about 500 miles from Nuremberg to Eckernfoerde, but over the war-torn roads with bridge after bridge dynamited and endless detours, it took me a day and a half to reach Gettorf, where I remembered from my May visit the turn off to Wulfshagenerhuetten. Winter had made road worse than I remembered. As I reached the house where I had delivered Ilse and her children in spring, a boy was playing in front of the place. It looked silent and gray with the leaves brown the trees bare. I asked the boy where Gerd could be found and he said "They moved away to Lindhoeft—about ten kilometers from here." Just to make sure I had the whole story, I asked, "And Frau von Schwerin, did she go with them?" "Yes, she did," he replied, "but she died from scarlet fever last week." I was close to tears as I made my way through the muddy road back to the highway. After some searching I discovered that Gerd was now located near the British Command Post where I had reported Ilse's arrival to Major Ormsby, the local commander.

I turned into a driveway. A long farmhouse was in front of me. Turning the corner, I stopped the jeep before the rear entrance to the building. A few empty milk cans stood on the cement floor leading into the house. Kids looked out of a window having heard the car stop in front of the entrance. I entered the house, knocked, stuck my head in the door and there was Alix, Gerd's wife, mending socks, surrounded by her own and Ilse's children. The two oldest girls ran to find Gerd. This is what I learned about Ilse.

She and her children had left Wulfshagenerhuetten with Gerd in May, when Major Ormsby made Gerd administrator of the farm of the former top Nazi of Holstein, Gauleiter Lohse. Alix and Ilse together had managed the eight children and had gotten along fine until October, when Ilse fell sick with diphtheria and Gerd had brought her to the hospital in Schleswig. She soon improved and the children had gone several times to visit her. Suddenly there was a complication; she had contracted scarlet fever which she had had as a child. The physician felt that she would be well soon and she seemed to get better. One afternoon, she just leaned back in her bed and died. She had no idea that death was coming and had not written a word for her children. The suddenness of the event had struck all of them and they appeared still dazed.

The girls found Gerd, who came and greeted me. He was very glad to see me. He told me that he had reported to Major Ormsby the day after I had delivered Ilse and been told that he would manage the former Gauleiter's farm. In the course of the interrogation, Major Ormsby had said: "If your brother is good enough to fight in the American army and can vouch for you, we shall be glad to help you." When he came to the farm to assume command, the man who had run it for the Gauleiter told him to go away, they did not need him and were managing just fine. Depressed as Gerd was, he was ready to accept that he had struck out. But Alix encouraged him not to give up but to go back to Major Ormsby. It worked. Gauleiter Lohse's man was thrown out and Gerd was able to start his job. His orders were simple: Produce as much food as you can squeeze out of the farm to feed a population swelled by thousands of refugees.

Considering what life in Germany was, he was doing surprisingly well. He had already planned for Joachim and Ehrengard, Ilse's oldest children, to be apprenticed as a carpenter and a seamstress, two professions that could help them if they ever had a chance to emigrate, which they were considering but with great reservations. Gerd was still hoping that he might be permitted to go back to Below and perhaps be allowed to farm one fifth of the land. Only the lack of information on what had happened in the Russian Occupied Zone of Germany could have made Gerd think of such a plan.

Now without Ilse's help Alix was trying to keep the crowd clothed. She looked weary with dark circles under her eyes. Gerd was spinning wool in the evening to provide thread so that Alix could mend. Their clothing had become rags and their shoes were in deplorable condition. What I had brought was immediately allocated and I promised to rally Marion and her family and our friends in Cincinnati to start collecting clothing. What was most needed were shoes, pants and shirts, sewing materials, and knitting wool.

Ilse's help was sorely missed and Claus and his wife Gisela, whom I had not as yet met, had promised to come to Lindhoeft to help. Talk and exchange of news continued uninterrupted. The good news was that Ruth, Margarete, and Armgard were safely in the British zone, and our parents had decided to stay in Stralsund. Hermann Brandes, Ruth's husband, about whom I will report later, was looking after them to provide provisions and heating material for the winter. By about 11:30, I crept into my bed roll. The children had been permitted to stay up. They regarded me as if I had arrived from Mars.

The next morning Gerd showed me Ilse's grave and told me that she had written an account of her trek from Iven. He gave me a copy, which I translated. It reads like the stories of the Mormon trip from Kansas to Utah. But the danger was from low flying planes not roaming Indians.

There was no more time. Having promised help, I left to find Ruth and Margarete, who lived in Arpke, a village not far from Hannover where Hermann Brandes' family owned farms. Arpke was a farming community with a population of 500 with about 15 farm units clustered around a church and a country inn. A farm worker at the entrance to the village had directed me to the farm of Heinrich Brandes. When I drove into the courtyard to enter the house I could sense fear and hostility. When I said that I was looking for my sister, Ruth, who was married to a man by the name of Hermann Brandes, their faces lit up. I had found Hermann's parents. They provided a guide who took me to a place that was known as the barracks. Driving through a wooded area we found ourselves in front of a small wooden building to which was attached a wood shed. A man came out of the house, and when I said, "You must be Hermann Brandes," he replied, "I know who you are." Ruth showed up a moment later and collapsed in tears. This I found typical. All of them had pushed themselves to their very limits time after time and then, when something unexpectedly nice happened they collapsed in a stream of tears, before they could again take control of their emotions. Ruth's two year old daughter, Christine, quickly responded to a chocolate bar and then I saw a nice looking young woman whom I did not know—it was Gisela, Claus' wife. I had missed Claus, who had left that very morning to go to Lindhoeft to work out their transfer so that they could help Alix and Gerd with their brood of eight children.

Hermann Brandes, 27 years old, was a strapping, powerful man with a noticeable limp. Wounded at Stalingrad, he was on the last hospital plane that made it back to Germany. A heavy leather and metal contraption supported his "withered" leg and protected him from arrest by the Russians on his frequent visits to the Russian Zone. Whenever they wanted to arrest him or put him to work, he hit his metal covered leg with his walking stick and said in Russian, which he had picked up during the campaign that had landed him in Stalingrad: "Bein (leg) kaputt." Never did he disclose that he could easily carry a 150 pound bag of coal or potatoes to keep his family comfortable, or walk 20 miles over war-torn roads. He had experienced the end of the war in Pommerania and had brought Ruth, who was pregnant, to Stralsund, so that she had access to medical help at the time of delivery. They reached Stralsund just as the Russians captured the town. Their second child, Claus, was born there. Hermann was still registered as a resident of Hannover and as an invalid. The Russians told them that he could not remain in their zone. Two months after Ruth's delivery they had to leave the Russian zone and go west. With their few possessions and their new baby in a baby carriage, they had set out on foot and in a week managed to cross the Elbe in a leaky boat and reach Arpke. Ruth was already making plans to resume her teaching career and hoped to find employment in the neighborhood.

While I was listening to Ruth's account of leaving Stralsund, Margarete, totally unchanged, appeared with her husband Karl von Larisch, whom she had married in 1940. Much older than she, he had served in WW I as a lieutenant and as a colonel in Hitler's Wehrmacht had commanded a tank regiment under Rommel in North Africa. Now he was unemployed and hoping for a small position in Holzminden where he had some connections. Listening to Margarete, it was obvious that as a colonel he had commanded a regiment, but with the war behind them she had now assumed command. All of them had stories of their flight from the Russians, of weeks on the road in horse-drawn wagons with strafings by planes and all the perils of that incredible westward migration. But I heard no complaint—they were determined to go to work and make a new life for themselves and their children.

There were several hints that none of their adventures could compare with the incredible dangers that Claus had survived. But I wanted to hear that story from him, and so I was satisfied to know that he and his wife were safe and would soon be in Lindhoeft trying to manage their future. In time I would be able to piece together what he had done in the six years after I had said good-bye to him in Dresden in March of 1939.

The next morning I left early to locate my cousin Armgard Seydel, reported to be in Schliekum, about an hour Southwest of Hannover. I found her with her five children, looking almost unchanged. How that small, frail woman managed to survive was a miracle, and so was the story of her escape.

After her husband had been killed in Russia in 1942, she had managed the Marienwalde farm, with the help of an uncle until the approach of the Russians forced them to flee. Feeling responsible for the farm workers, she had planned one large trek group of ten wagons for the employees, which she and her uncle would lead. For her family she had equipped two carefully prepared and loaded covered wagons, and put her sister Jutta in charge. Jutta would take her own two small children and Armgard's four, aged 6 to 14. The 14 year old Friedel drove one of the wagons until he broke a foot during an air attack. My sister Margarete with her two children, who had fled before the Russians from East Prussia, had reached Marienwalde just in time to join them. They moved west one day ahead of Armgard. That one day made the difference. Nothing went the way they had anticipated, but they managed to cross to safety before the Elbe crossings were closed to refugees.

Armgard and her uncle followed a day later with the large group, hoping to catch up. They didn't make it. The Russians overtook them and turned them back to Marienwalde. Armgard and her uncle were brought to a command post, where a Russian officer questioned her while her uncle was held outside. She heard two shots and never saw him again. The whole Marienwalde contingent was turned over as slave labor to Polish military forces. The Polish contingent had followed the Russian army to occupy all the lands east of the Oder River, which at Yalta had been allocated to Poland. Until August she worked 12 to 16 hours daily, plowing, planting, harvesting on very short rations. Determined to get back to help her children, she saved enough from her meager, daily bread ration to risk escape. She made it. In Schliekum she had leased to a local farmer the four horses that had brought Jutta's contingent to safety. That was the capital with which she would start the rebuilding of her family.

On the evening of the 19th after my eventful six day trip I was back in Nuremberg, weary but content. I was proud of my family. They had coped with enough adversity to fill a book like *Gone with the Wind*. Except for my parents and Claus I had seen them all. In Hermann Brandes, my newest brother-in-law, the family had acquired a man born for those times—without fear or qualms. He had demonstrated that to help his family he would dare to do things that none of us would ever have dreamt of. I had heard no complaints from any of the family and saw no self pity. Occasionally there was a wry acknowledgment of their fate: We had it coming! All of them realized that if there was to be a future for them they had to find it.

Col. Behle was delighted when I gave him a run-down of my "War Crimes Investigating Trip." The next day—November 20, 1945 the War Crimes Trials in Nuremberg opened. It was to be Jackson's greatest day.

We had managed to procure tickets for the opening session in the visitors' gallery from which we had a perfect view of the court, the defendants, their defense counsels and the large prosecution staff. I sat and waited for the great moment when Jackson would deliver his opening statement. Nobody knew what he would say. It was a perfectly kept secret. No advance copy had been leaked, we merely knew that the interpreters in their glass cages would find a copy of the text on their desks when they entered the booth, but they would have no chance to prepare their translations in advance. All of us felt the tension.

Jackson rose from his chair when the eight judges of the court entered the courtroom and seated themselves behind the long bench. Lord Lawrence, the British judge and president of the Tribunal bowed politely to the prosecution and the defense and asked Jackson to proceed. He rose, bowed in reply to the court, placed the folder with the text of his opening statement on the lectern and with a dignity acquired by years of practice before the highest courts, he commenced in a clear baritone voice with the classical, time honored phrase:

May it please the court:

The privilege of opening the first trial in history for crimes against the peace of the world imposes a grave responsibility. The wrongs which we seek to condemn and punish have been so calculated, so malignant, and so devastating, that civilization cannot tolerate their being ignored, because it cannot survive their being repeated. That four great nations, flushed with victory and stung with injury, stay the hand of vengeance and voluntarily submit their captive enemies to the judgment of the law is one of the most significant tributes that power has ever paid to reason.

Before I discuss particulars of evidence, some general considerations which may affect the credit of this trial in the eyes of the world should be candidly faced. There is a dramatic disparity between the circumstances of the accusers and the accused that might discredit our work if we should falter, in even minor matters, in being fair and temperate.

Unfortunately, the nature of these crimes is such that both prosecution and judgment must be by victor nations over vanquished foes. The worldwide scope of the aggressions carried out by these men has left but few real neutrals. . . . We must never forget that the record on which we judge these defendants is the record on which history will judge us tomorrow. To pass these defendants a poisoned chalice is to put it to our lips as well.

Before outlining the prosecution's case in detail, he made a few general observations to strengthen his argument that the defendants were not abused. He said:

"If these men are the first war leaders of a defeated nation to be prosecuted in the name of the law, they are also the first to be given a chance to plead for their lives in the name of the law. Realistically, the Charter of the Tribunal which gives them a hearing, is also the source of their only hope.'

He continued to put to rest the much repeated statement that every German was guilty and said:

"We should also make clear that we have no purpose to incriminate the whole German people. . . . If the German populace had willingly accepted the Nazi program, no storm troopers would have been needed in the early days of the Party and there would have been no need for concentration camps or the Gestapo . . . The German, no less then the non-German world, has accounts to settle with these defendants.'

Throughout the two hours in which Jackson presented the overview of the prosecution's case I was glued to my seat listening to the greatest speech that I had ever heard. I had seen the great orators of my time: Hitler, Goebbels, Roosevelt, and Churchill. What was presented now was different from any court proceeding I had ever seen. I was a privileged participant with a ringside seat witnessing a dramatic, historical event. Jackson showed in the span of not more than fifteen minutes, using simple words and compelling logic, that the difference between justice and vengeance is **fairness**. And, in explaining this assertion and summing it up he emphasized:

"We must summon such detachment and intellectual integrity to our task, that this Trial will commend itself to posterity as fulfilling humanity's aspiration for justice." For me this was precisely the affirmation of his command to Col. Story, given a few weeks ago, when he said: "The defendants **MUST** have the documents cited in the indictment."

Never before or since has an American judge or lawyer stated more persuasively what justice is all about.

With the trial now a daily event—five days a week, three hours in the morning and afternoon, a stream of visitors appeared in Nuremberg. Often Col. Behle was pressed into service to show them the historical environment of Nuremberg and the famous sites of Franconia. I remember particularly Senator Pepper of Florida and James Farley, the Postmaster General during the Roosevelt administration. Like all visitors they were most interested in learning of places where they could obtain gifts to take back to America. There was not much in that heap of rubble that they cared to acquire. But we gave them quick views of Nuremberg, Bayreuth and Rothenburg, certain that they would be reminded of their trip by the photos that we took of them with their own expensive cameras in front of such monuments as Hitler's stand from which he had addressed the Nazi Party Congress.

Three or four times more I obtained tickets to view the trial, but I missed the speed with which an ordinary trial proceeds and the tension that is created by rapid exchanges and challenges between prosecution and defense and the instant rulings of the court. I knew the basic story that the prosecution would deliver, and had myself received some of the proofs like Ilse Koch's lampshades to Nuremberg. The prosecution showed the tattoos of concentration camp victims whom she had killed to enlarge her collection of lampshades made from human skin.

Security at the Palace of Justice during the trial was strict. A tank with guns, ready to shoot, stood next to the entrance gate and military policemen checked everybody's credentials. Although I had entered the building daily, and often several times a day and knew the guards, I had to produce my identification card. Admission to the visitor's gallery was gained only by the possession of one of the specially printed admission tickets for that day. The MP guarding the entrance cautioned everybody that the taking of pictures was strictly forbidden. Since I knew several of the army photographers, and could obtain almost any picture I wanted, I was not even tempted to break that rule, but its existence, and its breach by an officer of high rank, provide an amusing story.

Having a front row seat next to an army Lt. Colonel, I was in a position to notice him reaching into his pocket and then leaning against the balustrade with a Minox camera hidden in his hand. By

November 1945 discipline in the army had vastly declined. During combat times no second lieutenant would have ever challenged a superior officer on such a minor matter as court security. But this was not combat, it was Nuremberg 1945 and so I gently touched his arm and waved my finger indicating: **Forbidden.** He responded to my warning with an amused smile, continuing undisturbed with his photos. After he had finished his film and put the Minox in his pocket, he raised his right lapel, so that I could see a German round identification badge reading: *Geheime Staatspolizei No. 2.*

During a short recess of the session he explained that the camera and the badge were war trophies. At the end of the war his unit had occupied the Berchtesgaden area and he and several other search teams combed the area for the many Nazis who had taken refuge there for the great last stand, which never came. He had studied pictures of the top Nazis and was sure that he would recognize any of them. With a small team of tough and ready men he had set out for the high mountains after he had been tipped off that some top Nazis had been sighted in a ski hut. When they reached the hut, the door opened and about ten men in worn civilian clothes opened the door and came out unarmed. The colonel instantly recognized Kaltenbrunner by the heavy scars on his left cheek but instead of arresting him, he said, "We are looking for some SS men and Kaltenbrunner. Have you seen him?" Kaltenbrunner replied, "No, we have not seen anybody but there are some men in uniform in another ski hut about two kilometers further up." The colonel turned to his men and said: "Lets go" upon hearing this agreed upon sign his crew raised their machine pistols and upon the command: "Haende hoch (Hands up)" the crew slapped handcuffs on their prisoners and the colonel personally frisked Kaltenbrunner, and removed the Minox and the Gestapo badge before he delivered him to his headquarters.

Thanksgiving in 1945 fell on 22 November. In the early afternoon we saw a football game between the teams of two divisions in the stadium that Hitler had built for the Party Congress of 1938. In the distance we could see the massive arena where under a dome of floodlights the Nazi faithful had massed at the Party Congresses and in a frenzy of enthusiasm had confirmed their eagerness to die for Hitler and Germany. They had received what they had asked for. That stadium was now empty and above it flew the Star Spangled Banner, as we sang the National Anthem before the game started.

The time for my orders to go home was getting closer. Col. Behle and I had become friends and we had one thing in common: Both of us were insatiably curious. Both of us thought that we could end our association by one glorious adventure—a trip to visit my parents in Stralsund. I am certain that I had provided the inspiration for this plan and suggested that we go to Stralsund via Berlin. Behle had gathered considerable experience with the Russians during his visit to Prague. He had manipulated his War Crimes Trial Investigating pass to great advantage. The Russians had not interfered with his sightseeing in the city and except for being stopped frequently, he had traveled much, even seen Lidice, the place where the Nazis had wiped out a whole village as retribution for the assassination of Reinhard Heidrich, the Governor General of Czechoslovakia. Before he left for Prague, he had established contact with the Russian Liaison Mission in Nuremberg who assured him that properly stamped orders stating that he came in pursuit of war crimes business was all that he needed.

Behle, an expert at preparing authentic looking military documents, had prepared innocuous looking travel orders for the two of us which merely stated that we were to proceed to Stralsund in connection with war crimes matters of the International Military Tribunal. To facilitate the contact with the Russians in Berlin he had returned to the Russian Liaison Commission in Nuremberg and obtained a letter of introduction to their Berlin group. The letter was in Russian, which he could not read and did not fully trust. So we had the letter translated by one of our Russian speaking friends. It was a simple letter of recommendation.

The trailer was loaded with our bed rolls and ample K- rations and gasoline for a week in Russian territory. The jeep was winterized, which meant that we would have little heat but would not get wet. We were dressed for cold weather as we left shortly after lunch on November 30. It had snowed and the roads were slippery. From Nuremberg it was Autobahn all the way to Berlin—only 500 miles away. But we had to make detour after detour with most of the bridges dynamited and out of commission. Behle, who loved to drive and did not trust my driving, demanded that I keep him awake and give him a good account of the area through which we were going. Since it was an area that I knew well I did not run out of entertaining stories.

It was quite obvious that we could not make Berlin that evening, so we turned off the Autobahn near Hannover and called on Armgard and her five children, whom I had seen only two weeks before. I had told Behle the story of her escape from the Poles and her return in August after her children had given up all hope of ever seeing their mother again. He was impressed with that story and was quite agreeable to meeting his first German family. They were asleep when we knocked at the door at about ten that night. I still have a picture showing her with 4 of her 5 children and Col. Behle. As always the opening of K-rations and the appearance of instant coffee, candy, cigarettes, cheese, ham and the dried fruit bar was for Germans a miracle. We talked till long after midnight, slept in our bedrolls on the floor, and took off the next morning for the remaining run to Berlin.

Just a few miles east of Braunschweig we had to stop at the Helmstedt Checkpoint, where all traffic to and from Berlin was halted by the Russians. Their soldiers examined our American orders and let us enter the 110 miles of Autobahn that separated the British Zone from Berlin. We were warned not to leave the Autobahn under any circumstance. In case of a vehicle breakdown military police would assist us, as the road was heavily patroled by Russian, U.S., and British military police who enforced the speed limit.

Col. Behle zoomed right to the headquarters in Berlin Dahlem and checked us in at the best VIP billet in Berlin, the Harnack House—until the war the main office of the Max Plank Foundation. As a second lieutenant I would never have been allowed in those reserved facilities, but Behle insisted that I be quartered there because of the (important!) nature of our War Crimes work.

When I presented my travel orders to the young German girl who made the room assignments, she looked at me with intensity as if she were trying to place me. Finally she said: "Lieutenant Von Rosenstiel, were you by any chance once an exchange student at the University of Cincinnati?" When I nodded, she continued: "I must talk to you because I have a message for you from Kienzler." When I replied: "Kienzler was no friend of mine—just give me the key to my room." She handed me the key and said: "I know." When I had reached the second floor I saw that she had followed me. She was determined to talk to me and I found it impossible to escape.

In spring of 1938 Kienzler had been selected to be the German exchange student at the University of Cincinnati for 1938-1939 and had visited me in Berlin to learn as much as he could about being in Cincinnati, how to deal with questions about Hitler etc. The SS button on his lapel identifying him as a party loyalist, had warned me to be cautious. I suggested that he not display the button at the university because the administration was anti-German and the climate, with a substantial Jewish population was not pro-German and certainly anti-Nazi. To give him a reliable contact I told him to telephone my girlfriend (later my wife) who could recommend conventional activities like participation in the Glee Club, etc., that would keep him out of political trouble. Within weeks of his arrival, she wrote me that he had joined a fraternity which, under his tutelage, engaged in active anti-Semitism and created difficulties that endangered the German exchange student program.

In August of 1939 the war in Europe had started and I was involved in starting my new life in the United States. On Columbus Day Marion and I returned to Cincinnati for a short visit. We had planned to visit an Austrian physician and his German wife in whose house I had been a frequent guest during my time in Cincinnati. As we were walking toward their house the door opened and out came Kienzler. He walked up to me grabbed my hand and said, "I'm so glad to see you. I know you have very good connections with the

Institute of International Education in New York and I want you to say a good word for me to have my scholarship extended for another year!" I was furious about this suggestion and merely said, "Kienzler, you do not belong here. You are an SS-man and you belong in the trenches!" With that I turned around and walked away with my wife.

Now the young woman clearly distraught and embarrassed yet driven by something that she must deliver said:

"Kienzler, as you know, was a convinced Nazi and SS-man when he was in Cincinnati. He believed in Germany's mission and had persuaded the Austrian physician whose house he had visited in October 1939 to sell his medical practice and re turn to Germany for a glorious future in the Greater German Reich. He had obtained forms for him from the German consulate and from Germany to carry out this project. Then Kienzler made his way back to Germany via the Far East, the South Manchurian Railway, and Moscow. He arrived some time in 1940 and immediately joined a Waffen SS unit as an officer. It did not take him long to see that the Germany of which he had dreamt in Cincinnati did not exist. The year in America despite all the trouble that he had caused, had changed him and he realized now what a ruinous mistake he had made recommending return to Germany to his Austrian physician friend. His sense of guilt never left him. Relations with Russia were still fairly good at that time. One close and trusted friend of his, on continuous courier service between Berlin and Moscow, had agreed to mail in Moscow a letter to the Austrian doctor urging him to cancel all plans for the return to Germany. The friend got the letter safely to Moscow and posted it after affixing Russian postage stamps.

"On June 17 Kienzler's unit commander called him to his office—he was stationed near Berlin. On the table lay the letter to the Austrian doctor in Cincinnati in the envelope with the Russian stamps. The officer told him that his Russian friends had returned the letter to the Gestapo to demonstrate how valuable they were as friends of Germany. The letter was treason. He would be brought before the Peoples Court, found guilty, and hanged. However, since he had been a member of the SS for a long time, there was an alternative—he could join a Himmelfahrts Commando (a suicide squad) leading the German attack on his Russian friends on June 21, 1941. If he would be interested in that proposition, he would be given a day's leave to say farewell to his family and would be listed as having died as a hero. He spent the night with the young woman who was relating this account. He had told her: 'If you ever meet a man by the name of Von Rosenstiel, who was an exchange student in Cincinnati, tell him how it all ended.'"

Never have I heard a story that describes more clearly how a year in America could open the eyes of even a devout SS-man to the pernicious nature of the Nazi system.

One of the first things I did in Berlin was to reestablish contact with Bill Dickman, whom I had met earlier during the summer in Hoechst. He came to join us at the Harnack House mess and told us of his life in Berlin. The headquarters of OMGUS (Office of Military Government of the United States) was located in the West, the least damaged area of Berlin, and General Clay had made a good start by showing that he was fully aware of the difficulties of working with the Russians. He warned us that relations with our Russian allies were by no means friendly and predicted that we would not be able to carry out our plans to visit Stralsund. But above all he stressed the need for caution in observing the numerous warning signs where the Allied sectors ended and the Russian Zone began. Even inadvertent crossing of the line had created incidents of shooting and arrests by over-anxious, trigger happy Russians who saw spies in every person wearing a non-Russian uniform. Their motto was: Shoot first—ask questions later.

At the Soviet headquarters' liaison office in West Berlin the next morning, we presented our orders and the letter from the Russian office in Nuremberg and were treated courteously. They wasted no time inquiring why we wanted to go to Stralsund and what war crimes had been committed there. Col. Behle with complete candor said, "Our purpose is to visit the parents of my lieutenant." The Russian officer smiled understandingly but said, "I am afraid we cannot grant permission for an entry into our Zone, because this is clearly for a compassionate purpose, and compassion is not a valid ground for entering the Russian Zone." There was a depressed silence. The Russian officer, obviously embarrassed by the harsh rejection of our request, offered an alternative. "Couldn't you think of some legitimate task that you could accomplish in our Zone like looking for Bormann?" Behle's face lit up and he said, "Yes, indeed we are also looking for Martin Bormann." Bormann had been indicted in Nuremberg and was being tried "in absentia," because no evidence of his death had been found and his whereabouts since leaving the bunker after Hitler's suicide were unknown. Our Russian contact man assured us that the matter would be referred to General Zhukov, the Russian commanding general. We should return after two days for a decision. We were not optimistic, but since we knew that everybody was looking for Bormann, we felt that our case was not hopeless.

For two days I became Col. Behle's Berlin tour guide, which I now revisited for the first time since 1939. Continuous, massive air raids by day and night over years had done damage that was beyond imagination. Yet six months after bombings had stopped life was returning. The sectors of the three Western allies had already achieved some normalcy. Of course there was shocking devastation everywhere and shortages of housing, food and coal, but stores were opening and some municipal services like gas and electricity had been restored. The determination to get on with the cleanup and salvage of bricks from bombed houses for rebuilding was visible everywhere. Women dressed in rags [the rubble women] with work gloves, were collecting bricks and stacking them up in neat piles to be ready for the rebuilding. A few street cars and some subways were running. The Russian sector of Berlin, which was freely accessible to us, seemed different. People had a haunted look having lived under the Russian rule since May of 1945. They did not know that worse was in store for them.

Berlin was deep in the center of the Russian Zone and all streets leading out of Berlin carried big warning signs for their American,

English and French war-time allies: STOP -WARNING -YOU ARE NOW LEAVING the American Sector and ENTERING THE RUSSIAN ZONE. Having been alerted by Bill Dickman to the danger of carelessness, we moved with caution—and stopped to read all signs.

In our jeep we headed first to the Brandenburg Gate, which had weathered the firestorm that had destroyed most of the buildings on the Pariser Platz and the Wilhelm Strasse, the government center. Hitler's Reichskanzlei, constructed from Swedish red marble, had been heavily damaged by bombs, fire, and artillery shelling. I remembered standing in front of that building, brand new in March 1938, when Hitler had returned triumphantly from Vienna after the Anschluss of Austria. Now it was a shell of a few cracked walls and bent steel girders. The explosions had scattered the red marble all over the area. We entered the bunker, with nobody stopping us. On the floor I picked up stray pieces of printed material attesting to the glory that this heap of rubble had once witnessed: The formal seating arrangements of Hitler's first (1933) and last (June 1939) formal state dinners honoring Prime Minister Stojadinovitch and Prince Regent Paul, both loyal Nazi supporters from Yugoslavia.

Our next stop was the Berliner Schloss (Berlin Royal Castle). To reach it we drove along what before the war used to be Berlin's show street, Unter den Linden. I could still recognize the classical elegance of Germany's most famous street. Surprisingly, bombing, shelling, and street fighting had nicked and damaged every one of those famous structures, but they still stood there- proud survivors, damaged but not gone. Most of the Linden trees had disappeared, many obviously had been cut down for firewood and the few that were left looked like hurricane victims. The famous statue of Frederick the Great, near the university, had disappeared. We passed the monumental structure of the Prussian State Library, with boarded up windows; the Humboldt University, where I had been a student; the State Opera House and Schinkel's Wache, converted after WWI into the Tomb of Germany's Unknown Soldier, where I had seen many foreign dignitaries pay homage to Hitler and his henchmen. The majority of the henchmen were now prisoners in Nuremberg.

We crossed the Spree bridge leading to the Berlin Schloss, a massive complex, covering almost 90 acres with its two large inner courts, spacious enough to allow horse drawn coaches to discharge their passengers in comfort. Bombs had ripped large holes in many of the walls, and many windows had been blown out, but it was far from being a ruin. As we got closer, I remember wondering if there would be anything worthwhile to show Col. Behle.

I had seen it last in 1939 before the war when I lived in Berlin. Whenever I had visitors from abroad, I never failed to take them to this place. My first visit had been at the age of 13 in 1924 when my father had taken me there to impress upon me its importance to German and particularly Prussian history. The castle had been started around 1400 as a modest residence of the Grand Electors of Brandenburg. As their power and territory grew with each generation, the castle was upgraded until it had reached, toward the end of the last century, the gigantic proportions that I remembered.

I never forgot the stories that my father had planted during my first visit. The Weimar Republic had then been the acknowledged German government for six years, but devout royalist that he was, he did not acknowledge this change and preferred to populate this place, which he had seen in its glory, with royalty and Prussian Army officers in glittering gala uniforms bedecked with orders, bowing politely to corseted ladies with enormous hats and lace handkerchiefs. Beginning in 1920 the elegantly furnished rooms had been used as a museum documenting the times of the ruling royal house.

As Marion and I walked into the castle to buy tickets for a guided tour I spied a man washing a large field grey vintage Mercedes-Benz in one of the courtyards. We went over to talk to him. Looking at the car I said that it looked as if it had been used as a command car during the war. The man smiled and told us that it had been the Kaiser's car, which he had used during the war. When Wilhelm abdicated in 1918 this man had driven him from his last headquarters in Spa to seek asylum in Holland. After they had reached the

Dutch border the Kaiser had instructed him to take the car back to Berlin, because it was government property. It had been here ever since. This man was now employed by the state as a groundskeeper and once a month he took it out of the garage to wash and dust it.

When Col. Behle and I got out of our jeep an old man approached and asked us what we wanted. It was the man who seven years ago had washed the Kaiser's car. I told him that I wanted to show the colonel the castle. He offered to accompany us, and we were glad to have someone knowledgeable along. There was much damage, much was burned out and blocked off completely, only a few sections could still be entered. When we offered him a cigarette he eagerly accepted, but instead of lighting it, placed it into an envelope in his pocket, as it was the currency of post-war Germany.

The Kaiser's chauffeur took us to a section that looked shabby but had all three floors intact. We climbed a staircase to the second floor. In front of us was a long row of perhaps 15 guest apartments from which all furniture had been removed. Each of these identical units consisted of a salon, a bedroom, and a small anteroom with washstand and commode. None of them had plumbing. Servants had carried water to the three floors from pumps at street level. The servants for each apartment operated from a butler's pantry. As we entered the undamaged floor we could see what seemed an endless row of pantries, each with a large window opening out on one of the courtyards, with high wooden cabinets on each side of the window and on the opposite wall. The cabinets had louvered doors and our guide told us they had held china, glasses, and linen during the times of the Kaiser.

Our guide would later show us at the very end of the floor the only "modern" bathroom with flush toilet, running water and a bathtub. It had been installed at great cost in the imperial quarters when Wilhelm II ascended to the throne in 1888.

As we were leisurely walking through this row of butlers' pantries, I grabbed an elegant knob on one of the cabinets and opened the door to reveal a collection of several thousand old letters in all languages, some with seals and florid signatures. I just couldn't close the door without at least making an effort to read one or two letters. The first letter was from Veit Stoss, Germany's most famous wood carver, who had divided his time between Krakau in Poland and Nuremberg. I have no recollection what was written in the letter but I recall that I was fascinated by a handwriting so uniquely personal that he seemed to have used his pen like a carving knife. I could decipher the letter written some 400 years ago without difficulty and wondered if anyone could read my handwriting in 2350. The next letter was as modern as any dunning letter I have ever seen. The owner of the famous Augsburg banking firm, The Fuggers wrote it. Addressed to Queen Isabella of Spain, it chided her for her tardiness in repaying a loan and demanded prompt payment in annoyed terms.

My art acquisitions in Wiesbaden, which I related earlier in this narrative, had whetted my appetite for letters and art objects of the past and I must say that I was sorely tempted to grab a handful of the letters and stuff them into my musette bag for later evaluation. But I did resist temptation. Instead, I put them back and closed the door. I often think that this treasure trove may well have perished when the East German government decided to dynamite the whole castle to free Germany from its past. What a pity! We walked on, and the realization of my stupidity began to nag at me.

The guide brought us to the Kaiser's bathroom. An area of about 12 x 12 had an elegantly tiled floor, a toilet and an enormous wash stand with two basins and faucets for hot and cold water. But the most impressive installation was the gigantic bathtub. When the bathroom was built, cast iron or steel bathtubs had not as yet been invented; at that time they custom made an over-sized tub from hammered tin. The rim of the tub consisted of a wooden edging that was braced by wooden supports resting on the floor. On the wall above the bathtub an enormous mural painted on 6" x 6" tiles displayed a German battle cruiser with pennants flying and guns spitting fire, cutting through the North Sea and bearing down on his Majesty as he was entering his bathtub.

The bathtub had not withstood the intense heat of fire from an air raid. The tin had melted and was now lying on the floor, the wood reduced to ashes and the tin resembled crumpled, dirty aluminum foil. Viewing the remains of this display of imperial bathing comfort and splendor, I wished for a small truck, so that I could dismantle the whole 6'x 8' mural and take it back to America for display in a bath parlor to be built for the purpose. But accompanied by two witnesses to a possible grand larceny, I scaled my greed down to manageable proportions. The mural was surrounded by a border of 3"x 6" tiles that displayed tiny fish of delicate colors, sea fans, sea horses, and shells. With my pocket knife I carefully loosened two tiles from the border of this majestic picture and put them into my musette bag. Upon my return to the States, I framed them and have proudly displayed them at my home ever since. I have admitted my 1945 larceny in writing, hoping that it can be forgiven, for if I had not taken the tiles, the East Germans, determined to remove all links to their past, would have demolished them in 1950 anyway. This way they will remain as incontrovertible proof that they have seen *The Emperor Without Clothes.*

Returning through the Brandenburg Gate, we encountered a milling crowd with a preponderance of U.S. and Russian soldiers. Accidentally we had come to the first of the many barter markets near the badly wrecked Reichstag. It was a short distance from the new Russian monument honoring the Russian soldiers who had liberated Berlin. Berliners had promptly dubbed it the Monument to the Unknown Rapist. This was the area where American and Russian sectors met and where soldiers of both nations congregated for trading purposes. The Russians had vast amounts of German Reichsmarks and Occupation money which they had printed from plates the United States had handed over to them. It was legal tender, although it never compared in value with the purchasing power of American cigarettes. American soldiers had soon discovered that the most prized possession a Russian soldier could acquire with his vast amount of German money, was a Mickey Mouse wristwatch with a black face and a sweep second hand with a tiny Mickey Mouse racing around the dial. GIs were quick to learn about this fad and had purchased these watches in quantity for about $5 each from Sears. The test that a wristwatch had to pass was surprisingly simple. After the watch had been wound to establish that its works had the energy to propel the second hand on its race around the dial, the Russian would grab the watch by its cheap band and place it in his mouth closing his lips tightly around the band. Then he would blow himself up, trying to force air into the moving parts. If the air could stop the moving hand of the wristwatch, this was proof that the watch was a worthless fake and would be rejected as a fraud. It was a delight seeing GIs getting rich as the Russians almost exploded.

The next morning at the Harnack House, as we were about to visit our Russian friends to inquire about the permission to enter the Russian Zone, an orderly delivered a TELEX message from the Office of the Chief of Counsel in Nuremberg to Col. Behle. The TELEX read:

> "Russian Liaison Office reports two U. S. officers seeking admission to Russian Zone in search of war criminal Martin Bormann. Request investigation and immediate report."

We were both stunned and felt a noticeable sickness in our stomachs. It could be embarrassing if we were caught in our joy ride. We needed to think, not panic. I remembered that during his visit at the Harnack House, Bill Dickman had told us that his office had an enormous library of Nazi literature, which he was using for much of his work. I proposed to Col. Behle that I find the library and do some fast research on Martin Bormann before we sent a reply to the TELEX. The library had been assembled for Professor Carl Schmitt, one of the notoriously aggressive Nazi lawyers, and now it enabled the United States Military Government in Berlin to have access to all the Nazi publications of the past 12 years. I found the library, introduced myself to the librarian, an American soldier, and asked him to let me see everything that he had on Martin Bormann.

The very first volume I saw made reference to Bormann's 1925 conviction for participation in a so-called "Feme Murder." They intimidated and killed people who testified in criminal cases conducted by the Allies after WW I. Bormann, who had killed a witness who had testified, had spent a year in jail after his conviction. Once the Nazis had assumed power he had proudly used this fact to give himself the nimbus of a hero. And, as luck wanted it, the conviction had occurred in Neubrandenburg, a town in Mecklenburg a mere sixty miles south of Stralsund. That was all the information I needed to answer the TELEX.

We produced a terse, convincing statement that we were the people who had sought access to the Russian Zone. It set forth the following:

"Bormann 1925 convicted murder Neubrandenburg. To preserve cover no advance disclosure feasible. Possibility of his hiding with friends in Neubrandenburg, place of his first crime, must be explored. Criminal theory supports concept that criminals return to places of their crimes. Stralsund named in orders instead of Neubrandenburg to preserve cover. Bormann's involvement with FEME murder known only to members of this War Crimes Investigating Team. Proceeding as planned."

Our visit with the Russians turned out very different from what we had hoped for. The Russian headquarters were convinced that Bormann was such a dangerous man that General Zuhkov had allocated two officers and 15 enlisted men to the project. We could offer only two seats in our jeep and told our Russian contact of this fact. We remonstrated that it was impossible to provide that sort of an excursion force. So the Russian Liaison people promised to make another try and see if they could reduce the force to one officer and one enlisted man, whom we were willing to support with transportation and rations. The time for this new undertaking was again, two days and we could see the handwriting on the wall.

Col. Behle and I crisscrossed Berlin for another two days, saw some castles and ruins, visited friends who had survived, and finally when the two days were up and General Zhukov had not yet decided, we returned to Nuremberg. We stopped at Wiesbaden for a night and received a TELEX that General Zhukov had granted our request: One Officer and one enlisted man—but the date of the TELEX clearly showed that the Russians had issued the order only after they knew that we had passed through the checkpoint at Helmstedt on the way to Nuremberg. We did not turn around.

When we returned to private life, Col. Behle and I continued our interest in Martin Bormann over many years. Whenever news appeared in the American or German press we exchanged clippings and information. Finally we accepted that a skeleton found near the Lehrter Bahnhof, where he had last been seen, was all that was left of him. His dentist was able to identify the skeleton by the teeth, so that put to rest our valiant search for Bormann.

Going Home

Before my orders for the return to the States were cut I had an interview with a recruiting officer of Justice Jackson's staff trying to persuade me to stay for a while longer, and dangling a promotion before me. I wanted to get home so I declined, but they gave me the name of their Washington contact in case I wanted to change my mind and return as a civilian. I left Nuremberg on December 22.

Except for Col. Behle and Col. Fairman, with whom I remained in contact, I lost contact with all the people with whom I shared those exciting months in Nuremberg. In March of 1996, I learned by accident that participants in the Nuremberg Trials had organized themselves into a survivor group and were meeting every five years in Washington—and that 1996 was the year for the meeting. Anne and I went and had a wonderful time. Whitney Harris was there and several other people whom I remembered.

Twenty enlisted men and I shared a freight car that took us from Erlangen to the so-called **Cigarette Camps** which the army had laid out near Le Havre to prepare the millions of soldiers for their return. Our freight car had straw on the floor and a little Franklin stove to spread some warmth and allow us to heat water for the coffee in our K-rations. The car had no windows and because of the cold, we opened the door only when the train stopped, which was fairly often. Except for wearing the same uniform there was no longer any common experience—our contact was the number of points that had brought us together—I had 74. The ride took 36 hours.

Our Le Havre camp was *Lucky Strike*. We were assigned to a company organized merely for administrative purposes. Suddenly I heard my name announced over the loudspeaker with instructions to report to the company commander, a captain. He told me that he was appointing me finance officer for the 250 soldiers in his company. It was my function to arrange for the conversion of the soldiers' accumulated pay as proven by their pay books—they all had been paid in German occupation money—into U.S. currency. Having been in Germany under this system, I knew that every one of these 250 men had been involved in some sort of currency and black market manipulations and had much more money to convert than could be proven by his pay book. Checking 250 pay books and listening to 250 long stories about how they had won all the extra money in crap games and now wanted to convert it into dollars made me think: "Why me?" But there was no way to get out of this mess. I went to the barrack where I was to hold forth and found a red-haired, tough looking buck sergeant about my age, perhaps a couple of years older, smoking a cigarette. He saw my dismay and said, "What's the trouble?" When I told him he laughed and said, "In my unit I worked with the finance officer. I know what is involved. Why don't you let me handle it for you. I'll get it done in a hurry. When I am finished I'll bring you the sheets, you sign them and we can forget about the whole thing."

It was an easy way out. He prepared the accounting sheets, I signed them and I thanked him. He was a remarkable man, with superior intelligence, good education, and organizational talent. So I asked him what he had done in civilian life. As a vice president of one of the big American airlines he had trained several of the young air force generals in traffic control, plane maintenance, etc. When his number for entering the service had come he had contacted all his pupils hoping that they would get him at least a captain's rating, but the best anyone was willing to get for him was a 2nd lieutenancy. So he had enlisted in the infantry as an enlisted man and had enjoyed that life. He had seen some combat but his most exciting experience had been the discovery of the German art treasures that had been stored in a salt mine. He was radiant as he told me that he had held the *Concordat of Worms* in his hands and had viewed more original Albrecht Duerer paintings than one could find anywhere. So, he thought that having taken a B.A. in Fine Arts at Princeton had well prepared him for his army life.

Before boarding the Mount Vernon, an enormous troop transport in Le Havre on December 26, I sent Helene the following cable:

INTL=HAVRE VIA MACKAY RADIO DEC 26
VLT MISS HELENE VONROSENSTIEL:
447 WARREN AVE CIN=
TELL MOTHER I SHALL REACH STATES ABOARD
MTVERNON 3
JANUARY LOVE—DADDY

The crossing was rough. I spent most of my time wondering how it would be to return to civilian life and work after three years in the army. Frankly I was also worried about my marriage. The first five years of our married life, where I had been a sort of endangered species, had brought us close together. How would I be able to cope with two children, whom I did not know? I had seen Helene in diapers in her crib when I left in 1944 and Paul was born while I was overseas. And there was the nagging question: How could I help my German family with the small job that would be waiting for me at Schering? In the back of my mind was also the idea that I could and perhaps should make a contribution to the reconstruction of Germany. I had seen so many people who were seeking jobs in Germany and was convinced that I could offer more because I had learned much in my three years in the army.

On reaching New York harbor on the evening of January 3, 1946 we were loaded on a train that took us to a staging area which was now performing the reverse function. A full course dinner was waiting for us along with endless rows of pay telephones. I reached Marion late at night and told her that I would be at Fort Dix in about a day and that the discharge process would take about four or five days. She promised she would come as soon as she could make it and would see if she could rustle up a car.

Friends in New York loaned Marion a car and she came to visit me at Dix. After a competent and rapid discharge procedure at Fort Dix on January 9, 1946, in which I received my final pay of $524.40, I left the army. We stayed for a few days in New York and saw most of our New York friends. My fears about my marriage proved unfounded. It was as strong as ever. Marion noted that my English was more fluent, but the vocabulary enriched by "colorful" army parlance would need adjustment. I was a civilian again.